IDEOLOGY, REASON, AND THE LIMITATION OF WAR

Ideology, Reason, and the Limitation of War

Religious and Secular Concepts 1200–1740

JAMES TURNER JOHNSON

PRINCETON UNIVERSITY PRESS, PRINCETON, NEW JERSEY

for my PARENTS

CONTENTS

MUCH OF my research on English and other concepts of just war and holy war and on Anglo-Spanish tension during the late sixteenth and early seventeenth centuries was done during three months' study at the Henry E. Huntington Library. For the helpful assistance I received there, and for the Huntington Library grant that enabled me to spend a productive summer in residence there, I am gratefully indebted.

Two Rutgers Research Council grants facilitated the last stages of study and the preparation of this manuscript by providing me with a year's leave and by underwriting some of the costs of research assistants and a typist.

To write out of a long tradition of thought like that of the search for justice in war means that one is deeply indebted to many who have gone before in that tradition. Those from past and present from whom I have learned, whether in the end we agreed or disagreed, I acknowledge below in the text (particularly the Introduction), the Bibliography, and the notes. But Paul Ramsey deserves a special mention, not just for the wisdom of his books but for the counsel of his conversation. His *War and the Christian Conscience* is, moreover, the nearest thing to a single point of inspiration for the present book.

I am also grateful to colleagues in the American Academy of Religion for constructive criticism of parts of the Introduction and Chapter II, which were read as papers at the Academy's 1972 and 1971 annual meetings, respectively. Some of the ideas that surfaced early in my research were published also in my article, "The Meaning of Non-Combatant Immunity in the Just War/Limited War Tradition," in the *Journal of the American Academy of Religion*, June 1971. The discussion of the ideology of Christendom and its effect on just war theory, contained in the Introduction (pp. 12–17, below) is taken from my article, "Ideology and the Jus ad Bellum," *Journal of the American Academy of Religion*, xli, no. 2 (June 1973), pp. 212–18, with the permission of the Editor. Opportunity to develop my thoughts on the twentieth-century *jus ad bellum*, out of which comes the Epilogue to this book, was afforded by an invitation to write for *The Monist* issue, *The Philosophy of War* (October 1973).

Lastly, for the persistent editorial advice of my wife Pamela I remain indebted but grateful.

JAMES TURNER JOHNSON

May, 1974

IDEOLOGY, REASON, AND THE LIMITATION OF WAR

A great deal has been written upon the Augustinian and medieval backgrounds of Christian just war doctrine, and likewise the lineage from this doctrine to the modern field of international law has been copiously explored. One of the best recent books on Christian just war thought, Paul Ramsey's *War and the Christian Conscience* (Durham, N.C.: Duke University Press, 1961), goes all the way back to Augustine to find the genesis of noncombatant immunity, and traces certain modern-sounding elements in the principle of proportionality back to Thomas Aquinas.[1] Other Protestant theologians have not always been so thorough; for example, the German ethicist Helmut Thielicke looks mostly to Luther for his wisdom from the past.[2] But Roman Catholic writers take the Augustinian-medieval etiology as commonplace, though they are willing to look for modification of the classic doctrine in the pronouncements of recent popes, as witness John Courtney Murray's *Morality and Modern War* (New York: Council on Religion and International Affairs, 1959). The most

[1] See Chaps. II and III.
[2] Helmut Thielicke, *Theological Ethics*, vol. 2: *Politics*, ed. by William Lazareth (Philadelphia: Fortress Press, 1969), sect. 25. Thielicke *does* treat Roman Catholic moral theology, the Church Fathers, and the Bible as sources for relative justification of war, but he does this only briefly, sketchily, and with apparently little understanding of the interaction of the elements making up just war doctrine. On the other hand, he stresses the contribution of evangelical theology (and particularly Luther) out of all proportion to its actual contribution to the tradition.

3

careful and sustained twentieth-century Catholic discussion of the growth of classic just war doctrine remains Alfred Vanderpol's *La Doctrine scholastique du droit de guerre* (Paris: A. Pedone, 1919), but among books in English perhaps the most helpful is another classic, John Eppstein's *The Catholic Tradition of the Law of Nations* (Washington: Catholic Association for International Peace, 1935), which besides commentary offers considerable excerpts from relevant documents not elsewhere translated, and moreover takes Catholic just war tradition up into the period between the two world wars.

When one turns to the relationship between international law and Christian war doctrine the landscape is equally full of worthwhile studies. At the head of the list should be the entire Carnegie series *Classics of International Law*, several volumes of which are noted in the bibliography to the present book. But in the space of one volume James Brown Scott's *The Spanish Origin of International Law* (Oxford: Clarendon Press; London: Humphrey Milford, 1934) is a seminal and comprehensive study of the relationship between the thought of certain Spanish theologians of the sixteenth and seventeenth centuries (most prominent of whom are Franciscus de Victoria and Francisco Suarez) and the new secular science of international law as set forth by such as Alberico Gentili and Hugo Grotius. A recent book that has had a wide readership, Telford Taylor's *Nuremberg and Vietnam: An American Tragedy* (Chicago: Quadrangle Books, 1970) derives the moral limitation of war in international law explicitly from Christian antecedents, even though Taylor is neither comprehensive nor particularly accurate in his historical sketch. Finally, one should not fail to mention certain

4

works on war itself in which the etiology of attempts to limit war is investigated. Two such standard works have been extremely helpful in the preparation of the present book: John U. Nef's *War and Human Progress* (Cambridge, Mass.: Harvard University Press, 1950) and Quincy Wright's *A Study of War* (2 vols.; Chicago: University of Chicago Press, 1942).

With so many acknowledgedly excellent books available (and there are a great many others, of varying scope and quality, which I have not mentioned here), why yet another? This book has two fundamental aims: first, to explore the nature of the interaction between religion and secular society, not just in the dissolution of just war doctrine but also in its formation; and second, to investigate just war doctrine as an ideological pattern of thought, expressive of a greater ideology. Neither of these aims has been pursued in the studies presently available.

None of the theological histories that trace just war doctrine to its Augustinian and medieval roots exhibits any particular concern with the effect of this doctrine on the society to which it was preached and on which it was imposed as a moral guide; nor do these studies examine the input of secular forces into the very making of just war doctrine (which, after all, did not simply spring full-grown out of the thigh of Augustine of Hippo). On the other hand, secular historians who grant willingly that the chivalric code stands in some important way behind the development of doctrine on limiting war in western Europe do not draw connecting lines between this knightly code and the war doctrine of the church. My first purpose in writing this book

5

might thus be put simply as an attempt to get the theologians and the secular historians who have written about this subject into a meaningful dialogue with one another—and incidentally to rewrite some of the history of the development of Christian just war doctrine.

My first concern with the development of doctrine out of the interplay between secular and religious forces derives from research into the growth of English Puritan marriage doctrine done while I was a doctoral candidate at Princeton University (see my *A Society Ordained by God: English Puritan Marriage Doctrine in the First Half of the Seventeenth Century* [Nashville and New York: Abingdon Press, 1970]). The social position of the Puritan spokesmen, as opposed to their more High Church contemporaries, greatly influenced which elements of the Christian tradition they chose to emphasize and which to ignore. Similarly, to anticipate later discussion (Chapter II below), the tendency of the English to draw the just war doctrine that they inherited over into a new doctrine justifying holy war (which they still called "just war") cannot be understood simply as a theological movement. The documents bear this out: social factors, such as an overpowering fear of Spain and a deep hatred of rebellion, had a great deal to do with the development of holy war thought in sixteenth- and seventeenth-century England. Sir George Clark's *War and Society in the Seventeenth Century* (Cambridge: At the University Press, 1958), which I encountered at about the same time as the first of the holy war documents, further fueled my interest in the relation of social forces to ideas in the particular case of war; yet Clark's book also begs the question of what was happening in theological thought

6

on war during the social changes, some quite massive, that he treats.

Final focusing of the ideas that led to the present book came after reading M. H. Keen's *The Laws of War in the Late Middle Ages* (London: Routledge & Kegan Paul; Toronto: University of Toronto Press, 1965). This book, a brilliant and insightful treatment of secular developments in the law of war between the thirteenth and the sixteenth centuries, would nevertheless if read alone leave one with the same question left by Clark's study: how does the development of Christian doctrine relate to secular developments? This present study has benefited from material not readily available to all students of seventeenth-century warfare: the works of Vanderpol and Eppstein, cited earlier; Keen's own acknowledgment of an influence of canon law on developing secular law; and perhaps most important, points of contact between the secular and religious traditions in the persons of certain late medieval writers, most notably Honoré Bonet, a cleric whose *L'Arbre des battailes* (*Tree of Battles*) was written as a guide to the nobility and was based in both Christian theory and secular law (Bonet is treated in Chapter I below). Keen provides the missing part of the picture painted by Vanderpol and Eppstein; or conversely they fill in the picture created by Keen. Yet alone neither offers a complete understanding of the development of just war doctrine in the late Middle Ages.

Those authorities who have traced Christian just war theory back to its Augustinian and medieval roots have overlooked one simple yet devastating fact: *there is no just war doctrine, in the classic form as we know it today*, in either Augustine or the theologians or canonists

7

of the high Middle Ages. This doctrine in its classic form, including both a *jus ad bellum* (statement on the right to make war) and a *jus in bello* (statement on what is allowable in the course of war), both in a reasonably elaborate form close to what twentieth-century commentators mean when they say "just war doctrine," *does not exist* prior to the end of the Middle Ages. Conservatively, it is incorrect to speak of classic just war doctrine as existing before about 1500. Earlier there exist *two* doctrines, a religious (*i.e.*, theological and canonical) one largely limited to the right to make war (*jus ad bellum*) and a secular one whose almost total content related to the proper mode of fighting (Law of Arms, *jus in bello*).

As the first stage in reconstructing the development of classic just war doctrine, Chapter I below explores the merging of the *jus ad bellum* provided by religion with the *jus in bello* provided by the knightly code and civil law. The gradual amalgamation of these two distinct traditions on war into one in the late Middle Ages has a counterpart in the gradual dissolution of classic just war doctrine in the century following the Reformation. This metamorphosis too has been improperly understood. Just as a religious and a secular source had come together in the formation of that doctrine, so in the post-Reformation century of political and intellectual instability the unified just war doctrine of the late Middle Ages divided along a line between the religious and the secular. The split was not, however, between *jus ad bellum* and *jus in bello* but between two divergent readings of the received *jus ad bellum*: one that took war for religion to be the purest, holiest, most just kind of conflict imaginable, and another that consciously and completely ruled out war for religion and emphasized as just causes of war those that could be put in natural-law (mainly political) terms. This latter tradition retained most of the classic provisions of just war doctrine and, in particular, kept a surer hold on the law of war (or *jus in bello*). This tradition, manifested most fully but not exclusively in the works of the Spanish theologians Victoria and Suarez mentioned above, is nevertheless *not* the classic doctrine because of the clear and uncompromising disallowance of any right to make war for religion and because of its exponents' concern with grounding their arguments in natural law rather than in revelation. This tradition, as I have already noted, further metamorphoses into secular international law. To distinguish it from the classic doctrine I call this position, treated below in Chapter III, "*modern* just war doctrine."

The other tradition that comes out of classic just war doctrine is the more controversial and the more misunderstood. For this line of thought, which emphasizes the place of religion in justifying war, I use the term "holy war" (following the usage of the sixteenth- and seventeenth-century proponents of the doctrine), but the "holy war" of the early modern period is both in derivation and in intention a just war doctrine. Much of the misunderstanding of this tradition of thought on war derives from the typology put forward by Roland Bainton in his book, *Christian Attitudes toward War and Peace* (Nashville, Tenn.: Abingdon Press, 1960), and in an earlier paper, "Congregationalism: From the Just War to the Crusade in the Puritan Revolution" (*Andover Newton Theological School Bulletin*, 35, no. 3 [April 1943], pp. 1–20). Bainton distinguishes sharply among the ideas of pacifism, just war, and crusade in Christian history and associates the crusade "type" directly with not only the medieval wars generally called crusades but also the English Puritans in particular. According to Bainton's typology the crusade (or holy war) has four distinguishing marks: a holy cause, God's direction and help, godly crusaders and ungodly enemies, and unsparing prosecution.[3] A full discussion of what is right and wrong with Bainton's thesis, in the specific case of the Puritans, is undertaken in Chapter II below, but the most important points in my criticism should be noted here. First, Bainton does not take into account that those whom he terms "crusaders" understood themselves to be squarely within the just war tradition, and in particular the Puritans derived their thought on war directly from the classic Christian doctrine. Second, to single out the Puritans as English "crusaders" is to overlook all the other classes of Englishmen who at about the same time were clamoring for religious war on the basis of their own various preferences in religion. Two obvious examples of the latter are those Catholic clergy in exile who attempted to stir up English and Irish Catholics to holy rebellion against the anti-papal royal authorities, and political advisers to Elizabeth I who, Protestant though not Puritan, counseled war with Spain not just because that country was powerful and predatory but because it was *Catholic*.

In short, a proper understanding of the post-Reformation development of just war doctrine, including the preparation for the new science of international law, must take into account the separation from the mainstream of that doctrine of an element that is very much a part of classic doctrine (and indeed ultimately de-

[3] Bainton's four defining marks appear in virtually the same form in the cited article (p. 15) and book (p. 148).

rives from Augustine): the allowance of war for religion among the just causes enumerated in the *jus ad bellum*. The holy war doctrine that resulted from taking this as the most just cause legitimizing war must be set in complementation to the modern just war doctrine, which allows only natural-law causes as justification for war. Only when *both* are understood as progeny of classic just war doctrine can the development of thought on limiting war in the modern period be understood for what it is: an attempt to eliminate the obviously ideological aspects of the inherited just war doctrine and to base all proposed limits on war squarely in the natural—reason, custom, positive law.

The second of the principal aims of this book is to investigate the ideology of just war thought in a crucial period of its development.

Since the term "ideology" has come to be employed in a variety of ways, some of them mutually contradictory, it is necessary to explain the usage in this book. Broadly put this term has a negative connotation when used to refer to the beliefs and ensuing behavior of a partisan group with which one disagrees. Thus rightists decry the "ideological" nature of Communism, while leftists respond with denunciations of "Fascist ideology." Both rightists and leftists here find in "ideology" something sinister, something to be avoided. Correspondingly, in speaking of their own convictions Communists refer to Marxist-Leninist "thought" or Maoist "thought"—not "ideology." This negative usage has had influential expression by Karl Mannheim in his widely read *Ideology and Utopia*.

There is, however, another connotation to "ideology,"

11

which can be traced to the writings of Max Weber and which is neutral in flavor. "Ideology" in this neutral or relativistic sense is used to refer to belief structures that are discretely based and different from one another, and no value judgment as to their contents is implied. In this sense of the term both Communism and Fascism are ideologies, and one may speak also of Puritan ideology, the ideology of the Pure Land School of Buddhism, or indeed the ideology of a world religion such as Christianity. Unless otherwise specified or clear from the context, "ideology" in this book has a neutral or relativistic sense.

In this sense, then, classic just war doctrine is inherently ideological. This doctrine, as already argued above and further probed in Chapter I below, developed within the ideological limits set by medieval Christendom. Two main factors defined these limits. The first, a theological factor, was simply Christian doctrine as it took shape in the West. But the second was geographical: the boundaries of Europe. Within these two limits Christendom came into being, not coterminous with the spread of Christianity over the world, not present in Europe either before or after it was gripped by a united faith, but a theologically and geographically defined entity unique in history. This was a community diverse in languages, physical types, local customs, and many other respects, but united in belief, moral code, scholarship (and scholarly language), and certain larger customs that affected the well-being of Christendom as a whole, among these the mode of waging war. We may speak of an ideological unity within this community; indeed, the ideological unity made community possible. When just war doctrine developed within this community it incorporated the values resident in the common ideology—not *Christian* ideology, which incorporated Byzantines and Copts as well as Catholics, but the ideology of *Christendom*, defined by geography as well as theology. Because it developed out of the community as a whole and not merely out of Christian theology or canon law this war doctrine had a relevance and an adequacy, both moral and political, that it could not have had otherwise. There is considerable evidence that so long as Christendom existed the developing just war doctrine did effectively limit conflicts within the community. Here the ideological nature of just war doctrine worked in its favor. The doctrine expressed "community law": the law of coordination.

Sociologists of law define three basic types of law, including the law of coordination.[4] Its most salient characteristic is given by the nature of community itself: a grouping of people sharing a common end who are internally driven to seek that end and help one another toward it. The family, especially in its classic Greek and Roman forms, is an example of a nearly pure type of community; the medieval monastery is another. In a community the coordination of effort is the primary function of law. Since everyone agrees as to the ends to be sought, law coordinates their activities so as to maximize attainment of those ends. Such was the character of just war doctrine in medieval Christendom.

At the opposite extreme from community law, the law of coordination, stands the law of power, or "society law." The outstanding characteristic of this kind of law

[4] For fuller discussion of this perspective see Georg Schwarzenberger, *The Frontiers of International Law* (London: Stevens and Sons, 1962), chap. i, "The Three Types of Law."

13

is the use of power—usually military force—by an elite to subjugate the other members of the society and ensure their cooperation in producing the ends the elite wish for themselves. Here "might makes right" is a truism. A slave-holding aristocracy offers one example of this; Hitler's "New Order" offers another.

Between the two extremes set by the law of coordination and the law of power stands a third kind of law, that of *hybrid groups*: the law of reciprocity. Consider the case of a society in which there exist two groups (two communities) of equal strength. Neither has the power to impose its will upon the other. Within each group community law has sway, but in the society as a whole the law of reciprocity must obtain. A state of affairs in which equilibrium of power makes it possible for power to be ignored is the most outstanding characteristic of hybrid groups. The United States, with all its pluralism, is one example of hybrid grouping, and much of American law is reciprocal in nature, with everyone reasonably content so long as he believes he has received at least as much as he has given. The international order, so far as it *is* an order, is a second example of hybrid grouping in the contemporary world.

What is the place of ideology *vis-à-vis* each of these types of human grouping, with their corresponding kinds of law? In communities the same ideology is shared by all; this is what is meant by the individuals' wanting the same ends. In "societies" the ideology of the elite is imposed upon those subjugated. Thus Hitler imposed Nazism upon the conquered peoples of Europe, whatever their own preferences might have been. In hybrid groups a plurality of ideologies coexist—one for each community participating in the grouping. Here

14

the imposition of ideology is frustrated by the balance of power, and community ideology tends, in the group as a whole, to be subordinated to those needs and desires amenable to satisfaction by bartering. Of course, even in hybrid groups some ends are held in common (hence the grouping); these tend to produce a group ideology in which elements of particular community ideologies may find expression. Robert Bellah's construction of a "Civil Religion in America" (*Daedalus*, 96, no. 1 [Winter 1967], pp. 1–21) out of elements of patriotism fused with beliefs drawn from the three major United States religions gives an illustration of this phenomenon.

Returning to the question of just war doctrine as a manifestation of community law in Christendom, the peculiarly ideological component of this doctrine is its notion of justice, conditioned both by theological and philosophical heritage and by common custom. The destruction of classic just war doctrine amounted to the removal of this component of justice, with no satisfactory replacement. This destruction or dissolution of the classic doctrine moved through two stages, which also marked the transformation of the community that was Christendom into the hybrid grouping that is international society today.

The first stage was the destruction of the theological, and to a lesser extent the philosophical, unity that characterized Christendom. I have already alluded to the immediate results of this: the creation of two communities, Catholic and Protestant, with conflicting belief structures that were taken by the two sides to be mutually exclusive. The concept of just cause was rent asunder. On the one side it was converted into a con-

15

cept of holy cause (as one Puritan preacher put it, "Whose cause is juster than God's?"),[5] and on the other an attempt was launched to find a more inclusive concept of justice (the natural) than could be any longer provided by religion. In the hands of the holy warriors just war doctrine became an ideological weapon to stir up the faithful against the infidel; and in the hands of the secularizers the *jus ad bellum* of the classic doctrine became increasingly formalized, and the doctrine as a whole increasingly reduced to a set of limits on the pursuit of wars between sovereign states. The ideological character of classic just war doctrine shifted when the unified community that had produced it split into two mutually antipathetic groupings—each with, nevertheless, the same heritage in the war doctrine of Christendom. With this split Europe ceased to be a community and became a hybrid grouping, and the law of coordination had to give way to the law of reciprocity. Secular naturalist international lawyers effected this change (though their way was prepared by the last great theologians of the Spanish school), and they did so by eliminating the concept of just cause, which had so easily been made to serve narrow, partisan ends. The *jus ad bellum* conceived as *compétence de guerre* was one result; by this doctrine each sovereign had the right and authority to decide when just cause for war existed, and the search for a definition of justice by an overarching ideology was in effect abandoned within international law. Another result of this transformation has been balance-of-power politics: reciprocity in action.

[5] William Gouge, *Gods Three Arrowes, III. The Churches Conquest over the Sword* (London: George Miller for Edward Brewster, 1631), p. 215.

16

The second stage in the destruction of classic just war doctrine was reached when the geographical boundaries of Christendom ceased to contain all relevant international intercourse. I wish here to skip over a stage in which the law of power obtained in European relations with the rest of the world and consider what has happened as a result of the end of the colonial era. This stage has been mainly completed in the twentieth century. The standard of "civilization" that had replaced the old notion of justice in traditionalist international law as the chief limiting principle on war ceased to obtain when "uncivilized" nations (many of them former colonies) were admitted to full status in the world. But because many of the new nations were, in regard to power, hopelessly inferior to the "great powers" of Europe, the United States, Japan, and China the doctrine of *compétence de guerre* no longer sufficed as an adequate statement of reciprocal law on war. This doctrine had, after all, made colonialism possible by permitting strong states to subjugate weak ones in the name of overriding national interest or an ostensibly altruistic desire to "civilize" the conquered peoples. The twentieth century has seen a cumulative attempt to restate the law of reciprocity on the right of resort to war, moving through the League of Nations Covenant, the Kellogg-Briand Pact, and the United Nations Charter, with mutual nonaggression treaties and mutual defense alliances springing up in train. As I have elsewhere argued, the result has been generally to outlaw all first use of force while normally allowing second use as defensive *per se*.[6] This avoids the ideological pitfalls

[6] See my article, "Toward Reconstructing the *Jus ad Bellum*," *The Monist*, 57, no. 4 (Oct. 1973).

17

presented by classic just war doctrine, but the question needs to be seriously asked whether this new doctrine is any longer a *just* war doctrine.[7]

The two main factors I have cited in the dissolution of classic just war doctrine do not, of course, comprise everything that can be said about the matter, even when the scope is restricted to that which has to do with ideology. Though these are the principal contributing factors, there is one other that is important enough to deserve mention here, though I do not treat it elsewhere in this book. That is the use made of even the secularized doctrine of *bellum justum* by sovereigns

[7] A certain irony exists with regard to Christian doctrine on war during the period of dissolution of classic just war doctrine. There is no discrete and recognizable Protestant war doctrine, except among the pacifist sects, after the post-Reformation wars have ended. In a masterpiece of syncretism, the state—and through the state, international law—is allowed to speak for Protestant Christians. On the other hand, by holding themselves aloof from the modern secular state Roman Catholic theorists maintained a just war doctrine fundamentally the same as that of the sixteenth-century Neo-Scholastics until the twentieth century. But in a hybrid-group world this latter doctrine was but the expression of one particularist ideology on how to conduct war and was not recognized as binding by members of other ideological faiths. When, in the late nineteenth and early twentieth centuries, the Roman church began to come out of its cloisters and meet the world, it began to abandon its classic war doctrine and to speak the language of international law—which, perhaps, it took to be the "community law" of the world. The teaching of recent popes makes this abundantly clear. But the world is not now a community, and it is the law of reciprocity that holds foremost place in international law, not the law of coordination. Thus the Roman church made a fundamental mistake, weakening her war doctrine to conform to international law. For fuller treatment of this see the article cited in note 6, above.

18

in the sixteenth and seventeenth centuries. I speak here of the doctrine as shaped by such theologians as Victoria and Suarez and such pioneering secular theorists as Gentili and Grotius. In spite of their different value bases these four men and others like them agree more than they differ in the just war doctrine that they proclaim, and in their writings the serious attempt to make war conformable to standards of justice, defined from nature by reason, reaches a zenith. But I wish to point to the way in which sovereigns applied the theories, not the theories themselves. The ideology of the just war was twisted out of shape to serve princes' own ends. Three cases will illustrate this point.

First, both Gentili and Grotius transform the medieval requirement of proper authority to wage war into the requirement that war be a public contest, solemnly declared. So long as this provision aided sovereigns to suppress civil wars and engage in wars of conquest against lesser lords—that is, until the absolutist state was firmly established—princes and their spokesmen could conveniently cite this requirement to "prove" the justice of this particular use of force, the injustice of that. With the absolutist state firmly established, however, other considerations of interest led sovereigns to ignore the need for a solemn declaration of war, and this provision lapsed into general disuse.

To take a second case: Victoria expressly forbids a state to make war to spread religion. Yet the Spanish colonizers of the New World evaded this point by looking to another one also in Victoria's theory: the insistence that peaceful missionaries and traders be given free passage wherever they went. If the Indians resisted the missionaries and the traders (and the soldiers who accompanied them), force could justly be used—not, indeed, to spread religion, but rather to insure the right of free passage.

A third case is provided by the use of the idea of simultaneous ostensible justice. Beginning with Victoria the possibility is admitted that, while one side may *actually* be in the right in a given war, the other side may, because of invincible ignorance, *believe* itself to be in the right also. In such cases, according to Victoria, only God can know which side really is fighting justly. The belligerents should be chastened by the realization that both sides might seem to be equally in the right, and so be especially scrupulous in observing the *jus in bello*, the rules of war. The doctrine of simultaneous ostensible justice was thus intended to affect the *conduct* of war, not the *resort* to war. The same is true in Grotius, who takes this idea over from Victoria and further develops it. But princes who had read Machiavelli as well as Victoria and Grotius applied the doctrine another way. *Any* resort to war could be justified, they argued, because invincible ignorance clouded men's minds and made all concerned in a dispute think they were right. The doctrine of *compétence de guerre* followed from such reasoning.

These three cases illustrate that sovereigns were all too ready to use just war doctrine to provide an ideology to excuse their resorting to war, not, as was intended, as a set of moral limits on the use of war. Thus what had been a universal ideology was transmuted into a particularistic one—an ideology in the negative sense, because it excuses *my* actions while condemning *yours*. Perhaps the most important phenomenon exhibiting this tendency was the hundred years of war for religion that followed the Reformation, including the German civil wars between Catholic and Protestant

20

leagues, the French Wars of Religion, the first English Civil War (the Puritan Revolution), and the Thirty Years' War. In all these conflicts holy war advocates on either side sprayed streams of invective against their opponents as being in league with the Devil—and therefore without a just cause for fighting—and cast themselves as children of righteousness who implicitly possessed true justice in all that they did. Here, in a curious twist, the doctrine of invincible ignorance is made to prove the *injustice* of the other side (the ignorant, anti-Christ side) and becomes an apologetic for subjecting it to the harshest possible prosecution of war—the exact opposite of the way the idea of simultaneous ostensible justice was originally intended. Here just war doctrine, a body of thought fundamentally aimed at limiting war, is turned into an apology for unlimited ideological war (in the narrow, negative sense of ideology).

In Chapter I of this book the theological and secular bodies of doctrine that come together to form classic just war doctrine are treated. On the theological side are two separate bodies of writing: canon law and scholastic theology. On the secular side two traditions, with corresponding documents, are also found: the chivalric code, representing the knightly class, and the *jus gentium*, mainly a lawyer's statement in its more precise forms. Each of these four lines of thought is ideological in a narrow, exclusivist sense as well as in a broad, inclusive sense. Narrowly conceived, each of these traditions represents the position of one class of medieval men: canon lawyers, theologians, soldiers, secular lawyers. But broadly they all belong within the unity that

21

was Christendom. All four developing traditions have to be considered to fill out the entire picture, and when a final unified just war doctrine is achieved toward the end of the Middle Ages it contains elements of all four streams of thought, joined together in what is perhaps the best possible expression, for the case of war, of the synthesis of many factors that forms the ideology of medieval Christendom.

In Chapter II the exaltation of a purely theological component of the *jus ad bellum*, war for the cause of religion, is explored in the particular case of England, which was a kind of crucible for developing holy war thought. With the ideological unity of Christendom gone, the ideological character of the just war doctrine bequeathed by Christendom was transformed into an exclusivist expression of the rights of the righteous against all other men. Though mainly concerned with analyzing the development of English holy war doctrine as the result of social as well as theological influences, this chapter also explores the concept of holy warfare to illuminate the problem of limiting ideological war today.

Chapters III and IV examine the developments in just war doctrine most clearly opposed to holy war, that is, those developments that begin by seeking a more inclusive value base for the concept of justice in war and end by attempting to root out the ideological (that is, the value) component of just war doctrine altogether. Chapter III is devoted to analysis of five theorists who remain close to the classic doctrine and form a bridge between it and the overtly secular war doctrine of modern international law. The five are the Spanish theologians Franciscus de Victoria and Francisco Suarez, mentioned above; the English Puritan theologian William Ames; and two other contemporary Englishmen who were not theologians: Matthew Sutcliffe, an adviser to Queen Elizabeth I, and William Fulbecke, a jurist. In the writings of these men three common characteristics emerge: the value base informing the concept of justice in regard to war is clearly naturalist, though here natural law continues ultimately to draw its sanction from God; the *jus ad bellum* is modified so as definitely to exclude the possibility of just war for religion; and the balance between *jus ad bellum* and *jus in bello* within the overall doctrine begins to be tipped in favor of restraining wars already begun, away from limiting the resort to war. A fourth characteristic, found in Victoria, Suarez, and Fulbecke, is the admission of the possibility of simultaneous ostensible justice, which contributes to the undermining of the classic *jus ad bellum* in these authors and their disciples. In the works of these five theorists taken together, a modern just war doctrine, derived from the classical but distinct from it, emerges.

In Chapter IV three secular figures are treated who are clearly well over the bridge from the Middle Ages into the modern period. Hugo Grotius, John Locke, and Emmerich de Vattel take modern just war doctrine, which in the form treated in Chapter III still retains a medieval flavor and most of the medieval form, and change it into a doctrine based entirely in nature and agreements among men, with no backwards glances to search out divine approval. In the theories of these men the doctrine is set forth as universal and non-ideological, with what remains of the idea of justice traced to man's nature and his positive decisions. Here the *jus ad bellum* becomes essentially formalized, but especially in Locke and Vattel the *jus in bello* is expanded con-

23

siderably beyond the limits reached either in the classic doctrine or in the modern doctrine treated in Chapter III. This continues the trend toward unbalancing the two components of the overall doctrine and sets the pattern for further development of war doctrine in international law during the eighteenth and nineteenth centuries.

In schematic form the plan of the central chapters of this book is as follows:

Chapter I:

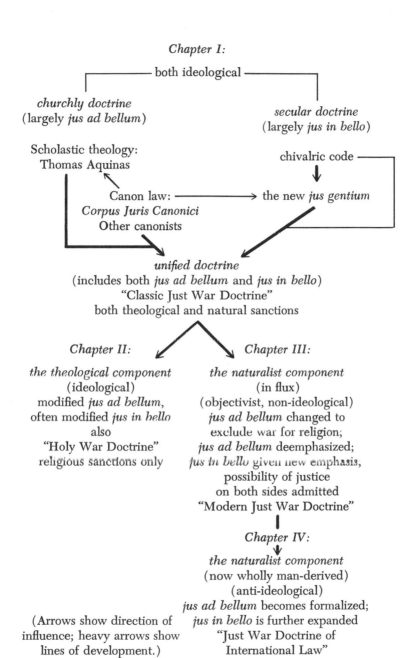

both ideological

churchly doctrine
(largely *jus ad bellum*)

secular doctrine
(largely *jus in bello*)

Scholastic theology:
Thomas Aquinas

chivalric code

Canon law: ──────────→ the new *jus gentium*
Corpus Juris Canonici
Other canonists

unified doctrine
(includes both *jus ad bellum* and *jus in bello*)
"Classic Just War Doctrine"
both theological and natural sanctions

Chapter II:

the theological component
(ideological)
modified *jus ad bellum*,
often modified *jus in bello*
also
"Holy War Doctrine"
religious sanctions only

Chapter III:

the naturalist component
(in flux)
(objectivist, non-ideological)
jus ad bellum changed to
exclude war for religion;
jus ad bellum deemphasized;
jus in bello given new emphasis,
possibility of justice
on both sides admitted
"Modern Just War Doctrine"

Chapter IV:

the naturalist component
(now wholly man-derived)
(anti-ideological)
jus ad bellum becomes formalized;

(Arrows show direction of
influence; heavy arrows show
lines of development.)

jus in bello is further expanded
"Just War Doctrine of
International Law"

25

CHAPTER I

War for Church and for Prince
in Late Medieval Just War Theory

AMONG those who have written on just war doctrine from the standpoint of theological ethics during the past twenty years a consensus exists as to what that doctrine, in its classic form, provides. There is first a *jus ad bellum*, composed of the requirements that a just war be one fought on proper authority, for a just cause, and with a right intent, with the further requisite that the end of such war always be peace. Second in order, though not in importance, comes the *jus in bello*, which is alternately described as providing for noncombatant immunity and weapons restrictions, or as exhausting itself in the principles of proportionality (of use of force) and discrimination (in choice of those against whom force is used). To conceive the classic doctrine in this way is essentially correct, but it is *incorrect* to find the doctrine in this highly complete and sophisticated form in the writings of such seminal figures in the history of just war thought as Augustine or Thomas Aquinas. Nor is it correct to claim for the classic doctrine a parentage wholly Christian, if by "Christian" is meant "biblical," "theological," or "canonical." What recent writers rightly identify as just war doctrine in its fullest form was the result of forces from outside as well as within the walls of the medieval church; classic just war doctrine was a product of secular and religious forces together, and in this fact lay its function and its strength: its relevance for both personal and political morality during the age in which it reached full expression.

The two mistakes made by recent commentators (to regard the just war doctrine of the high Middle Ages and earlier as having the unity and sophistication of the classic doctrine they define, and to regard this classic doctrine as being uniquely the product of Christian thought) have their antecedents in the writings of earlier students of the just war. One of these, the French commentator Alfred Vanderpol, deserves a close look because of the degree of influence that his writings have had.

In one of his two major treatments of Catholic doctrine on war, *La Doctrine scholastique du droit de guerre*, Vanderpol summarizes as follows the history of this doctrine prior to the modern period:

> . . . [T]here was professed in the Catholic Church, up until the seventeenth century, a doctrine of war of which St. Augustine had posed the principles, of which St. Thomas had given the formulas, and which can be summarized as follows:
>
> The prince (or the people) that declares war acts as a magistrate under the jurisdiction of which a foreign nation falls, *ratione delicti*, by reason of a very grave fault, a crime which it has committed and for which it has not wished to make reparation. As the depository of authority to punish a guilty subject, he pronounces the sentence and acts to execute it in virtue of the right of punishment that he holds from God: "Minister enim Dei est, vindex in iram ei qui malum agit." ["He is the minister of God to execute his vengeance against him who does evil."][1]

[1] Alfred Vanderpol, *La Doctrine scholastique du droit de*

This passage makes clear two elements that Vanderpol thinks essential to the presence of a just war: an actual fault on one side, coupled with a pure act of vindicative justice in God's stead on the other.[2] It is further Vanderpol's position that just war doctrine, as professed in the Catholic Church, is essentially all of one piece throughout the Middle Ages, until it begins to deteriorate in the early modern period, when part of the very core of the church's doctrine is excised by theorists outside the church who are not concerned with preserving continuity of doctrine.[3]

Vanderpol's interpretation must be taken with utmost seriousness, because his is almost the only detailed study of scholastic just war doctrine available. But close attention should be paid to what he does *not* say as well as to what he says, for the limits of his reach have made for a narrow, if orthodox, content in what he has grasped. In the passage cited, as well as throughout his book, he is concerned only with Catholic doctrine; more

---

guerre (Paris: A. Pedone, 1919), p. 250. In citations from this book I translate from the French text.

The quotation beginning "Minister enim dei . . ." is from Romans 13:4 and is given by Thomas Aquinas (from whom Vanderpol here draws it) in the *Summa Theologica*, II/II, Quest. XL, Art. 1.

[2] Vanderpool continues, in the section to which the passage cited above forms the introduction, with a damning criticism of those theorists of the just war who, in the sixteenth and seventeenth centuries and after, had ceased to require that there be fault on one side, justice on the other, and had introduced the pernicious notion that in a just war, justice might sometimes be recognized as existing on both sides. This possibility of simultaneous ostensible justice will be treated in connection with those who develop it in Chaps. III and IV below.

[3] Vanderpol, *La Doctrine scholastique*, pp. 260–75.

specifically, he focuses principally upon the scholastic theologians, involving earlier Christian thinkers only because they provide the raw materials that the scholastics refine, and prolonging his investigation into the sixteenth and seventeenth centuries only because the theorists he treats there (Victoria and Suarez chief among them) were themselves engaged in trying to recast scholastic modes of thought for their own time. By limiting himself so narrowly to scholastic war doctrine Vanderpol completely misses the impact of the other medieval streams of tradition that ultimately join with that of the church to produce just war doctrine in its most classic and complete form. Likewise the narrowness of his scope has made it necessary for him to speak as if there were but one just war doctrine in the period he treats, when in fact there were three positions, all related, that went by the name "just war doctrine": the modern doctrine, which began to be formulated in the sixteenth and seventeenth centuries and which developed into secular international law; the post-Reformation holy war doctrine, in which the term "just war" is applied to what Roland Bainton and others have described under the term "crusade"; and the parent of them both, medieval just war doctrine, itself the product of two distinct traditions on war that can broadly be labeled as "churchly" and "secular." Far from being all of a piece, medieval just war doctrine was gradually constituted over several centuries out of elements of great diversity; moreover, this doctrine itself, on the surface so complete, contained the seeds of the bifurcation that was to take place in the sixteenth and seventeenth centuries.

At the center of both the constitution and the dissolution of classic just war doctrine lies the concept that

Vanderpol named as fundamental to the idea of just war: that there must be a fault on one side and, on the other, an act of vindicative justice undertaken by prince or people acting as "minister of God." This concept has a twentieth-century parallel in the idea that war should not be fought unless it is in defense of one's own national rights or those of another nation threatened by the unjust aggression of a predatory power. It is possibly not entirely by accident that Vanderpol, a Frenchman, published his interpretation of medieval just war doctrine in 1919, when French feeling still ran high against Germany for having begun the war only recently and at great cost concluded. The idea that fault should be followed by vindicative justice was certainly characteristic of French opinion at the close of World War I. Likewise, there is no doubt that this was *one* of the central characteristics of the just war doctrine of the medieval church. But was it *the* central concept in the definition of that doctrine? The evidence suggests not. Rather, another idea must be placed alongside this one for a true appreciation of what constituted the specifically Christian medieval war doctrine. This second concept is that justice, being informed by charity, expresses itself through mercy and not only through vindication. The just war doctrine of the medieval church not only declared that princes and people may take up the cause of justice as ministers of God; it also set certain limits on what they might do in that capacity.

Three points should be kept in mind about this second characteristic of the churchly just war doctrine in the Middle Ages. First, it provided an internal constraint within the doctrine itself on the theme of vindicative justice. Left to itself this latter idea could easily become a basis for a kind of obligatory war: wherever there is fault, the godly prince should go to war to avenge it. This is precisely what happened in the birth of holy war doctrine in the aftermath of the Reformation. There the themes of fault and vindicative justice were magnified, as the next chapter shows, by being made, respectively, into offense against God and defense of true religion. In the most radical holy war proponents, the theme of limitation was almost completely lost. On the other hand, in conscious reaction against holy war tendencies, the modern just war doctrine, which began to develop in the sixteenth century, played down the themes of fault and vindicative justice and stressed the limits of what can be done in a just cause. Because of these opposing tendencies the bifurcation of classic just war doctrine in the sixteenth and seventeenth centuries can be conceived as the pulling apart of two characteristics—vindication and mercy—that had existed together in medieval just war doctrine.

Without the characteristic of restraint in the church's war doctrine there would have been no room for the development of a *jus in bello*. Zeal for vindication of harm done implies strict prosecution of the war effort and does not appear to leave room for truces, humane treatment of prisoners of war, and general respect for the rights and persons of noncombatants. It is in fact the case, as I show below, that the churchly just war doctrine as it began to take definite shape in the thirteenth century had only a rudimentary and truncated *jus in bello*. Nevertheless, the germ was there, and it requires us to recognize that this doctrine was concerned with limiting the ravages of war as well as with compelling godly folk into battle against wrongdoers.

Third, and related to the second point, the theme of

31

restraint in the churchly doctrine provides the vehicle by which secular medieval just war doctrine is amalgamated with churchly to produce, by the end of the Middle Ages, a just war doctrine in what we today would identify as classic form: a complete and sophisticated doctrine including both *jus ad bellum* and *jus in bello*, as described above. This is not to say there has been no further development since the classic doctrine took shape but rather that before the end of the Middle Ages there was no unified and complete doctrine dealing with both the resort to war and the waging of war. The *jus in bello* especially was to see further change in the direction of fullness and explicitness; by the sixteenth century it comprised only a fairly inclusive list of noncombatants and certain other limits on what could be done even to the combatants against whom one was fighting. The three main requirements in the *jus ad bellum* of the classic doctrine come straight from Augustine via Thomas Aquinas and the code of canon law; the two parts of the *jus in bello*, conversely, come mainly from the residue of the chivalric code and developing European custom on the fighting of wars expressed in a growing body of "common law" or *jus gentium*. (I set aside "common law" to avoid confusion with the English common law tradition; the medieval *jus gentium* is not related to the English common law, but in both the way they came into being—out of common custom—and in their functioning the two traditions are similar.)

One of the chief aims of this present chapter is to investigate this amalgamation of churchly and secular war doctrines into one. Were the former conceived as having only to do with the vindication of fault, it might still be possible to show that the churchly and secular

32

traditions *did* come together, but it would be impossible
to understand much of *how* or *why* the amalgamation
took place. The limitation of cruelty against enemies,
which is characteristic of Christian thought on war as
far back as Augustine, provides, in the late Middle
Ages, the opening into which the two secular traditions
on *jus in bello* fed, thereby expanding and making more
explicit the church's doctrine, with the result that by
the end of the Middle Ages there is a single, unified just
war doctrine.

In this chapter three separate but related investiga-
tions are conducted. There is first the matter of how
the church's own particular just war doctrine came into
being in the high Middle Ages, what it provided, and
what diversity characterized the interpretation of its
provisions. Second, the same questions must be asked
regarding the development of secular just war doctrine.
And third, the points of contact between the churchly
and secular doctrines must be explored to explain why
and how the doctrines came together. There is finally
a fourth question, to which all three of these investiga-
tions help to contribute the answer: why did classic just
war doctrine come to pieces shortly after it reached full
expression, and why did the split, when it occurred,
come on grounds of religion (or particularist ideology)
versus the natural (or a generalist ideology)?

A THIRTEENTH-CENTURY BENCHMARK

Christian just war doctrine goes back at least to
Augustine; since Augustine takes pains to base his own
position in evidence drawn from the Bible, it can be
argued that there is a just war doctrine in the Bible.
But it is not until recently that the attempt has been

made to base a full-blown doctrine on his writings. For the theorists of the early modern period it was not the teaching of the Bishop of Hippo that was most important, but rather the just war doctrine as they inherited it, in its classic form, shaped over all the intervening centuries since Augustine's time, but particularly given form by canonists and theologians in the immediately preceding three hundred years. Though no one in that period used the term, it is meaningful to think of a "benchmark" in just war doctrine placed to mark the thirteenth century, when serious attention began to be given to the problem of consolidating and clarifying the church's position on war. Composing this benchmark are two documents, the *Corpus Juris Canonici* or code of canon law, which included the *Decretals* of Gratian and further compilations of law done under Pope Gregory IX; and the *Summa Theologica* of Thomas Aquinas. Of these it is undoubtedly Thomas' *Summa* that has best stood the test of time, for he is still cited as a source for twentieth-century just war doctrine. But in the immediate medieval context it is Gratian's *Decretals* that stand out; here Augustine's teaching is repeated in capsule form—even Aquinas may have drawn his understanding of Augustine's teaching from Gratian. Here also is the first successful attempt at a consolidated canon law. Both the theological and the legal streams of thought on justice in war in the late Middle Ages seem ultimately to flow from Gratian.

The *Corpus Juris Canonici* and the *Summa Theologica* together form a benchmark in the church's war doctrine because of their position in regard both to what had gone before and to what was to come. These documents drew (as best as possible) into coherence the fragments of war doctrine taught in the name of the church during the disorder of the previous centuries, all the way back to Augustine at the beginning of the fifth century. From these documents flow two intermingled but fundamentally distinct streams of thought that shape just war doctrine during the rest of the Middle Ages: scholastic theology and canon law. This latter stream, indeed, is also intermingled with that of secular law, an increasingly important factor in the late fourteenth century and throughout the fifteenth century. But for now our concern must be focused on the development of the church's doctrine only. Even among Protestant theorists in the immediate post-Reformation era, such as those treated in the next two chapters, this doctrine, the common possession of Christendom for centuries, provided the basis of thought about justice in war—though the diversity and ambiguity of the doctrine meant that they would almost of necessity develop it in many different directions. Medieval thinking, moreover, conditioned both the English Protestants who formulated a theory of holy war and the Spanish Catholics who initiated the move to modern international law. It is the development of just war doctrine by medieval canonists and theologians, then, that must be investigated at this point.

GRATIAN'S *Decretals* AND THE DEFINITION OF THE RIGHT TO MAKE WAR

The just war doctrine of Augustine, though clearly not this alone, is at the bottom of the teaching on war in Gratian's *Decretals*, published around 1148 and a primary source for both kinds of ecclesiastical commentators on just war. Much of Gratian's treatment of the question of war has to do with whether any participation in war at all is allowable for Christians. His evidence on this need not concern us here, however, for it is after he concludes that war is not absolutely and always ruled out for Christians that just war doctrine properly begins. The only wars in which Christians may legitimately take part are those that are "just." From the first, then, Gratian's concern is whether or not a Christian may go to war, and the idea of "just war" in his understanding is a set of limits on Christian resort to war. To put this another way, from the very first Gratian's just war doctrine is a doctrine of the *jus ad bellum*.

Two definitions of just war are provided in the *Decretals*: one from Isidore of Seville (560?–636), and through him from Cicero, the other from Augustine. Isidore's is given first: "A war is just when, by a formal declaration, it is waged in order to regain what has been stolen or to repel the attack of enemies."[4] Augustine's differs slightly: "Those wars are customarily called just which have for their end the revenging of injuries, when it is necessary by war to constrain a city or a nation which has not wished to punish an evil action committed by its citizens or to restore that which has been taken unjustly."[5] Aside from these definitions, perhaps the most significant statement is one from Augustine, which Gratian quotes: "The enemies of the Church are to be coerced even by war."[6] Gratian thus allows war for the sake of religion, though his emphasis is upon

[4] *Corpus Juris Canonici*, Pars Prior, *Decretum Magistri Gratiani*, Pars Secunda, Causa xxiii, Quaest. ii, Can. i. Hereafter cited as CJC, *Decretum*.

[5] *Ibid.*, Can. ii.

[6] *Ibid.*, Quaest. viii, Can. xlviii.

defense. Justification for war, according to the *Decretals*, definitely requires a fault on one side, plus action to correct the ensuing injustice on the other side—elements that Vanderpol later cites as essentially characteristic of just war doctrine. But the Pauline phrase terming the wronged party God's "minister" is lacking in this context, as is the concept of war commanded by God. An element is added to the Augustinian formulation by Isidore's requirement of a "formal declaration"; though not a part of Augustine's war doctrine, this stipulation became one of the necessities for a just war in medieval thought.[7]

The distance set, in the *Decretals*, between war in defense of religion and offensive war against those not of the Christian faith is indicated by Gratian's comment after the passage from Augustine on coercion of the Church's enemies. If just war is that which is declared by an edict and which has the purpose of revenging injuries, Gratian questions, then how can the children of Israel be said to have undertaken just wars? Many of their wars, after all, have the flavor of aggression. Gratian's answer also comes from Augustine: when the Israelites fought the Amorites, it was because the latter had refused the Israelites the right to pass in peace through their territories. Denial of the right of free, peaceful passage is thus defined as the wrong needing to be revenged, and the case fits under the definition at which Gratian has already arrived. Since there is in

[7] By its attribution to Roman origin (Augustine's debt to Cicero having been forgotten) this requirement also points to that hidden reality in the formulation of canon law: the influence of the study of Roman law that was carried on throughout the period being considered here.

37

Augustine clear support for the justice of wars commanded by God,[8] and since examples of this sort of war are plentiful in the Old Testament—and are likely the cause of Gratian's question—the clear inference is that Gratian does not wish to put forward a concept of commanded offensive holy war to add to the ranks of the faithful or to eradicate any and all who are not Christians for the "crime" of disbelief.

A just war according to the *Decretals* thus must be declared beforehand and must be fought to redress a wrong already performed, including wrongs done to the church. The emphasis is on defense of one's own rights, implying assertion of them if denied; protection of one's own property, implying regaining it or just payment for it if unlawfully seized; and punishment for wrongdoing if the other nation has taken no steps to exact punishment of its own. The issues of commanded war and offensive war are left aside, with the exception that some of the above types of wars might seem to be offensive if the antecedent wrong done were not known to the observer. Actual wrong must have been done, moreover; it is not enough for evil *intentions* to have existed. Preemptive redress of wrongs or punishment of sin (which to the medieval mind was an instance of redress of wrongs) is ruled out. The significance of this point will become obvious in the next chapter, where the serious advocation of the use of war to forestall evil intent is discussed.

THOMAS AQUINAS' THREE CONDITIONS FOR JUST WAR

Gratian's *Decretals* can fairly be said not to have stated briefly the essence of the idea of just war, owing

---

[8] As, for example, in *Contra Faustum*, xxii, 74–79.

to the method he used of laying excerpts from diverse sources side by side out of context. Thomas in the *Summa Theologica* reduced the concept to three conditions: that a just war be fought on right authority, have a just cause, and be waged with a right intention. As with the definitions provided in the *Decretals*, the three requirements pertain directly to the question of whether to begin war, the *jus ad bellum*. This is, during most of the history of just war doctrine from Augustine to the sixteenth century, the principal—almost the only—content of Christian just war doctrine. Though in Thomas the beginnings of a *jus in bello* can be discerned, his stress on the question of the right to make war deserves first attention.

In explaining his three conditions for just war, Thomas makes explicit the two ideas that for Vanderpol sum up the essence of the church's doctrine: just cause, says Thomas, exists where there is some fault to be punished, and right authority exists where the magistrate is acting (in Paul's words) as "minister of God to execute his vengeance against the evildoer."[9] This puts the *jus ad bellum* succinctly, but it does not go further, into the question of what is right in war. For Thomas, in just war there has to be a just side, the vindicator, fighting against an unjust side, which has perpetrated some evil. Besides setting a clear distinction between the two sides, this also implies the condition that just war shall always be of a defensive or retributive nature only. This does not, however, mean that the just side must always wait until the wrongdoer strikes the first blow in arms, for certain kinds of offense are not military in nature but still justify use of force to set things

[9] See note 1, above.

right. Heresy offers an example of an offense against God deserving to be avenged, no matter how unwarlike the heretics are; similarly, failure to pay a just debt is an offense that a creditor may take up arms to correct. Thomas does not rule out first use of force in his doctrine, either implicitly or explicitly; yet his *jus ad bellum* retains the fundamental character of requiring that some fault exist that in justice must be corrected.

Right intention, the third of Thomas' three requirements for just war, is especially interesting because, while it pertains in context to the question of a *jus ad bellum*, it also contains implications important for the development of a *jus in bello*. Thomas draws the concept of right intention from Augustine (the source also of Thomas' other two primary conditions), and he defines the concept in Augustine's own words: "The desire for harming, the cruelty of avenging, an unruly and implacable animosity, the rage of rebellion, the lust of domination and the like—these are the things which are to be blamed in war."[10] The passage from Augustine from which this is taken is cited by Gratian at greater length than by Thomas; in the *Decretals* the context is the general question of whether Christians may without sin participate in war, and right intention pertains directly to the idea of a *jus ad bellum*.[11] Another passage from Augustine repeated by both Thomas and Gratian gives insight into the reason it is good to have right intention in warfare: "For peace is not sought in order to the kindling of war, but war is waged in order that peace may be obtained. Therefore, even in waging war, cherish the spirit of the peacemaker, that, by conquering those whom you attack, you may lead them

[10] Aquinas, *Summa Theologica*, ii/ii, Quest. xl, Art. 1.
[11] CJC, *Decretum*, Quaest. i, Can. iv.

40

back to the advantages of peace. . . ."[12] Here the requirement of right intention is justified first on purely pragmatic grounds, and once again the most direct reference appears to be to the question of whether in the first place to make war. But it is "the spirit of the peacemaker," however, that epitomizes right intention, and this relates closely to the negative definition given by the listing of attitudes to be avoided (or in Augustine's more pointed words, "to be blamed") in fighting a just war. Both characterizations connect this third of Thomas' requirements directly to the Christian idea of charity, which is itself expressed through peacemaking and which wishes good, not harm, to the neighbor. The requirement of right intention in just war doctrine is thus the requirement that Christians who make war do so with love for their enemies, to correct their errors and not simply to hurt them or dominate them. This realization opens Thomas' doctrine in the direction of a *jus in bello*, and even though he does not develop his thought further in this direction, later writers do so. The concept of right intention can properly be conceived as an important source for the *jus in bello* in Christian theological thought.

Implications for Christian conduct during war can certainly be drawn from elsewhere—for example, from what Thomas Aquinas or Augustine has to say about self-defense—but just war doctrine, that doctrine which has specifically to do with war, is until the end of the Middle Ages focused foremost on the question of whether Christians may ever in the first place take up arms, not on the related question of what they may

[12] Aquinas, *Summa Theologica*, II/II, Quest. XL, Art. 1; CJC, *Decretum*, Quaest. I, Can. III; Augustine, *Ad Bonifacium*, CLXXXIX.

legitimately do after war is begun. Today the situation is reversed: principal focus, in both Christian thought and international law, is upon what weapons may be used and against whom they may legitimately be employed. Where it is assumed that modern war necessarily implies thermonuclear war, the moral prohibition of such weapons is read back to prohibit war itself. Thus today the tendency is to derive a *jus ad bellum* (or rather, as Paul Ramsey has called it, a *jus contra bellum*) from *jus in bello* limitations.[13] In the Middle Ages exactly the opposite obtains. For this reason it is important that a germinal idea of *jus in bello* can be found in Thomas' three conditions for a just war, but at the same time too much must not be made of it for Thomas' own time.

Is there anything in Thomas' discussion of the question of war that goes directly to the matter of limiting prosecution of war and that the late Middle Ages understood as such? The answer is a very small yes. Both Thomas and, before him, Gratian prohibit warfare to certain churchmen.[14] Later in this chapter we shall see how the list of those to be spared the ravages of war was expanded to include women, children, the aged and infirm, and others. But in Thomas and Gratian only clerics and bishops are mentioned. They may not make war, and so they may not have war made against them. Though this clearly pertains directly to the *jus in bello*, I suggest that it is only in retrospect that it can be viewed as the beginnings of a doctrine of noncombatant immunity. As M. H. Keen has pointed out (in *The Laws*

[13] Paul Ramsey, *The Just War: Force and Political Responsibility* (New York: Charles Scribner's Sons, 1968), p. 190.

[14] Aquinas, *Summa Theologica*, ii/ii, Quest. xl, Art. 2; CJC, *Decretum*, Quaest. viii, Cans. iv, xix.

of War in the Late Middle Ages), medieval warfare was conducted among members of a warrior class and those who directly supported them;[15] clerics and bishops— those specifically mentioned by Gratian and Thomas— belonged to a different class. Keen traces the rise of noncombatant immunity to two principal factors: a kind of snobbishness among knights, which led them to want to fight only against those of their class; and a residue of the older sense of what is chivalrous, which made at least some knights conceive themselves as protectors of the innocent. Though Keen means to speak only of the secular law of arms, both of the factors that he mentions are to be found also in ecclesiastical writers, and the prohibition of war to clerics and bishops appears a likely manifestation of the class distinction. War is not the business of priests; therefore they should be spared its inconveniences. But this is a derivation from the form used by Thomas and Gratian, who simply prohibit the named churchmen from entering into war in any fashion. The implication runs two ways: they should be spared, because it is not their business to fight; yet if they do fight, they have no claim to immunity because they are being faithless to their calling.

NONCOMBATANT IMMUNITY IN *De Treuga et Pace*

For a clear statement of the idea of noncombatant immunity in the high Middle Ages one must look elsewhere than to Gratian or Thomas Aquinas. The earliest authoritative pronouncement appears to be that of the treatise *De Treuga et Pace* (*Of Truces and Peace*)

[15] M. H. Keen, *The Laws of War in the Late Middle Ages* (London: Routledge & Kegan Paul; Toronto: University of Toronto Press, 1965), pp. 2–3, 189–90.

added to the growing body of canon law under Pope Gregory IX in the thirteenth century. Here eight classes of persons are listed as having full security against the ravages of war: clerics (presumably including bishops, though they are not specifically named), monks, friars, other religious, pilgrims, travelers, merchants, and peasants cultivating the soil (as opposed to peasants in the army of their feudal lord, who were combatants). Animals and goods belonging to the innocent are also protected here, as well as the land upon which the peasants work.[16] The paragraph giving this listing is short, and no reasons are appended for the inclusion of the named classes or the non-inclusion of others. Reasons may, however, be inferred. First, such protection of the innocent obviously embodies the proscription of various kinds of wrong intention defined in the Augustinian tradition, which stands behind all medieval thought on war. Charity demands that the innocent be spared. But perhaps more directly to the point is the canon of Gratian, also repeated by Thomas, forbidding clerics to bear arms, which the listing in *De Treuga et Pace* presupposes and expands upon.[17] This strongly suggests that it was the business or function—Keen might add, the class—of clerics that gave them immunity in war, as we have already seen. Such reasoning— since they are forbidden to take up arms, they are not able to participate in war, and so they are not to be treated as combatants—would encompass as well all the other classes of persons listed in this thirteenth-century collection of canons. It might even be correct to read this listing as naming *only* those noncombatants

16 CJC, Pars Secunda, *Decretalium*, Lib. I, Tit. xxxiv.
17 CJC, *Decretum*, Causa xxiii, Quaest. i, also Quaest. viii, Cans. iv, xix.

44

who were granted immunity because of their function in society. If so, this would explain why those other types of noncombatants—women, the aged, children, the sick and the blind—are omitted in this particular listing. They might have been understood as noncombatants because of "negative" function—inability to bear arms. But it might also be the case that they did not have to be specifically named because they were protected by the residue of the chivalric code: the traditional ideals of the knightly profession.[18]

It is interesting as well as significant for the history of the portion of the just war doctrine concerning *jus in bello* that only a century after the *Corpus Juris Canonici* was composed Honoré Bonet's *L'Arbre des battailes* gives a list of noncombatants that draws together both these types, those excused because it was not their business to make war, and those excused because they were too weak to bear arms.[19] Bonet's mem-

---

[18] This is the suggestion offered by Keen and by J. R. Hale in the *New Cambridge Modern History* (Cambridge: Cambridge University Press, 1957), I, 291.

[19] J. H. Stevenson, ed., *Gilbert of the Haye's Prose Manuscript*, vol. I: *The Buke of the Law of Armys or Buke of Batallis* (Edinburgh and London: William Blackwood and Sons, 1901), p. 236. This version of Bonet's *L'Arbre des battailes* is in a Scottish translation dating from the fifteenth century, and in spite of the difficulty sometimes encountered in making sense of the translation, I cite this version here because of its historic importance as the vehicle by which Bonet's treatise entered the English-speaking world. A far better and more accessible English version, with critical apparatus, is now available in G. W. Coopland, ed. and trans., *The Tree of Battles of Honoré Bonet* (Cambridge, Mass.: Harvard University Press, 1949). I have used this translation as a check on the content of the Scottish version in my treatment of Bonet's position in this book, and most of the remainder of my citations from Bonet are from Coopland's translation.

bership in the Benedictine order together with the fact that his book was one of the most widely read and influential chivalric treatises during the period of the Hundred Years' War are circumstances that provide clues about the dual nature of the sources of the *jus in bello*. His contribution is discussed at more length later in this chapter.

SUMMATION AND ASSESSMENT

In a certain sense it might be legitimate to stop investigation at this point, with the authoritative compilation of canon law under Gregory IX and with the publication of Thomas Aquinas' *Summa Theologica*. To do so would, however, be to place on these works the emphasis that at the beginning of this section was denied to Augustine. The just war doctrine was modified later in the Middle Ages by ecclesiastical and secular canonists, theologians, and others who wrote in the chivalric tradition, and it is this modified doctrine that is the classic just war doctrine that conditioned the thinking of the sixteenth- and seventeenth-century theorists discussed in the following chapters. Yet it is also true that by the end of the thirteenth century a benchmark had been erected that defined how far subsequent writers might go without leaving just war doctrine behind.

Engraved on this benchmark are three requirements for a just war—right authority, just cause, and right intention—along with definitions of a certain precision including limiting factors: a just war must be declared in advance; it must be undertaken for the end of peace. Implied throughout is the condition that just war be of a defensive or retributive nature only; offensive wars and wars of preemptive retribution are not permitted.

46

Just war may be undertaken for the sake of the church, though churchmen are forbidden to take up arms or declare war. Left ambiguous is the question whether what is to be defended is Christian religion or the Roman church, along with its intricate interrelationship with the state in the medieval world. (In such a world this ambiguity is absolutely necessary, as no medieval man could easily have distinguished between church and religion; the difficulty arises in a later age, three centuries after, when a large portion of the population of Europe could no longer *fail* to make that distinction.) Nearly all that is found on this benchmark pertains to the *jus ad bellum*; only the beginnings can be found of limits on what can be done *in bello*: notably the characterization of right intention, which applies to both parts of just war doctrine, and the truncated list of noncombatants given in *De Treuga et Pace*. And even this list derives from the prohibition of war to clerics and bishops, which in turn follows from their function as understood in the light of the *jus ad bellum*: they do not have the authority to wage war, as their business is not temporal.

Implicit in this thirteenth century benchmark definition of just war doctrine is Vanderpol's dichotomy between the unjust side, which has committed some fault, and the just side, which acts to repair the injury and to punish the guilty. The statement of Paul regarding the magistrate occurs explicitly in Thomas: "He is the minister of God to execute his vengeance against the evildoer." The question of God's role in just war is thus raised, but the development of that role follows a peculiar pattern. Rather than exalting the presence of God behind the magistrate (Vanderpol's interpretation), tradition after the thirteenth century increasingly sepa-

47

rates God and the magistrate as motive forces for just warfare. On the one hand the magistrate's authority is gradually elevated as one who acts in God's stead (even if with his blessing; the implication is that God chooses magistrates and then leaves them to do their duty as they see it); on the other hand, the effective presence of God is gradually restricted to the portion of the doctrine that relates to war for church or religion—matters in which, one might almost say, God has a direct concern. These twin developments, growing increasingly throughout the late Middle Ages, are the roots of the bifurcated just war doctrine of the early modern era— a result that no man of the thirteenth century, including the benchmark figures, would have anticipated.

JUST WAR DOCTRINE IN CANON LAW:
WAR FOR THE FAITH AS JUST CAUSE

To pursue the lines of development of separate elements in the just war idea requires temporarily putting aside the concept of a benchmark on which is engraved the essence of just war as defined in the *Corpus Juris Canonici* and the *Summa Theologica* of Thomas Aquinas. It is only in retrospect that such a benchmark takes on a definite outline. To the men of the Middle Ages the documents composing it were, though authoritative, not the final authority that later ages have often taken them to be. In the growth of canon law on war there existed a particularly vigorous ferment; in this period canon law influenced both the theologians and the secular science of law.

The canonist Raymond of Penafort (ca. 1175–1275), an older contemporary of Thomas Aquinas, is a significant figure for the developments we are investigating.[20] Raymond lists five conditions, all of which are necessary, for a war to be just:

1. The person making war must be a layman and not an ecclesiastic, since the latter may not draw blood.
2. The object must be to recover goods or defend one's country.
3. The cause must be to obtain peace after all other means have failed.
4. The intention must include no hatred, vengefulness, nor cupidity and must be to obtain justice.
5. The authority may come from the church, when the war is of the faith, but otherwise it proceeds from the order of the prince.

Raymond also mentions "the case in which war can be fought without a special order from prince or Church; this is when it is a matter of defending one's goods or his country. It is a principle of law that one may repulse force by force, on the condition that it be done after [force has first been applied] and with moderation."[21]

Most portentous is the fifth condition enumerated above, which a later age was to read rather differently than Raymond likely intended. One must, according to the second condition, fight in defense or to recover goods. But in the fifth condition the Christian faith becomes one of the goods, the only one for which the church can give authority to fight. The crusading route is thus opened. Neatly separated off are all other sorts

[20] Vanderpool, *La Doctrine scholastique*, pp. 55–56, 63.

[21] *Summ. Ram.*, Lib. II, tit. v., 12; Vanderpol, *La Doctrine scholastique*, p. 55.

of goods and the authority to fight for them, which must come from the prince except when the case is that of repelling force by force, which is permitted by "a principle of law." Here Raymond does not speak of church law but of ancient Roman law, the common law of the empire, with its elements of natural law and *jus gentium*.

A similar position, except for the possibility of the church's declaring war, is taken by Raymond's contemporary Hostiensis (ca. 1200–1271), who ascribes this position, moreover, to "several authors."[22] Vanderpol comments that it "scarcely differs" from the formulation of Thomas, and then ascribes the same conditions to eight other medieval writers.[23] Later he lists eleven causes that, according to Guerrero (one of the eight writers Vanderpol cites) may justify war:

1. If a province blasphemes God by the cult of idols;
2. If it departs from the worship of God;
3. If it ceases to be faithful to its temporal lord;
4. If it rebels against its sovereign;
5. If it defends evildoers;
6. If it is guilty of an injury to a prince or his legate.
7. A prince may make war to free himself from an unjust tribute;
8. In order to deliver a friendly or allied nation from its enemies;
9. To recover the freedom of its subjects;

[22] *Summa Aurea*, lib. i, rub. 34; Vanderpol, *La Doctrine scholastique*, p. 56.

[23] Vanderpol, *La Doctrine scholastique*, pp. 55–56. The eight named include Sylvester, Monaldus, Carletti, Guerrero, Bellini, and Lupus.

10. To recover the integrity of his kingdom.
11. A war against one who aids an enemy may also be declared a strong duty.[24]

Here religious and secular reasons for war are lumped together in a *mélange* with no apparent rationale except Guerrero's perception of the tradition. For our purposes the first two, which define possible causes for war for religion more precisely than does Raymond's phrase "for the faith," are the most interesting. Guerrero's listing comes from a period when support for the crusades as wars for religion figures in many works on war. This reasoning was never admitted officially by the church; the papally accepted apologetic for the crusades always strongly emphasized the temporal injustices perpetrated by the infidels upon nations and pilgrims who just happened to be Christian. However, the possibility of war for religious reasons only was supported by numerous theologians and canonists,[25] and—the most important consideration—though war against infidels *qua* infidels was condemned by Innocent IV, the continuing discussion of the meaning of war for the sake of the faith kept such ideas in the just war tradition as it developed throughout the late Middle Ages.

The piety of the would-be crusader leads always to the same conclusion: if worldly goods can be defended by war, if the unlawful seizure of such goods can justify rising in arms to take them back, meanwhile punishing the thief so that he will not give trouble again, then things that pertain to God, which partake of something

---

[24] Guerrero, *De Bello Justo et Injusto*; Vanderpol, *La Doctrine scholastique*, p. 63.

[25] Vanderpol admits this; see p. 57.

beyond this world, must all the more zealously be defended against attack and seizure by the unfaithful; the truly faithful must be all the more ready to take arms to restore the church where it has been suppressed or cast out. The infidel who has done evil against God's honor, moreover, deserves a much harsher punishment than someone who has insulted a mere earthly prince or one of his ambassadors. The crusader's piety follows naturally from a world view that includes two spheres, nature and *super*nature (literally, that which is *above* nature), the latter being God's immediate dwelling-place. That peculiar logic of the Middle Ages whereby injury to a more important person was conceived as more serious than similar injury to someone less important is also a supporting factor here: God being the highest person of all, injury to him was conceived to be far worse than insult to even the highest temporal lord. The Pope, as God's viceroy on earth, was a natural beneficiary of such reasoning.[26]

In the sixteenth century a widespread movement began to take shape composed of men who advocated forcible unification of Christendom by war. These men naturally turned to the branch of just war tradition that embodied most clearly the piety of the crusader. They looked particularly to the benchmark documents, the *Corpus Juris Canonici* and the *Summa* of Thomas Aquinas, to search out those elements most favorable

[26] The classic example of such logic is Anselm's theory of the atonement. Since God is an infinite person, the insult sin has given him is an infinite insult requiring an infinite expiation. Man, being finite, cannot provide this. So Christ, God become man, is necessary both to supply an infinite expiation (through his godly nature) and to insure that it is a human expiation (through his human nature).

to their ends. Thus Augustine's statement that "that kind of war is undoubtedly just which God himself ordains," tucked in by Aquinas at the end of a paragraph that begins with quite another thought—namely, that some fault has to be present to justify a war— becomes the first, and not the last, thing to be said.[27] This development is already present in the list of causes for war given by Guerrero, as it is in another medieval list, this one classifying wars into types, ascribed by Vanderpol to "some canonists." Here the type of just war named first is that against infidels.[28]

THE GROWING INFLUENCE OF *Jus Gentium*: WAR FOR PRINCE AS JUST CAUSE

THE SEPARATION OF WAR FOR CHURCH AND WAR FOR PRINCE

A similar movement to the above, though one that proceeded from a fundamentally different set of concerns, resulted in the exaltation of the secular prince's authority to judge and punish wrongdoers in the temporal sphere. When, in the sixteenth and seventeenth centuries, Cajetan (1469–1534) and Bellarmine (1542–1621) set down what they considered to be just war doctrine, it was the prince's execution of vindicative justice that stood at the center of their arguments. This line of reasoning, as we shall see below in Chapter III, is carried furthest by the Spanish theologians Victoria and Suarez. Cajetan's statement is a strong assertion of princely authority: "[The prince] can *of his own authority* use the sword against internal or external disturbers

---

[27] Aquinas, *Summa Theologica*, II/II, Quest. XL, Art. 1.
[28] Vanderpool, *La Doctrine scholastique*, p. 57.

of order; [his] reason is the perfection of the State. It would not in fact be a perfect state which did not have the power to punish, according to justice, those who trouble its tranquility, whether they are citizens or foreigners."[29]

A more moderate position, though it proceeds from the same presupposition, is that of Bellarmine: "[The prince] may not punish all the faults of other men, but only those that prejudice the people who submit to him; for he is not the ordinary judge of these others, [but] he is the defender of his own, and because of the necessity of defending them, he becomes, up to the point of using the sword to punish those who have violated the rights of his subjects, the judge [of the former]."[30]

What happens to the just war doctrine after the thirteenth century that allows Cajetan and Bellarmine to make such statements? They are not drawing upon the same background as Thomas Aquinas, a theorist upon whom both later writers greatly depend. Between Aquinas' age and their own a kind of continental drift sundered the idea of natural law from the idea that God is the author of all law. Not only the pious but all Christians still, in the sixteenth and seventeenth centuries, accepted the *concept* of an overarching sphere of divine law within which the natural law, including as one of its elements the *jus gentium*, is enclosed. But the significant fact about the early modern age is that *for practical purposes* this did not matter. The sense of the immediacy of God's presence behind the prince,

[29] Cajetan (Thomas de Vio), *Summula*, v, Bellum; Vanderpol, *La Doctrine scholastique*, pp. 65–66. Emphasis added.

[30] Robert Bellarmine, *De Controv. Christ. Fidei*, ii, cont. ii, lib. iii, *de laicis*, cap. xv; Vanderpol, p. 61.

present in medieval theology and canon law, had by this time eroded to the point that "the divine right of kings" could be taken to mean that a king could do whatever he pleased. The focus in this later age was not upon the donor of authority but upon the person who wields it, who *has* it; the right to use the sword against malefactors, wrote Cajetan, is the prince's *own* right. During the three centuries separating Aquinas from his sixteenth- and seventeenth-century commentators a new emphasis on the natural law fundamentally altered the meaning of the very language of just war doctrine, making it not primarily an assertion of God's judgment against evildoers but a description of the right of princes to retaliate against troublers of their own domains. In this manner just war doctrine was pulled in a way opposite from that of the crusade theme, with the result that in the sixteenth century these two disparate elements broke apart into just war doctrines of quite different thrusts.

Two factors contributing to the secularization of the power of the prince need to be pointed up here: the idea that the prince's power comes from below, that is from the community, tended to supplant the idea that it comes from above, that is from God; and the waxing concept of *jus gentium* as the body of custom and agreements among peoples modified the notion that *jus gentium* is dictated from above as part of a hierarchy of laws within divine law. The first factor allowed the prince to act in the name of his people rather than in the name of God, and the second allowed wrong to be defined not in terms of an absolute morality but in terms of violation of customary or mutually agreed upon rights.

The political community of the sixteenth century, Bernice Hamilton writes,

> . . . was not created by a pact of men, but was a natural association, exercising its inherent right to govern itself. This God-given right or authority could not fail to be exercised; *i.e.* a community without a government was as inconceivable to [the] Spaniards as to Hobbes. Even in a state of nature those with ability to rule would be sure to organize the rest; but in a political community that power resided in the community, which might exercise its own authority, or transfer it to designated rulers.[31]

As Hamilton earlier makes clear,[32] this idea of community had been building throughout the later Middle Ages. The old Roman doctrine of the sovereignty of the people was being asserted: the idea that, since the perfection of the state is the aggregate of that of its citizens (since the goal of the state is the common welfare) and since each person has the right to seek his own good, the political community has that right as well and on a grander scale. It was this idea, which comes ultimately from Aristotle but is found more immediately in Cicero's *Republic*, which in the late Middle Ages prepared the way for such opposite political doctrines as democracy and divine right of kings.

As the late medieval canonists knew, Isidore of Seville had grounded his position on just war in Cicero and in Roman law in general. "Just war must be waged on valid authority, either to regain things lost or to drive

[31] Bernice Hamilton, *Political Thought in Sixteenth-Century Spain* (Oxford: Clarendon Press, 1963), p. 160.

[32] *Ibid.*, see chap. II.

out invaders," Isidore declared in his *Etymologiae*; and again, "Unjust war is that which results from passion, not from lawful reason."[33] Knowledge of justice is the result of the work of reason, and it is thus reason that drives the prince to war in a just cause. This gave a natural-law coloration to the definition of just war that Isidore contributed to the code of canon law. It was to Isidore that later canonists looked when they began to move in the direction of an authority for war that derives from the natural order. The antecedent of the positions of Bellarmine and Cajetan was not only Thomas Aquinas but also this of Isidore regarding the judge: "The judge is so called because he speaks *the people's law*, or because he pronounces on the law. To pronounce on the law is to judge with justice; for there is no judge if he does not have justice in him."[34]

After Isidore, these ideas about the rational—or natural—source of the judgment exercised in a just war still had to be decisively separated from the theological affirmation that all reason comes from God. The move in this direction was a practical and not a theoretical one. Thus the canonist John of Legnano (d. 1383), whose influence lies heavy on Honoré Bonet, divided just wars into four types. His "Roman war" is that waged by the church's authority against infidels. This type stands apart. The other three types of war are clearly justified without any reference (even implicit) beyond the natural order: war levied on the authority of a prince, war levied on the authority of a judge (some objective third party; this assumes that the party

[33] Isidore, *Etymologiae*, xviii, i.
[34] CJC, *Decretum, Pars Secunda*, Causa xxiii, Quaest. ii, Can. i.

in the wrong has refused to accept the outcome of arbitration), and "necessary war" waged in self-defense.[35] John's is not a unique case. Vanderpol reproduces a seven-type classification of just wars, which he abstracts from a number of canonists, in which the first named is "Roman war" as defined by John, and the remainder are all clearly based in natural reason.[36] Leaving aside the case of self-defense, which as "necessary war" is not even included among types of just wars by many writers on the subject, the wars levied by higher authority for redress of grievance or punishment of evildoers fall into the category that the canonist Bartolus of Sassoferato (d. 1387) called "public war, which is declared by the Roman people, or by the emperor on whom their entire authority has been conferred."[37]

In fact, then, at the end of the Middle Ages just wars may generally be described in three distinct ways:

1. War against enemies of the church—blasphemers, idolaters, heretics, those who would set up a new cult in place of that of Rome. Such war is waged on the authority of the church.
2. Wars of self-defense, which are generally regarded as involuntary and waged on one's own authority. One who comes across a thief in the act of stealing one's goods needs no outside authority to oppose him, with force if need be; the same is true of the prince who acts in behalf of his people to oppose outsiders who are caught in the act of enslaving them or stealing their goods or their lands.

[35] John of Legnano, *Tractatus*, cap. 76; Keen, *Laws of War*, p. 67.

[36] Vanderpol, *La Doctrine scholastique*, p. 57.

[37] Bartolus, *Comment in Dig. Nov.*, xlix, Tit. 15, lib. 24; Keen, *Laws of War*, p. 70.

3. Wars of restitution or punishment. These are declared and waged by the prince on his own authority and volition after he discerns, with the help of his counselors, that an injustice has been done to him or his people and has not been set right. Many divisions of this general type of just war are offered by different commentators.

On the practical level God's honor was deemed to be at stake only in the first of these cases. In the second case it is one's own honor, while in the third case it is the prince's, both of which derive from nature and the *jus gentium*. A similar division may be noted with respect to authority: in the first case it is God's, manifested through the command of his earthly viceroy, the Pope; in the second it is one's own authority, known by reason to be naturally vested in every man; in the third case it is this natural authority of each man aggregated together in the political community and wielded by the prince, who exercises it according to his own lights and those of his counselors. The stage was thus set for the bifurcation of just war doctrine in the sixteenth and seventeenth centuries, when religious war and political war go their separate ways.

THE NEW SHAPE OF THE *Jus Gentium*

The canonists were aided in their separation of war for church from war for prince by a growing secularization in the concept of *jus gentium* as a body of custom and agreements among peoples and their sovereign princes. In ancient Roman law the latter had been one of two thematic ideas together defining *jus gentium*, the other being the concept of a positive law deducible by reason from the general principles of the natural law.

This double parentage led to a certain ambiguity in application. When the medieval canonists began to try to make of the *jus gentium* something far more specific than any Roman had ever attempted, they were often puzzled by the confluence of two quite different concepts. As Keen puts it, their problem was that "their antique authorities seemed sometimes to speak of the *jus gentium* as a law common to all men, and sometimes merely as the common law of the Roman empire."[38] Their method of resolving the problem was characteristic. Since the Romans had not pursued to any distance the rational deduction of the *jus gentium* from the natural law, the medieval writers had recourse to the Old Testament, using the Israelites' laws and practices as their guides to the content of the *jus gentium*. The laws and practices of Israel, ordained in some immediate manner by God, became an authoritative statement for medieval lawyers of the *jus gentium*, a concept inherited from Rome. After all, it was argued, God, who had made the natural law, is all reason. How could he give the people of Israel a law that does not correspond in reason to the natural order of things? This reasoning gave to medieval law a certain minimal body of propositions within the *jus gentium*.[39]

These minimal propositions were not, however, the entire content of this body of law. The task of how to conceive the common-law element became most interesting to the canonists of the late Middle Ages, and in this area the drift toward a modern conception of international law took place. To specify the common-law element within the *jus gentium* meant not only historical research to see what ancient Roman writers had

[38] Keen, *Laws of War*, p.12.
[39] *Cf. ibid.*, pp. 12–13.

included in this category but also the task of studying contemporary European society to discern and specify the customary, though unwritten, behavioral links that bound together the people of Christendom; it meant looking beyond the Christian world to study behavior in other cultures; and, perhaps most importantly for the present purpose, it meant studying written treaties and agreements made among men. It is specifically this study of treaties among sovereign lords that has developed into international law as it is known today.

As the common-law side of the *jus gentium* increased in importance, so also did the concept of the prince as deriving his power and authority from the community: from the community of all Christian Europe, which appointed princes to keep the general peace and to serve as checks on those who would endanger that peace, and from the national community, which empowered and authorized its prince to maintain the customary laws and practices of his people against disturbers of the peace both external and internal. Agreements between two princes, in such a system, had more weight when they were founded in both the general and the particular bodies of custom and practice, and less weight when they were founded in one of these alone. Thus during the Middle Ages, to give an example, the common custom of all Europe protected heralds in time of war, no matter which side was theirs, since they belonged to an international fraternity and not one narrowly identified with the interests of this or that prince or people.[40]

---

[40] In the Hundred Years' War, Keen writes, "They all, English and French alike, belonged to one single and special fellowship, with its own ranks and ceremonies. Throughout the battle of Agincourt the heralds of both sides stood together on a hill, away from the fighting in which their order had no part; and

With truces and safe-conducts, to move down the scale in military customs and practices, matters became progressively less absolute. The latter, often written by inferior commanders, were valid only within territories controlled by the writer, though in some cases agreements could be made to honor safe-conducts reciprocally. More interesting for present purposes are truces, since a truce between two princes had, in the late Middle Ages, rather far-reaching effects, amounting to complete suspension of the state of war.[41] This contrasts sharply with practice during the Thirty Years' War, when truces were generally regarded as worthwhile only to the extent that one's own side could increase its advantage (or lessen its disadvantage) by what it could accomplish during the truce. Modern practice has proven to be a continuation of this latter trend.

The difference between the fourteenth and the seventeenth centuries (or between the Hundred Years' War and the Thirty Years' War) regarding practices during a truce illustrates in a particular way the general point made above: as *jus gentium* became more a matter of agreements according to custom, the power and authority of the prince tended to be enhanced. Another factor operates as well: the breakdown of the unity of Europe as a result of the Reformation, so that European customary law ceased to have as much weight as that derived from the particular community at whose head was the prince. In 1340, at the start of the Hundred Years' War, both sides could still reasonably believe in war as a corporate trial by battle, in which God would grant

afterwards it was Mountjoy King of Arms of France who told Henry V that the day was acknowledged his." *Ibid.*, p. 195.
[41] *Ibid.*, p. 207.

victory to the side with justice behind its claims. Thus a truce was like an adjournment in a court of law; when it ended, the suits were to take up where they had been left when the truce began. But two centuries later, beginning with the Dutch War for Independence and continuing as common practice during the Thirty Years' War of the next century was the utilization of truces for tactical purposes, to gain something that could not be gained while fighting continued. Though men of this latter time continued to use language presenting war as an international trial by combat, hidden beneath their words was a fundamental shift in expectations as regards justice. In this latter age justice was always assumed to lie with one's own side. A medieval man, though believing earnestly in the rightness of the cause for which he fought, could at the end of the battle accept the outcome as just, so long as the battle had been conducted fairly by all on both sides. But the post-Reformation man was incapable of believing in such an operation of justice; if his side lost, it was manifestly because the other side had acted unfairly and treacherously, or because God wished to keep his chosen ones from pride by delaying for a time their ultimate victory.[12] Since the cause of one's own community was

[12] *Cf.*, for example, the "Letter, Lately Written by a Spanishe Gentleman, to his Friend in England" (n.p., 1589), which chides the English for giving glory to God for their victory over the Armada. "God hathe punished us for our sinnes which are great, but the punishment of our faultes, excuseth not your far greater offenses . . ." (p. 4). The Spanish *people*, the author continues, have suffered great injuries at the hands of the English *Queen*, who is guilty of "dooble dealings" (pp. 10–11). This juxtaposition of people and government allows him to argue that no animosity to the English *people* was intended by the Armada. Finally, the author accuses the English government of following

universally deemed to be the highest, the prince at the head of that community, who had responsibility for securing its rights in the international arena, had to be given all the power of the community in order to act effectively.

The definition of *jus gentium* in terms of community practice, together with the assumption to one's own community of the only truly *right* practice, is thus at the beginning of the movement toward the doctrine that "might makes right." In the period treated by this book, the thirteenth through the seventeenth centuries, this doctrine does not clearly emerge. Significantly, during the cooling-off period after the horrors of the Thirty Years' War, the period when modern international law began to take shape, the great theorists laid considerable emphasis on the development of *jus gentium* as a truly universally binding law. It is the work of Grotius and his successors, then, to provide after the holocaust of a hundred years of religious war that shattered the unity of Europe a new basis for conceiving that unity, along with a new basis in custom and mutual self-interest for mitigating the harshness of war.

THE ABSORPTION OF CHIVALRIC IDEAS ON WAR

Great changes overtook the chivalric ideal on warfare during the later Middle Ages. It could almost be

---

the principles of Machiavelli—in the context of the times, one of the worst things he could say. Numerous examples of this manner of sentiment can be found from all the nations of Europe during the late sixteenth and early seventeenth centuries. The irony is that *all* rulers were at this time beginning to act according to the principles of Machiavelli, and ceasing to act according to those that had moved princes during the Middle Ages.

said that the chivalric ideal itself perished that day at Agincourt when so many of the most noble representatives of French knighthood were cut down by English yeomen armed with longbows. But such a description, while dramatic, would not, of course, be true. It requires only a casual reading of the history of the Hundred Years' War to realize that by its end the method of warfare and the chivalric ideal were both much changed from what they had been during the very earliest campaigns. But while the chivalric ideal was profoundly affected during this period (the Hundred Years' War ended in 1453), it did not utterly perish. The high ideals persisted, but their increasing irrelevance to actual conduct, whether in war or out, became more and more apparent until they could be held up to ridicule in *Don Quixote*, written only a century and a half after the last blows were struck in the Hundred Years' War—the climax of warfare on the chivalric model. The chivalric law of arms remained, but it was extended, simplified, and regularized to apply to the common soldier as well as the knight; either abstracted from the chivalric ideals and made into a strictly military code of discipline, or else joined to even higher ideals and made a part of the church's developing just war doctrine. Nor is this latter dichotomy a complete one, since the military and ecclesiastical laws of arms continued to influence each other reciprocally well on into the modern period.

Our concern here is limited to the relation between the decaying chivalric code and the just war doctrine, which was growing toward its classic form. The waning moral influence of the chivalric ideals and the growth of military codes of discipline out of the knightly laws of arms are outside the scope of this book. I

65

shall further narrow our focus by discussing but two authors who both illustrate and accomplish in their writings the intermingling of churchly and chivalric themes. These two authors point to all the principal factors contributing to this joining of doctrines, and their books moreover provide two examples of how the intermingling occurred. Honoré Bonet wrote as a cleric knowledgeable in canon and civil law, especially the work of John of Legnano, and thus he represents the thinking that was joining canon law and *jus gentium.* Yet he obviously also knew a great deal about chivalry, and this affected the readership of his book profoundly; as Keen puts it, "[f]or heralds and soldiers, [his] book was a work on chivalry."[43] Christine de Pisan wrote explicitly for the soldier class, where she had a wide readership and influence; yet she drew copiously from Bonet, taking over many of his theoretical formulations and canons hardly changed. These two authors are thus on a boundary: one leans toward the churchly body of law on war, and the other leans toward the chivalric. Yet together they illustrate and exemplify the interweaving of the two sources into what by the beginning of the sixteenth century was a single body of doctrine on war.

HONORÉ BONET's *L'Arbre des battailes* (*Tree of Battles*)

Bonet, writing between 1382 and 1387, reflects the completion of the *Corpus Juris Canonici* as well as a climactic era in the growth of the chivalric code—the beginning of the Hundred Years' War. His *L'Arbre des battailes* is divided into four parts. The first sets the problem of war within an apocalyptic framework; the

---

[43] Keen, *Laws of War*, p. 21.

second traces the history of warfare; the third relates the practice of war to virtue; and the fourth, the lengthiest part, takes up numerous cases (132 in all) of the sort normally encountered in medieval war. It is the last two parts of this book, and above all the fourth part, that are most instructive in the matter of the relation between the teaching of the church and the chivalric law of arms in the fourteenth century.

At the beginning of part IV Bonet inquires, "From what law does war come?" and answers: from divine law, from the *jus gentium*, and from the law of nature. He expends by far the greatest effort on explaining the allowance of war according to divine law. In this regard Bonet makes two chief points: that war is a positive good, and that God has ordained war. He is thus notably more disposed toward accepting war as an institution than the benchmark authors of the century before had been. For Gratian and Thomas, as well as for Augustine, war is something to be excused, something to be permitted Christians only as a final resort, when all peaceful means have failed. But for Bonet (and this is one sign of his proximity to chivalric patterns of thought) war is much more; it is one of the good things God has given to his creatures.

Some argue, Bonet allows, that war is an evil thing because so much evil is done in battle. Yet this argument, he retorts, is spurious: "I tell you that this argument is worthless; for the truth is that war is not an evil thing, but is good and virtuous; for war, by its very nature, seeks nothing other than to set wrong right, and to turn dissension to peace, in accordance with Scripture."[44] Bonet explores the background that makes

[44] Bonet, *L'Arbre des battailes* (Coopland, ed.), p. 125.

possible this assertion of the virtue embodied in war in part II, and what he says there is a song of praise for chivalry. What is to be admired in the true soldier is the union of strength of soul and strength of body, both of which come from God. Yet the former strength is of much more value, since (as in the case of David and Goliath) God gives "victory to him who is His friend, though he be very feeble in body, rather than to him who is very strong in war yet is without love to God."[45] In this Bonet did not simply express the piety of one who had taken holy orders; the oath of knighthood too was holy, and the importance of ordering one's service toward godliness was deep in the chivalric tradition. Bonet underscores this: a man who is truly strong is marked by two signs. "As a first sign you will observe that he finds all his pleasure and all his delight in being in arms, and in just wars, and in defending all just causes, quarrels, and holy arguments. The second sign is that such a man, seeing the great ill and peril incurred in such a war, or maintaining such quarrel, should yet not quit his purpose, nor for any labour or travail fear to expose his body to fair fight and strict justice."[46]

Within this context the meaning of Bonet's statement that war is virtuous "in accordance with Scripture" takes on a special coloration. Not only is the virtue of justice associated with war, but also that of strength, the particular virtue of the soldier, a fortitude of both soul and body. When knights act virtuously—that is, according to the traditions embodied in their profession—war itself is virtuous and good. Bonet makes this point negatively: "And if in war many evil things are done, they never come from the nature of war, but

---

[45] *Ibid.*, p. 120.   [46] *Ibid.*

from false usage; as when a man-at-arms takes a woman and does her shame and injury, or sets fire to a church [notably he does not say "a knight"; men-at-arms did not take the knightly oath]. Such cases do not come from the nature of war itself but from false usage of battle and war, and from war wrongly conducted."[47] The position is clear: war in itself is good; it only needs to be conducted by virtuous men.

Bonet's argument for the goodness of war, it must be remembered, was meant to refute the argument that war is evil because of the bad that accompanies it. If war is good, moreover, "we must understand that [it] comes from God, and not merely that he permits war, but that He has ordained it."[48] God's aim in ordaining war is the right government of a world infected by sin; it is his means, through virtuous servants, "to wrest peace, tranquillity, and reasonableness, from him who refuses to acknowledge his wrongdoing."[49]

In his derivation of war from divine law, then, Bonet relies on two traditions: that of medieval chivalry, expressed through praise of the virtuousness of war and the truly strong knight, and that of the church, expressed in his statement of the end of war as justice and the punishment of sinners. Here the two traditions join in mutual support, and it is clear that to Bonet's mind they are saying much the same thing.

But in his detailed treatment of the practical matters of war—who may be held prisoner, who is obliged to do military service for another, who is not required to go to war, the rights of those in a battle zone, the pay (or lack of it) soldiers should receive, and many other such

[47] *Ibid.*, p. 125.   [48] *Ibid.*

[49] *Ibid. Cf.* the language of Thomas Aquinas, borrowed from Paul: "to execute [God's] wrath against the evildoer."

topics—Bonet enters a field scrupulously avoided by medieval theologians and treated very carelessly by many canonists. It is not, in fact, until the sixteenth and seventeenth centuries that such problems are set within a comprehensive theological framework; Suarez stands out for his concern with the day-to-day conduct of war in his disputation *On Charity*, vii.[50] But in his own time Bonet's interest in such matters is, for a churchman, a lonely one.

The closest point of contact between the ecclesiastical and chivalric traditions in regard to the practical conduct of war comes in connection with the question of noncombatant immunity. It has already been noted that Bonet expands the list of noncombatants given in *De Treuga et Pace*; we have now to discover whom Bonet would include and what reasoning stands behind his list. Most instructive in this latter regard is his question "Whether in time of war the ass should have the privilege of the ox," which was by canon law to be spared. "[W]e must consider for what reason oxen are privileged. Certainly the only reason is that they plough the soil. Now if a poor man has only one ox, and harnesses his ass along with the ox to plough, then, considering that the ass does the work of an ox, I hold that he must have the same privilege, for he takes an ox's place."[51]

One can only guess whether Bonet meant this passage to sound as humorous as it does. What is clear is that he is utterly serious about this line of reasoning: in

[50] James Brown Scott, ed., *The Classics of International Law, Selections from Three Works of Francisco Suarez, S.J.*, vol. 2 (Oxford: Clarendon Press; London: Humphrey Milford, 1944), pp. 836–54. Cited hereafter as Suarez.

[51] Bonet, *L'Arbre des battailes* (Coopland, ed.), p. 188.

countries where men use mules or horses instead of oxen, they take on noncombatant status; a similar extension, moreover, includes certain people. An ox-driver's helper has the same immunity as the ox-driver; a farmer's wife carrying food to him in the field has the same immunity he possesses; and in general anyone who carries on business analogous to the peaceful plowing that an ox does ought to be granted immunity from war. Bonet calls upon all kings to enforce this immunity, for not to do so removes from war its virtue: "[T]hat way of warfare [which has no strict observance of noncombatant immunity] does not follow the ordinances of worthy chivalry or the ancient custom of noble warriors who upheld justice, the widow, the orphan and the poor."[52] Thus Bonet regards the immunity from war of the classes of people he names, as well as their possessions, and other people like them and their possessions, as deriving ultimately from the laws and customs of chivalry. It is the concern of a knight for the welfare of the innocent that defines the immunity of those Bonet lists, and yet he has no compunction about adding them to those named in the canon law of the church. In this case the supplementation goes largely one way: from law of arms to church doctrine.

Bonet's list and the reasoning behind it (which implies extension of noncombatant immunity to considerably more persons and things than he actually names) comprehend far more than the rather meager provision in *De Treuga et Pace* (not to mention the even narrower listings of Thomas and Gratian) for the immunity of those with religious tasks to perform. The *jus in bello*, as it is formulated as part of classic just war

[52] *Ibid.*, p. 189.

71

doctrine, owes far more to the chivalric tradition of protection of the innocent than to the doctrine of the church as expressed in thirteenth-century canon law.

CHRISTINE DE PISAN's *Les Faits d'armes et de chivalrie* (*Acts of Arms and Chivalry*)

Pisan (ca. 1361–ca. 1431) is not the theorist Bonet is; her book, while heavily dependent on Bonet's, abridges his arguments again and again in the interest of presenting a more colloquial, even chatty, treatment of the subject of war. She writes as if in a conversation with intimates: now she speaks with Bonet on some point, either to acknowledge her dependence or to express some minor disagreement; now she turns to her reader, drawing him into the subject with a combination of flattery and practicality. Both Bonet and reader are addressed from time to time as "Dear Love" or "Fair Love"; Bonet, in addition, is throughout the book deferentially called "Master." Pisan is what we today would call a popularizer, and for her day she was a good one. The proceeds from this book and other writings allowed her to support herself and her three children after the death of her husband. She was a champion of the rights of women in an age when women were expected to belong by nature in second place after men. Her activities in making her own way in a man's world perhaps contributed to the favor and patronage she received from the other great champion of the rights of women in her time, Queen "Isabeau" of France.

Pisan's defense of war derives ostensibly only from the scriptures; she does not mention the *jus gentium* or the law of nature. Yet it is obvious from the flow of her argument that she is abridging and paraphrasing Bonet. Even so, it is interesting that for her God only

72

permits war; he does not, as Bonet asserts, ordain it. To put Pisan's theory of warfare briefly, she would allow only wars that are waged for the sake of justice and undertaken by sovereign princes for the protection of their subjects.[53] Only three categories of just cause for war are named: to sustain the church, to defend vassals, and to help allies. But Pisan expands this last category by adding, "& in this point be comprised women, widows, orphans & all them that may have necessity."[54] This reading of "ally" only chivalry could have comprehended: it is an inversion of the idea that the knight is the ally of the weak and innocent. Yet the only named source is scripture.

For Pisan the sources for a common law governing warfare have become so close as to be almost inseparable. In her book elements from religious law (protection of the church), feudal civil law (defense of vassals and allies), and chivalric code (defense of the helpless) are set side by side with no qualifying words, no indication whatever that they derive from diverse segments of the medieval experience of life. Because of this Pisan is, for all her attempts to write for the nobility of her time, closer to the just war theologians of the sixteenth and seventeenth centuries than is the churchman Bonet.

A similar confluence of sources is apparent in Pisan's treatment of noncombatant immunity. Whereas in

[53] Christine de Pisan, *Les Faits d'armes et de chivalrie*, rendered in a rather literal fashion into English by William Caxton, translator and printer, in 1490 as *The Book of Fayttes of Armes and of Chyvalrye*. The original by Pisan dates to 1408–09. The edition of Caxton's version cited here is that of the Early English Text Society (London: Humphrey Milford, 1937), a reissue of that of A.T.P. Byles (London: Oxford University Press, 1932). See pp. 9–11.

[54] *Ibid.*, p. 12. Spelling modernized.

73

Bonet the distinction is still fairly clear between those
who are immune because of their office (priests, bishops, religious, *etc.*) and those excused because of their
not having risen in arms, including those not able to
bear arms (peasants, merchants, women, children, *etc.*),
in Pisan such a distinction has almost disappeared. This
is the more significant since the first class of persons
derive their immunity from canon law, while the second
receive theirs from the chivalric law of arms.

> I ask whether a king or prince . . . may by right over-
> run the country of his enemy, taking all manner of
> folk prisoners, that is to wit them of the common poor
> people as be laborers, shepherds and such folk; & it
> should seem that nay. For what reason ought they to
> bear the penance of that [wherein] they meddle not
> themselves; whereas they cannot the craft of arms,
> nor is it not their office, nor they be not called for to
> judge of wars; & also wars come not by such poor
> folk, but they be full sorry for it, as they that full
> fain would always live in good peace, nor they ask
> no more. So ought they then as me seemeth to be
> free thereof, like that of right be priests, religious &
> all folk of the church by cause that their estate is not
> to [involve themselves with] war.[55]

Once again the canon law and the chivalric code are
drawn together with the emerging *jus gentium* to excuse
what are essentially disparate groups of people from the
ravages of war.

Pisan's book received wide distribution during the
last part of the fifteenth century and the early part of

[55] *Ibid.*, p. 224. Spelling modernized.

74

the sixteenth, a hundred years after it was written.[56] By this later period, it is safe to assert, there is but one doctrine of war for medieval Europe, whether it be called just war doctrine or law of arms. Pisan's treatment of her sources so as to obscure their distinctness is a factor in producing this unified doctrine.

CONCLUSION

By the end of the Middle Ages, though not before— and certainly not in the benchmark documents of the thirteenth century, the *Corpus Juris Canonici* and the *Summa Theologica* of Thomas Aquinas—a just war doctrine had evolved that included, in rough and preliminary form, all of the elements that today would be cited as characteristic of just war doctrine. It had two portions, one governing the right to go to war (*jus ad bellum*), the other governing what is right to do in war (*jus in bello*). The former derived principally from ecclesiastical sources, and the latter chiefly from secular sources: the remnants of the decaying chivalric code and the increasingly comprehensive and authoritative *jus gentium*.

The *jus ad bellum* in this doctrine requires proper authority, just cause, and right intention for there to be a just war, with the addition that the person in authority should declare his intention by an edict before proceeding against the enemy. These are all elements

[56] Christine de Pisan was widely read among the nobility both before and after her death in 1429. After considerable circulation in manuscript form, *Les Faits d'armes* was printed in French in 1488 and again in 1527, both times in Paris. Caxton based his version on the 1488 French edition. (See also note 53, above.)

drawn directly from thirteenth-century documents. But by the sixteenth century new interpretations had been applied that gave the *jus ad bellum* a somewhat different thrust from that of three centuries before.

First, by the end of the Middle Ages, proper authority had come largely to mean the authority of the secular sovereign prince, which was understood as deriving from the community he represents. This concept came about as a result of two principal developments: a practical distinction between wars for religion or church and wars for protection of the rights of the community, based on who—either pope or prince—could authorize just wars for these reasons; and an increasing emphasis on *jus gentium* as a body of customs and agreements among sovereigns, not a divine dispensation. Since disputes among secular princes during the late Middle Ages were virtually continual and affected the whole of Europe, and since the church was in practice denied any role in them (though the church continually tried to assert its claims to being the highest judge among secular princes), the authority of princes to wage wars for what we would call "reasons of state" tended to be limited only by their power to gain their ends. This tendency existed in a relationship of mutual reinforcement with the growth of *jus gentium* into the precursor of international law—political agreements, based on reasons of state, among sovereign princes. The authority of the church to decide on the justice of wars thus tended to become increasingly limited to matters of protection of religion.

Second, just cause had, along with the above movement, become bifurcated into the religious and the political, with the latter category obviously, from the relative amounts of literature on these two subjects, increasing greatly in importance. Punishment in the name of God of those who have done some wrong, which Vanderpol took to be the essence of the just war, had in the late Middle Ages been reduced to worldly size. Vanderpol thought of the wrongdoer as morally culpable, guilty before God and man alike, but by the time of Bonet there was already a sense in which, though God might know of the guilt of one side, so far as men were concerned both sides might fight honorably. This is the only way the chivalric ideal of fighting could be maintained. Such a possibility was made reality for men of the late Middle Ages by the Hundred Years' War, in which an objective judgment of the justice of one side and the fault of the other was impossible owing to the tangled nature of the claims of the two sides.[57] In any case, chivalric tradition called on all knights to treat each other with courtesy and fairness until a dispute between them was settled, by combat if need be. The stage is thus set for the development, in the sixteenth century and after, of the concept of a war to be regarded as just on both sides—an idea that is

[57] To exemplify somewhat this complexity: the English King was a vassal of the French King because of holdings in certain parts of France; yet he had a claim on the French throne that was valid according to English civil law on royal succession, but according to French law was invalid. Should the English King do homage to the French King as his liege lord? Or should the French King submit to the English King his very crown and do homage to him? The problem was rendered still more complex by the fact that a number of English noblemen in addition to the King had possessions in French territory (some dated to the time of William the Conqueror, and others had been acquired more recently). Who was to be *their* liege lord?

pure anathema to Vanderpol.[58] Because of the increasing importance of war for purely political reasons among men who shared a common faith, war for religion tended to become a separate category. Thus in the sixteenth century a dual phenomenon emerges: a resurgence of the idea of religious war in the new form of a doctrine of holy war, side by side with assertions by influential theologians that *no* just war may be waged for the sake of religion. (These developments are the subjects, respectively, of the next two chapters.)

Third, right intention had, by the end of the Middle Ages, largely divided into its component parts, one pertaining to the *jus ad bellum*—namely, the provision that the aim of war should be peace—and the other to the emerging doctrine of *jus in bello*. This was a substantial shift from the thirteenth century, when right intention was almost exclusively a matter to be decided about prior to beginning a war. In the thirteenth century, it was the responsibility of the person authorizing the war to examine his motives to see if any of the evil intentions that Augustine had named were present. But in the sixteenth century and after it was the responsibility of every man fighting a just war to keep it just by rooting out from his own soul the motivations that Augustine had disallowed.

In the long run it was the growth of the *jus in bello* that was most significant for just war doctrine in the modern period. Twentieth-century developments in the laws of war have focused almost entirely on limiting the harshness of war, except for the notable production of the Kellogg-Briand Pact (called "the agreement to end war"), one of the most conspicuous failures in

[58] Vanderpol, *La Doctrine scholastique*, pp. 265–75.

modern diplomacy. In the immediate perspective of the sixteenth and seventeenth centuries, however, the integration of a law on what is right *in bello* into just war doctrine proved significant in the following ways. In wars that were regarded as just, so far as man could judge, on both sides, it was this residue of the chivalric code that required every soldier to treat those on the enemy side with the least severity possible. Further, the presence of a concept of *jus in bello* made it possible to judge the relative justice of the opponents in a war on the basis of the manner in which each side fought for its cause. Though just *cause* might apparently be present to both sides, the undisciplined *conduct* of the soldiers on one side, for example, might be relatively unjust when compared to the conduct of their opponents. A way was also opened to definition of an absolute standard of justice *in bello*, eventually including a notion of war crimes. Finally, the presence of restraints on conduct in war helped to mitigate, at least in some quarters, the harshness with which wars for religion were prosecuted in the post-Reformation period. The concept of *jus in bello* served to counter, with varying effectiveness, the argument that an absolute end, the defense of Christian faith, required the use of unlimited means or unrestrained harshness against the enemy. Had limits on the prosecution of war still been in the secular law of arms only, it is doubtful that they would have served in any way as effective restraints on warfare for religion. Paul Ramsey has effectively traced the principles underlying the *jus in bello* to Augustine;[59] I have here shown its more immediate roots in the con-

[59] Paul Ramsey, *War and the Christian Conscience* (Durham, N.C.: Duke University Press, 1961), chap. II.

cept of right intention and the declaration of the immunity of churchmen in canon law; but the fullest source of this portion of classic just war doctrine is the secular law of arms bequeathed by the chivalric code. It is indisputable that by the sixteenth century Christian theologians were using the *jus in bello* as an authoritative portion of their just war doctrine.

From Just War to Holy War
Rationale in English Thought

THE tendency toward bifurcation within just war doctrine produced, during the late sixteenth and early seventeenth centuries, two conceptions of just war that point in fundamentally opposite directions. The two religio-political doctrines, directed to the problem of justifying war, utilize similar or even identical conceptual forms and terminology; both derive from classic Christian just war doctrine as it had taken shape by the end of the fifteenth century, and yet neither doctrine is compatible with the other. Both the likenesses and the disparities must be taken seriously. The pacifism–just war–crusade typology (notably as formulated by Roland Bainton and discussed in the appendix to this chapter) is a misleading conceptual tool for understanding the developments I am describing, despite its wide currency and general acceptance. Holy war doctrine in the early modern period is fundamentally a form of *just war* doctrine inherited from the late Middle Ages, and it takes its bearings from the idea, at least as old as Augustine, that God himself inspires and commands some wars. Also a form of medieval just war doctrine is the position taken by such theorists of international law and relations as Victoria, Suarez, Ames, and others (discussed in the next chapter) who explicitly rule out war for religious causes and require, for a war to be just, the presence of certain naturally defined,

81

politically manifested criteria. This position, which further metamorphoses into secular international law, is the one I call in this book "modern just war doctrine." It represents what most moderns take to be the content of Christian thinking on justice in war, and it does indeed preserve more of the classic doctrine than does the contemporaneous holy war concept. But *all* of the classic doctrine has not been preserved in modern just war thought; the fundamental rationale behind holy war thought in the early modern age, the idea that God is "a man of war" who directs his people into certain battles in the service of their faith, has been omitted. This is the ideological component of classic doctrine that the secularizers find unacceptable.

Holy war doctrine and modern just war doctrine developed out of their common source during the same period of time—the approximately one hundred years of serious and virtually continuous warfare between Catholics and Protestants, the end of which might be put at the close of the Thirty Years' War, but which in truth did not finally conclude until the Puritan Revolution was fought in England. Because these two just war doctrines developed simultaneously there is no chronological reason to treat one before the other. I have chosen to put holy war thought first because it is, for this period at least, a phenomenon of relatively limited duration, with no direct progeny. When Catholics and Protestants leave off fighting each other for reason of religious belief, holy war theorizing ends. But this date, the mid-seventeenth century, barely marks the beginning of the tradition that attempts to ground the limitation of war solely in secular considerations. By treating modern Christian just war thought secondly and specifically relating it to the work of early secular theorists of international law on war, I intend to direct attention to the elements of continuity in this intellectual tradition. Similarly, by separating treatment of holy war thought from this tradition I mean to indicate discontinuity between early modern holy war theory and the way we in the twentieth century generally think about justice in war.

For a number of reasons English culture provides a useful crucible within which to view the development of holy war thought. One of these is, of course, the fact that Bainton drew attention to the Puritans as examples of his holy war type. But the English affair with holy war thought is especially accessible, and most important of all it represents in microcosm what was happening all over Europe as reasons were advanced to justify going to war for religion. During the various exiles under Edward, Mary, and Elizabeth, Englishmen came in contact with Continental ideas on holy war and circulated these among their fellow countrymen. Continental humanists and ecclesiastical reformers visited England, spreading their ideas there. English mercenaries fought in Continental wars in which religious difference was a serious factor, then included in their memoirs their judgments on the allowability of this factor in answering questions about justice in war. Finally, in attempts to get England to enter this or that war on one side or the other, great amounts of propagandistic literature, written by Continentals who exercised special pleading in the cause of their own faith, were circulated among Englishmen during the Dutch War for Independence, the French Wars of Religion, and the Thirty Years' War. One specifically English factor cannot, however, be overlooked, for it played a considerable part in motivating English writers on the subject of holy war:

the rivalry between England and Spain. The English
feared the Spanish—as nominal lords of the Netherlands, not far distant, as adversaries in the New World,
as the most powerful nation in Europe, as the possessors
of the largest fleet in the world, as a staunchly Catholic
nation. The significance of this specifically English factor will be apparent in the discussions of the following
pages.

Interest in the subject of holy war[1] finds expression
in writings of Englishmen of a broad spectrum of abili-
ties, concerns, and occupations during the century run-
ning approximately from 1560 to 1660—that is, from
the onset of the Spanish threat to the end of the Puritan
Commonwealth. This widespread and cosmopolitan interest was not, as Roland Bainton and others (notably
Michael Walzer in his recent study) imply, limited to
Puritans. Indeed, the term "interest" may be too weak
for what was in fact a transmutation of categories of
demonstrably far-reaching significance: a change in the
fundamental concepts informing English thought about
morality in war. This metamorphosis was not merely an
English phenomenon but was part of a more general
shift resulting from the breakdown of a unified Christendom after the Protestant Reformation. What is specifically English is not the categorical and attitudinal
shift away from just war and toward holy war doctrine
but the particular circumstances in English political and
religious life that colored it. All the more important,
then, is the realization that it was not just a reformist
wing—the Puritans—that evinced this transformation;
rather, all kinds of Englishmen were redefining the tra-

[1] "Holy war" and not "crusade" is the term of preference of
English writers during this period. The two terms have the same
meaning, and I use them interchangeably here.

dition on warfare that had guided Christians for centuries, making of the just war doctrine their own version of a doctrine of holy war.

FRANCIS BACON:
HOLY WAR AS STATECRAFT

Francis Bacon is neither the earliest nor the latest holy war theorist in the period under examination; nor does he present a fully developed doctrine on holy war. But two factors make consideration of his position appropriate for first entry into this investigation of English thought on war. Bacon embodied much of what was best in English intellectual life in his day: breadth of interest and ability, openness to truth wherever found, concerns both practical and theoretical. *Considerations Touching a Warre with Spaine,* one of the two pieces in which he expresses his favorable disposition toward holy war, was prepared in 1624 as a study document for the King while Bacon was serving as a special royal adviser. Bacon was not a religious zealot; he speaks with a voice of calm reason from his base as an "establishment" intellectual and thus demonstrates that advocacy of holy war could, in the historical context of his day, emerge from this most unexpected quarter. Also, Bacon indicated the spectrum of types of persons who to his knowledge were concerned with advancing holy war ideas. This he did through the first of his writings on this subject, a dialogue called *An Advertisement touching an Holy Warre,* begun in 1622 and left unfinished. Here Bacon identified six characters typical of men writing on war in his own time: "a Moderate Divine," "a Protestant Zelant," "a Romish Catholic Zelant," "a Militar Man," "a Politique," and "a

Courtier."[2] There are numerous instances of representatives of each of these classes arguing the subject of holy war in print—among them the men whose arguments are treated in this chapter. Bacon was aware that persons from all these classes had a stake in advancing holy war ideas in Stuart England, and not just the Puritans (Bacon's "Protestant Zelants") whom Bainton identifies as crusaders.

In 1622 Bacon had no royal commission to write down his thoughts on the subject of holy war, and the dialogue form of the *Advertisement* suggests that it was intended for a general readership among the educated classes of English society. Though it is incomplete, this work yields important clues both to the state of English attitudes generally toward holy war and also to the direction in which Bacon's own thought on the subject was moving. Among the most interesting of these clues is the speech of the "Catholic Zelant" early on the second day. In order to advance the discussion and simultaneously to justify the cause of holy war as he understands it, this character enumerates six cases in the scholastic manner:

1. Whether war is lawful for a Christian state solely to propagate the faith;
2. Whether war is lawful to free Christians from servitude to infidels;
3. Whether war is lawful to recover countries once Christian, though no Christians now live there;

[2] Francis Bacon, *An Advertisement touching an Holy Warre*, in *Certaine Miscellany Works of the Right Honourable, Francis Lo[rd] Verulam, Viscount S. Alban* (London: I. Haviland for Humphrey Robinson, 1629), p. 93. Hereafter *Advertisement*.

4. Whether war is lawful to recover and purge consecrated places that have been profaned;
5. Whether war may be waged to revenge blasphemies to God and Christ and anti-Christian cruelties and bloodshed;
6. "Whether a Holy Warre, (which, as in the Worthiness of the Quarrell, so in the Justnesse of the prosecution, ought to exceed all Temporal Warres,) may be pursued, either to the Expulsion of People, or to the Enforcement of Conscience, or the like Extremities."[3]

Three observations will serve to indicate the significance of this listing. First, it has obvious application to wars fought against false Christians as well as to those fought against non-Christians. The great medieval crusades, the war against the Albigensians, wars against the Indians in the New World to convert them to Christian faith, and the post-Reformation wars of religion are all equally holy wars by the criteria implied in this list. Second, if all the above questions are answered by a yes, the limits of just war are entirely cast aside—both those defining the *jus ad bellum* and those defining the *jus in bello*. Even if yes is the answer only to some of the above, just war doctrine is seriously altered from the form it had generally taken more than a century before. Yet on the other hand, the questions are posed in a way that presupposes the content of late medieval just war doctrine; items 1–5 pertain to the *jus ad bellum* and may be read conservatively as tending only to broaden the reasons for justifiably going to war, and item 6 pertains to the *jus in bello*, questioning

[3] *Ibid.*, pp. 115–16.

87

how severely war for holy purposes may be pursued. The relation between classic just war doctrine and holy war thought in England at this time is obscured if they are conceived as two ideal types quite distinct from each other. Rather they interpenetrate each other, with holy war ideas emerging as redefinitions of certain of the categories of the just war tradition. Without the habits of thought created by the just war tradition, holy war thought in England in the sixteenth and seventeenth centuries would have been much different—if indeed it had come to exist at all. The list of questions posed by Bacon's "Catholic Zelant" is a reminder of the tension between holy war ideas and the inherited just war tradition. The third reason for the significance of this list is its universality. Though Bacon has the Catholic character introduce the questions to be considered in judging the morality of holy wars, the questions themselves are not peculiarly Catholic. Just as a wide variety of wars might be called holy, so also a wide variety of writers on holy war attempted to answer such questions as these. Puritan divines did so no less often than did Catholics, and indeed Bacon himself appears to have recalled his earlier listing when he returned to the subject of holy war in his 1624 study paper, *Considerations Touching a Warre with Spaine.* The questions posed by the "Catholic Zelant" are general questions defining the concept of holy war; the questions were Bacon's own, just as they were those of others treating this subject in the cultural context of the late sixteenth and early seventeenth centuries.

Though the *Advertisement* provides some interesting clues to Bacon's own position on holy war, it is necessary to turn to the *Considerations* to find his conclusions set out fully. In this later work Bacon is concerned with the problem of war in general, not just war for religion. But he devotes considerable space to this latter topic, an economy perhaps necessitated by the attitude of Protestant England toward Catholic Spain. Moreover, his very definition of war reflects holy war thinking: "Warres are Suits of Appeale to the Tribunall of Gods Justice, where there are no Superiours on Earth to determine the Cause."[4] This understanding of war was not unknown in the Middle Ages, and it also worked its way into secular international law as that began to be formulated in the seventeenth and eighteenth centuries. Both Grotius[5] and Vattel[6] thus describe war as the final arbitrament among nations that have no superiors. But in the context of Bacon's time defining war in this manner meant obscuring the essence of just war doctrine, in which the *limitation* on the Christian's right to make war was at least as strong as the *permission* he received to go to war. Bacon calls up the memory of trial by combat, in which the more righteous was thought to be protected by God against the onslaughts of the less righteous. Though he does not in this study paper suggest that God fights on the side of

[4] Francis Bacon, *Considerations Touching a Warre with Spaine*, in *Certaine Miscellany Works*, p. 3. Hereafter *Considerations*.

[5] Hugo Grotius, *The Most Excellent Hugo Grotius his three Books Treating of the Rights of War & Peace*, tr. from the Latin by William Evats (London: n.p., 1682), bk. ii, chap. i; p. 76. Hereafter *Rights of War and Peace*. I cite Grotius by book and chapter as well as by page to facilitate use of other editions of his work.

[6] Emmerich de Vattel, *The Law of Nations; or Principles of the Law of Nature: Applied to the Conduct and Affairs of Nations and Sovereigns*, tr. from the French (London: n.p., 1760), bk. ii, chap. v. Hereafter *Law of Nations*. I also cite Vattel by book and chapter to facilitate use of other editions.

89

---

the more righteous, it is but a short step from Bacon's definition of war to that claim, and less cautious writers take that step. Though Bacon writes judiciously and carefully, himself very much the "Politique," his own theoretical position is unmistakably favorable to holy war and is remarkably close to that of less restrained writers who openly advocate holy war.

Bacon defines his aims in this way: "I shall make it plaine; That Warres Preventive upon Just Feares, are true Defensives, as well as upon Actuall Invasions: and againe, that Warres Defensive for Religion (I speake not of Rebellion) are most just; Though Offensive Warres, for Religion, are seldome to be approved, or never, unlesse they have some Mixture of Civill Titles."[7] Bacon was concerned with changing the acceptance of defensive war in the just war tradition by broadening the category of what might justly be defended against. Religion, he argues, and not merely matters concerning the state, may be defended against external threats. Or perhaps this is an incorrect way to put the matter: in Bacon's time, as had not been the case when just war doctrine was being codified in the twelfth and thirteenth centuries, religion *was* a matter of state; with Protestant England set against Catholic Spain, overthrowing the religion meant overthrowing the state itself. In this historical context religion provided the ideology by which the state understood itself, and in the end the two cannot really be separated. It is the ideological functioning of religion in this period that gave rise to holy war rationales. I return to this problem in a broader context in the Epilogue to this book.

Bacon's ready acceptance of defensive war for protection of religion is more understandable if this relationship between the church and state is considered.

[7] Bacon, *Considerations*, p. 4.

Why else would a political adviser argue for religious war? Bacon the statesman arrived at advocacy of holy war in a context in which religion was subordinated to the state. Precisely the opposite is true of Catholic and Puritan spokesmen for holy war; for them the state had to serve the end of true religion. I suggest that this difference in orientation alone tends to explain much of the difference between the "Politique" Bacon and the writings of such figures as the Puritan divine William Gouge and the Catholic Bishop William Cardinal Allen, two strong advocates of holy war treated below. The difference is mainly one of tone, however, for Bacon goes quite far in advocacy of war for religious reasons. For him not only the actual attack against a state but the fear of subversion of the religion of a nation was sufficient cause to go to war. A war waged out of fear was not, to Bacon's mind, offensive but defensive, provided of course that the fear rose out of the proven evil designs of a potential enemy. Bacon envisioned such an enemy in the act of preparing to launch an attack upon one's own nation, and argued for a preemptive strike. Such, of course, was his reading of the relationship between Spain and England.

> For certainly, as long as Men are Men, (the Sonnes, as the Poets Allude, of Prometheus, and not of Epimetheus,) and as long as Reason is Reason; a just Feare will be a just Cause of a Preventive War; but especially, if it be Part of the Case, that there be a Nation, that is manifestly detected, to aspire to Monarchie, and new Acquests; Then other States (assuredly) cannot be justly accused, for not staying the first Blow; or for not accepting Poliphemus Courtesie, to be the last that shall be eaten up.[8]

[8] *Ibid.*, pp. 20–21.

Bacon's acceptance of the idea of preemptive war undertaken out of well-grounded fear for the safety of the nation and its religion to a large extent undercuts his reluctance to allow offensive war for the sake of religion. The distinction between offensive war and preemptive defensive war rests on a decision whether fear of another nation in fact rises out of that nation's intent to make war. Bacon's judgment was that since the Spanish had proclaimed themselves generally the protectors of the Catholic world, the English had a just reason to fear Spanish subversion of their religion;[9] also, they had just reason to fear an attempt at conquest. For Bacon, it was "[a]s if the Crowne of Spaine has a little of this; That they would plant the Popes Law by Armes, as the Ottomans doe the Law of Mahomet."[10] Spain had set herself on a course leading to offensive war against England for the sake of religion; now that that had been discerned, England could justly make a preemptive strike against Spain in defense of religion.

The distinction Bacon attempts to make between offensive war and preemptive defensive war is, in the end, unworkable. It requires the assumption that, at some previous time, a condition of peace existed in which neither of the two nations now about to fight had any reason to make war on one another. This is a dubious assumption but a necessary one to determine the origin of evil intent. Also, the judgment about whether a nation preparing for war is a potential enemy is always in part a subjective one. The arming of one's own nation may appear to be a justifiable act of defense, but to one's neighbor it may appear as an expression of unjustifiable hostility. Thus preparation for a preemptive war, once begun, must appear as a just cause for fear

[9] *Ibid.*, p. 31.   [10] *Ibid.*, p. 32.

on the part of the nation against whom it is to be
directed, spurring it, in turn, to redoubled efforts in
arming its soldiers in order to be the first one to strike.
The problems in sorting out evidence tending to support a just fear are intensified when there are no longer
only two nations involved, but when each one has
numerous alliances, overt and covert, and many conflicting interests.[11] In a climate of mutual distrust such as
that prevailing between England and Spain in 1624,
when many were still alive who could remember the
Armada (Bacon among them), calm judgments about
the potential use of new arms, armies, and ships were
next to impossible. Finally, it must be recalled that
Bacon advocated preemptive war not for the protection
of English maritime interests, not for the sake of friendly continental states then at war with Spain, not because
another armada lurked ready to attack English shores,
but only for the sake of religion. Indeed, just war doctrine by Bacon's time would have allowed England to
make war in these other cases, but *not* in this one case,
for religion. The next chapter makes this point clear.
In justifying preemptive war for the protection of religion Bacon was thus in direct opposition to the main
currents of the Christian tradition on war—which had

[11] Similar considerations had already led the Spanish theologian Francisco de Victoria to conclude that there exists the
possibility that two nations at war could, so far as their claims
on each other are concerned, be fighting in equally just causes.
So far as *human* judgment could tell, in some cases the *jus ad
bellum* would be equally great on either side, though God, according to Victoria, could still discern which side had *true* justice. This doctrine of simultaneous ostensible justice is of great
importance for the development of the *jus ad bellum* in the
modern period. For Victoria's treatment see below, Chap. III,
second section.

93

also become the accepted convention between nations. One might well ask, leaving aside all considerations other than religion, what conditions would have been required for Bacon *not* to judge that England had cause for just fear of Spain; the answer could only be, in the context of the times, that the two nations professed the same version of the Christian faith. To be believable, Bacon's criterion of judgment as to whether a fear is just must allow for both positive and negative judgments. Yet in this case, so long as England remained Protestant and Spain Catholic, a negative judgment was not possible. Bacon is thus in fact justifying not the case for preemptive defensive war, but rather that for offensive war for the sake of religion, or holy war. These words of his do not now appear so out of place: "I doe wonder sometimes, that the Schoole Men want words to defend that [holy war], which S. Bernard wanted words to commend."[12] Bacon must be classed among the advocates of holy war in early seventeenth-century England.

Though in the *Advertisement* Bacon raises both sets of issues inherent in just war doctrine—*jus ad bellum* and *jus in bello*—in the *Considerations* he restricts himself to broadening the concept of *jus ad bellum*, not even broaching the issue of *jus in bello*. Whether wars for religion are to be fought by the same rules as just wars for secular reasons thus remains ambiguous in Bacon. But in other writers advocating holy war the traditional limits of the *jus in bello* are challenged also, with the result in some cases that these limits are discarded. Two elements of the movement in English thought about war from the received just war doctrine

[12] Bacon, *Considerations*, p. 30.

to all-out advocacy of holy war are present in Bacon's writings: expansion of defensive war to include war for the sake of religion, and the claim of a right to wage offensive (or, to stay closer to Bacon's words, if not their implications, preemptive defensive) war for the sake of religion.

Bacon formulated his apology for war for religion in the context of a pervasive English fear of Spain. By the time he wrote the two treatises here discussed, this fear had become an ingrained habit, and it remained an important influence in English foreign policy decades after Bacon's death. A clash between the great Catholic continental power Spain and the Protestant island kingdom England seemed inevitable, and in some quarters more touched than others by radical Protestantism this imminent conflict was identified with Armageddon.[13] One of the chief causes of English interest in holy war and approval of wars fought for righteousness' sake is undoubtedly this heavy atmosphere of fear, envy, and distrust between England and Spain.[14]

[13] Though the perpetrators of such views may be loosely termed "Puritans," main-line Puritanism wished to have nothing to do with them. A signpost to this effect is William Perkins' attack on popular apocalypticism in two treatises: *A Godlie and Learned Exposition upon the Whole Epistle of Jude*, in Perkins, *Works* (Cambridge: John Legat, Printer to the University, 1605), and *A Fruitfull Dialogue Concerning the Ende of the World* (n.p.: W. Welbie, 1613).

[14] It must be pointed out that *interest* in holy war on the part of Englishmen in this period did not always imply *approval* of holy war. Two cases in point, one written before, the other after Bacon's treatises, are Sir Walter Raleigh's *A Discourse of the Original and Fundamental Cause of Natural, Arbitrary, Necessary, and Unnatural War*, in Raleigh, *Works* (Oxford: Oxford University Press, 1829), vol. viii, pp. 252–97, and Thomas Fuller's *The Historie of the Holy Warre* (Cambridge: Thomas Buck,

STEPHEN GOSSON:
PREACHING HOLY WAR AS JUST WAR

Fear of Spain is certainly the central issue in Stephen Gosson's sermon, *The Trumpet of Warre*, preached at Paul's Cross Church in 1598. This sermon is interesting theologically, because it manifests an explicit move from just war to holy war teaching, and politically, because it was preached by an invited speaker in a parish

---

Printer to the University, 1639). Though unrelated these two works take essentially the same position on holy war, and it is the reverse of Bacon's. Clearly, however, both Raleigh and Fuller are concerned with rejecting war for religion as preached and practiced by the Catholic Church only. To such war Raleigh gives the name "unnatural," meaning not to suggest that it is supernatural (higher than man's nature), but that it is beneath human nature. Though the Pope might declare such war to be not only "free from worldly ambition, just and honourable, but holy and meritorious," Raleigh argues, it is in fact none of these; the Pope uses such wars to satisfy his own ambitions (*Discourse*, p. 264). Later Raleigh specifically denounces the Pope's encouragement of Catholic forces against Protestant in the war of the Dutch rebellion and in the French wars of religion (*ibid.*, p. 276). That he considers holy war a Catholic perversion only is further emphasized in *A Discourse Touching a War with Spain, and of the Protecting of the Netherlands* (*Works*, vol. VIII, pp. 299–316). Addressing himself here to the same problem as Bacon in his *Consideration*, Raleigh too favors England's making war against Spain. His reasons, however, are quite different from Bacon's. England should help the Dutch against Spain because the Dutch are industrious and would be a benefit as friends, because if Spain wins her forces will have a refuge only 24 hours from England, and because, at the time of Raleigh's writing, Spain could not hope to overcome the combined might of the English and Dutch fleets and retaliate against England proper. Unlike Bacon, Raleigh stresses the advantage to be gained by England in such a war, and minimizes the fear that

where high members of government worshipped. In the present context it is significant further because Gosson, though a "Moderate Divine" and not a "Politique," arrives at a position that is a foretaste of Bacon's.

The sermon is divided into two main parts, the first concentrating on just war doctrine in an attempt to show how Christians may participate in warfare, and the second an outright exhortation to war with Spain. For present purposes the first part deserves much closer scrutiny than the second.

The wars in which Christians may participate, asserts Gosson, must be "just in reason, in religion, and in the practice of the church."[15] But, he continues, in the case of a just war all three coincide, so that they are but alternative ways of saying one thing: reason, religion, and church practice all concur in approving Christian

Englishmen ought to have of Spanish power. In this latter treatise Raleigh does not even consider religion as a possible motive factor for the English.

Thomas Fuller's position is essentially the same as Raleigh's. Fuller, however, offers a much more lengthy analysis of the subject of holy war, one directed toward proving such war to be rooted in papal arrogance, greed, and ambition. His repudiation of holy war is, however, limited to those crusades fought in the past; he leaves open the possibility of accepting war for religion as legitimate in the future, provided it is managed properly. He moves in this direction by recalling Bacon's "worthy" *Advertisement*, which, Fuller avers, if completed would have given ample advice on the management of holy war in the future (see Fuller, particularly bk. i, chaps. 9, 10, and bk. v, chap. 9).

When Raleigh and Fuller reject holy war, then, it is the Catholic use of religious pretenses for war that they reject, and not the *idea* of war for religion. I know of no English writing from this period that rejects holy war *per se*, as an *idea*.

[15] Stephen Gosson, *The Trumpet of Warre* (London: U. [or V.] S. for I. O., 1598), Sig. B3.

97

participation in "necessary" wars. What wars are indeed necessary is left unexplored; Gosson is rather concerned to prove that when there is necessity, Christians may do things they would not do in less demanding circumstances. A statement from Thomas Aquinas, "Nature is not wanting in things necessarie,"[16] is interpreted by Gosson to mean that man has the natural right to contrive weapons and engines of war, even those used offensively: "Nature not being wanting in things necessary, there may be a time wherein it shall be just and necessary for the soule of man to contrive weapons, & engins of offence, . . . and to put them in execution: such is the time of warre." These arguments derive directly from the just war doctrine as formulated in Scholastic theology and in canon law. But Gosson forges on, adding justifications that are a clear departure from the received doctrine. Acts of war in time of necessity, he asserts, are "Just in religion" because God, in the Psalms, "is saide to teach the fingers of the warrier to fight, and to cover his head in the day of battell." Moreover, "in the time of warre the battels fought, are saide to be Gods battels, and the overthrows given, are saide to be given by him. . . . The Lorde is a man of warre." That necessary wars are just in the practice of the church is proved by Deut. 20:2, in which "God commaundes the priest to stand forth and encourage the souldier."[17]

Religious justification of war, according to Gosson, goes beyond mere permission for Christians to participate in certain wars. Rather God himself engages actively in what Gosson continues to call "just" wars, aid-

[16] *Ibid.* Gosson cites Thomas' *Summa Theologica*, I, Quest. 76.
[17] *Ibid.*

ing the soldiers to fight more fiercely, protecting the righteous in battle, giving victory to his chosen side, and visibly underwriting the entire enterprise by commissioning his priests to encourage the fighting! This is no longer the traditional doctrine; it is holy war that Gosson is proclaiming. Such warfare is "just" in a sense quite different from that intended in just war doctrine. There "just" means principally "justifiable," with the emphasis equally on *permission* for Christians to participate in certain kinds of war and on *limitation* of their participation in even such war. There the soldier could still be called upon to do penance for the killing and other uncharitable acts he had performed, even though they had been done in course of a "just" war. But for Gosson the term "just" has taken on a new meaning, one more developed by extremely radical advocates of holy war, less developed by those less radical: a "just" war is not merely "justifiable"; it is "justified." Even as the true Christian stands before God a "just" (in the sense of "justified") man, certain wars are "just" before God.[18] This shift in meaning is crucial and de-

[18] In defining holy war in the English context as war justified by God and fought by justified Christians in his name, nothing is to be gained from raising the celebrated Reformation question whether "justified" means *made* righteous or *pronounced* righteous. Important as this distinction may be for distinguishing theologically between two types of justification doctrines, both themes are mixed together in the melting pot of English religion, and both appear together in English holy war theorizing. In Gosson, for example, God's teaching "the fingers of the warriers to fight" appears to illustrate God's making righteous those who participate in wars of which he approves. But that the Bible declares God's approval of such wars, calling "the battels fought, . . . God's battels," appears to exemplify forensic or pronounced righteousness. This same dual thrust shows up in other writers

ceptive. Because the term "just war" is used by even the most zealous proponents of holy war, those who have departed farthest from the received Christian teaching on war, their writings have the superficial air of belonging within a developing just war tradition; such is emphatically not the case.[19]

---

as well. Holy war as defined in the English context is justified war, but no meaningful distinctions can be made as to whether God *makes* or *pronounces* such wars righteous. In fact he appears to do both.

[19] Some recognition must be made at this point of the fact that Augustine, the father of Christian just war doctrine, is frequently cited by holy war proponents as approving the sort of war they advocate. This is true of the whole range of those calling for holy war in the context here being considered. Investigation of Augustine's teaching on war reveals that there is indeed an element in his thought that seems to accept the crusading theme. It is equally true that Thomas Aquinas read Augustine as allowing warfare in God's stead, though Thomas has much less to say on the matter than has Augustine. It is, as John Eppstein writes, "in the interests of historical accuracy . . . necessary to give its proper prominence to St. Augustine's doctrine of wars commanded by God" (*The Catholic Tradition of the Law of Nations*, [Washington: Catholic Association for International Peace, 1935] pp. 66–67), for it is this doctrine to which advocates of holy war in the sixteenth and seventeenth centuries looked for support. To return to the two senses of meaning implied in the term "just," *permitted* war as Augustine defines it can be described as "justifiable," while *commanded* (or holy) war is that I have called "justified" above. Both senses of "just" are thus present in the thought of Augustine. Holy war teaching in the writings of the Bishop of Hippo must, however, be kept in proper perspective—and that is an extremely narrow one. By the sixteenth century, moreover, the presence of holy war elements in Christian just war doctrine had been reduced to virtually nothing. It is important for proper understanding of English propagandists for holy war that they were going counter to what was in their time the accepted reading of just war doc-

Gosson anticipates Bacon in arguing that offensive war for religion is not to be allowed, while approving defensive war, even if preemptive, for protection of religion. Notably he identifies the Spanish as offensively promulgating religious wars, while he paints the English as beleaguered defenders of all they hold sacred. Ruled out are wars for cause of infidelity, revenge of injury done to God by idolatry, claims of supreme authority as vested in Pope or Emperor, and claims that the invaded is inept as governor.[20] In this

trine—and that though they were faithful to the letter of Augustine's teaching, they had lost the spirit. Eppstein catches this spirit in the paragraph following the citation given above:

. . . [T]he true emphasis in the Saint's writings as a whole is far less upon righteous battles than upon peace and mercy, forbearance and long suffering. It is by his praise of efforts to compose wars by reason; his exposition of peace as the greatest good of this life, proper outcome of man's natural sociability; his definition of that peace as the tranquility of order; his linking of human tranquility as by a mystic ladder to the peace of the heavenly City—it is by these contributions to the spiritual heritage of men that St. Augustine is now remembered. If his vindication of holy war had a potent influence upon the conduct of nations, still more had his grand conception of the City of God (*ibid.*, p. 67).

The just war doctrine as it stood in the sixteenth century was the product of three hundred years of development in a context provided by the presence of the Holy City on earth in the unity that was European Christendom. In this context the holy war elements progressively diminished in import. Only as a result of the disruption of the unity of Christendom caused by the Reformation did holy war elements again achieve any prominence in the thought of Christan men on war. And when such elements did appear, the tension that Augustine had maintained in his own doctrine proved no longer possible. Discrete holy war and just war doctrines resulted.

[20] Gosson, *Trumpet of Warre*, Sig. B4.

101

list the first two causes disallowed are direct references to the pattern of Spanish aggression against England, while taken together the four disallowed causes summarize the case for Spanish aggression on the continent. Nothing in this list characterizes England's claim to holy war, which is fundamentally defensive. Defensive war may be undertaken if "the losse of the church" is imminent, Gosson asserts.[21] England must fight only "in defence of the innocent, . . . that the King of Glory may come in, or in defence of your selves, your wives, your children, your lands, your lives, your countrie, and an innocent Maiden Queene. . . ."[22] Here the traditionally allowed defense of life, country, and property is extended to include defense of true religion. Since England was not at the time of Gosson's preaching at war with Spain, this sermon must be understood as a call to preemptive defensive war. The parallel to Bacon's argument is obvious.

Though Gosson, anticipating Bacon, expands the received *jus ad bellum* to include war for religion on princely authority, he does not go beyond the classic limits on the *jus in bello*. Gosson explicitly addresses the issue of what may be done in war, restricting himself to the traditional limits, though more zealous crusaders than he modify or remove them from their writings.[23]

---

[21] *Ibid.*, Sig. B14.   [22] *Ibid.*, Sig. C8.

[23] To classify Gosson as an advocate of holy war while admitting that he did not remove the just war limits of the *jus in bello* is to abandon the definition of crusade as formulated by Roland Bainton. "The crusading idea," Bainton writes, requires four characteristics: "that the cause shall be holy (and no cause is more holy than religion), that the war shall be fought under God and with his help, that the crusaders shall be godly and their enemies ungodly, and that the war shall be prosecuted unsparingly" (Roland Bainton, *Christian Attitudes toward War*

Gosson is, then, among the proponents of holy war because of his emphasis on the *jus ad bellum* as including warfare for religious reasons. But since he retains the classic limits in regard to the *jus in bello*, he can criticize the Spanish for fighting wars he calls "as unjust as they are uncharitable," which all men can observe in "the rough regiment of his warriers, that brake all the ancient lawes and privileges of the Countries where they enter, and turne the glorious and golden administration of justice into a hard and yron governement of war, administered by violence of arms. . . ."[24] The English, conversely, he can commend for fighting charitably, with greater care for loss of enemy life than he deserves, at the same time praying for victory with the least possible cost of English blood.[25]

The second part of this sermon, "The exhortation to the action of warre,"[26] includes nothing of interest in our present connection except for what appears to be Gosson's general concern throughout: he takes special care to assure his auditors that if England goes to war in a cause so just God will certainly be on her side. This

---

and Peace [Nashville, Tenn.: Abingdon, 1960], p. 148). A proper understanding of English attitudes in the late sixteenth and early seventeenth centuries requires a less rigid and more sophisticated cataloguing of characteristics, one that accepts a spectrum of holy war advocacy in English thought and allows finer differentiations than does Bainton within that spectrum. In brief, such cataloguing is possible through the identification of modifications of just war doctrine in given holy war proponents, with differentiation between those modifications that pertain to the *jus ad bellum* and those that pertain to the *jus in bello*. To develop such a catalogue of characteristics is one of the aims of this chapter.

[24] Gosson, *Trumpet of Warre*, Sig. C8.
[25] *Ibid.*   [26] *Ibid.*, Sig. C12ff.

will be so in spite of all the successes of Spain heretofore, which suggest that the Spanish are divine favorites. But such assurances only reiterate the point Gosson has so forcefully argued earlier: that God favors the righteous in battle.

In summary, besides those already identified in Bacon, two more characteristics of English holy war thought emerge out of Gosson's position: a shift in the meaning of "just" war from "justifiable" to "justified" war, together with the implications that follow for the righteousness of the cause and those who contend for it; and the idea that God actively fights on the side of right, a modification of the just war conception that God does not condemn certain wars or acts of war if they are performed in a just cause.

Two further characteristics of English holy war thought emerge in some Puritan writers of the 1620's and 1630's: the idea that God commands certain wars, which it then becomes a Christian duty to fight; and the idea that holy war has no limits, but is an unrestrained, all-out struggle of good against evil. These two concepts have already been introduced in the notes. They do not appear in the writers considered thus far; nor do they appear in most other discussion of holy war in the period here being considered. It is not, therefore, correct to say that these two characteristics *must* be present in holy war thought; these and the other characteristics identified above may be used to indicate *degrees* of advocacy of holy war—or to point up the intensity of conviction of personal or national righteousness experienced by particular writers broaching the subject of holy war.

A deeper penetration into the roots of the English fascination with holy war thinking needs to be made before this movement in its historical context can be fully comprehended. Bacon has been introduced to show the breadth of English concern with holy war; Gosson's sermon has been examined to demonstrate in microcosm the way in which just war doctrine is turned into a doctrine of holy war. Gosson thus reminds us more pointedly than Bacon that a major root of holy war thought in England is the received Christian doctrine on war, which set up the conceptual framework within which English advocates of holy war remained. But both Gosson and Bacon reveal another source of this sort of thinking: Englishmen feared Spain both as a powerful predator and as a great Catholic nation; thus their Protestantism was for them an aspect of their patriotism.

But why was there such widespread fascination with holy war ideas in this period? And why did fear of Spain manifest itself in this way rather than in the more rational, political manner exemplified by Sir Walter Raleigh's *Discourse Touching a War with Spain*, which is a study much more easily comprehensible to a political realist of today than is Bacon's study paper? At least partial answers are to be found in the figures examined in the next section.

FRENCH INFLUENCES

Any reasonably complete account of the genesis and growth of English holy war thought in the sixteenth and seventeenth centuries must take into account the influence of ideas born in France during the wars of religion and transmitted into English thought by friends of one side or the other in the French struggles. French treatises were translated, French ideas discussed in print, and developments in the wars chronicled either for propagandistic purposes—in an attempt to secure English support for this or that side—or as a prelude to modifications in English political forms. That partisans of both sides in the French wars at different times advocated holy war, and that treatises expressing this advocacy were translated into English from the French without doubt contributed to the development of English thinking about holy warfare. This pattern of influence has been investigated by J.H.M. Salmon in *The French Religious Wars in English Political Thought.*[27] Here it is necessary to look only briefly at two documents originally written in French and translated into English for popular circulation.

The Politicke and Militarie Discourses of the Lord de la Noue[28] is an excellent specimen of the thought of an educated and sensitive "Militar Man" (recalling again Bacon's characters), one who fought valiantly on the Huguenot side in the wars of religion. La Noue's *Discourses* form an interesting counterpoint to the works discussed above, since La Noue avoids questions of *jus ad bellum* and concentrates on what he perceives as inhumane violations of the *jus in bello* by soldiers in the religious wars. He passionately denounces those who would, while cynically crying, "C'est la guerre!" abandon all restraint in war: to do as they do would require "confound[ing] crueltie and justice with equitie and humanitie."[29] Again, he paints a vivid scene in which

[27] J.H.M. Salmon, *The French Religious Wars in English Political Thought* (Oxford: Clarendon Press, 1959).

[28] *The Politicke and Militarie Discourses of the Lord de la Noue*, tr. from the French by E. A. (London: T. C. and E. A. by Thomas Orwin, 1587).

[29] *Ibid.*, pp. 220–21.

a beleaguered peasant steps forth to challenge a soldier in the French wars; the peasant describes a ravaged people and land, then demands what cause can drive the soldiers to such cruelties. "Who will beleeve that your cause is just," he questions, "when your behaviours are so unjust?"[30] This fictional peasant is, of course, speaking La Noue's mind; yet his question must have been asked countless times by common people in the regions where the wars of religion raged, for both Catholic and Protestant armies committed numerous atrocities against the population on the pretense that they belonged to the contrary religion and so could not be trusted to live in peace—a practice that was to reach a kind of macabre perfection in the ill-treatment of the people of Germany during the Thirty Years' War. La Noue, the professional soldier, thus appears to yearn for a time in which warfare was conducted only between armies on the field of battle as he presents a picture of religious warfare in which the limits of the *jus in bello* have been forgotten, so that there are no noncombatants and the land is ravaged indiscriminately. His message is clear, though it is best formulated as a question: cannot war for religion—the most just kind of war—be fought according to the limits set by just war tradition and long accepted in European warfare?

A more theoretical work in the context provided by Christian theory on war is that of François de Saillans, writing under the pseudonym of Bertrand de Loque in his *Discourses of Warre and Single Combat.*[31] Saillans lists six justifications for warfare for Christians, the first

[30] *Ibid.*, p. 225.

[31] François de Saillans (Bertrand de Loque), *Discourses of Warre and Single Combat*, tr. from the French by I. Eliot (London: John Wolfe, 1591).

107

four of which tend directly toward a doctrine of holy war:

1. God has expressly commanded some wars.
2. God has instructed his people in the arts of war.
3. God is given the name "God of Hostes" in the Bible.
4. The Bible commends many kings and princes who have fought valiantly against their enemies.[32]

The ideas of commanded war and of God's aiding the righteous should especially be noted. The remaining two justifications offered are drawn from the traditional apologetic for just wars:

5. Jesus and his disciples do not prohibit just wars but in fact approve them, as witnessed by the story of Peter with the centurion Cornelius.
6. The law of nature gives a prince the right to make just wars.[33]

Saillans makes no distinctions between these two types of justifications; he considers them all to legitimize for Christians what he would term "just" war. That is, he does not seem conscious of any deviation from the Christian doctrine accepted in the past, but rather he tries, like Gosson seven years later, to justify warfare for religion within the context of just war theory. Thus when he considers the just causes for war, he first names the traditional ones: defense of the state and aid of an ally unjustly attacked.[34] But then he adds that Christians may also go to war for the sake of religion. They may make offensive war against apostates, defensive

[32] *Ibid.*, p. 1.   [33] *Ibid.*   [34] *Ibid.*, pp. 4–5.

war to protect the church against those who would establish "a fained religion."[35] His *jus ad bellum* is thus quite broad enough to accommodate the position of a Gosson or a Bacon.

In regard to the *jus in bello* two points need to be noted. First, Saillans, like La Noue, does not accept the argument that in war for religion soldiers must fight unrestrainedly. Rather they should fight valiantly, with an intent to avoid unnecessary harshness. Against non-combatants (and for Saillans there are such even in holy wars) soldiers are to observe the laws of the land that were in force prior to the war. That soldiers when not actually in battle had to obey and support the civil law and customs of the region in which they found themselves was a commonly accepted convention in European warfare in the century before the religious wars. Saillans condemns those who reject this convention, even as Gosson a few years later indicts the Spanish for overthrowing "all the ancient lawes and privileges" of the Netherlands and instituting arbitrary rule by force of arms. The second point to note in the context of the *jus in bello* is Saillans' introduction of the idea that "the armies [must] above all thinges be Godly and holy, if wee will have them worke good effect." This is necessary to God's continued support; since God walks in the midst of the camp of the side that is in the right, all soldiers must keep themselves pure to avoid giving some offense that would cause God to turn away in anger.[36] A "just" war (as Saillans conceives it) must be fought by the just.

[35] *Ibid.*, pp. 6–7.
[36] *Ibid.*, p. 29.

THE BEGINNINGS OF ENGLISH HOLY WAR
THOUGHT: HENRY BULLINGER AND
WILLIAM CARDINAL ALLEN

Propagandistic works by foreigners like La Noue and Saillans do not, for all their import for English holy war thought, constitute the first point of entry of holy war ideas into English minds. For this we must look yet earlier into post-Reformation history.

Perhaps the single most significant source for holy war ideas in English thought in the sixteenth century is Henry Bullinger's sermon "Of War," one of those included in his *Decades*.[37] This sermon is one of the opening arguments in the battle of ideas that climaxes in the holy war doctrines of Puritan writers in the 1620's and 1630's, discussed below. Its importance as a source is increased by the wide circulation given the *Decades*. In 1586, after the convocation of Canterbury, John Whitgift, then Archbishop of Canterbury, ordered that every minister with the degree of M.A. or LL.B. should possess a Bible, a Latin or English copy of Bullinger's *Decades*, and a notebook. Each one was every day to read one chapter of the Bible and every week one sermon in the *Decades*, taking notes on the readings in the notebook. Once each quarter the notebooks were to be examined by a person appointed for that purpose. So far as Whitgift's order was carried out, there is an identifiable point of entry for holy war ideas in the context of Reformation England.

[37] Henry Bullinger, *The Decades*, ed. by Thomas Harding, *The First and Second Decades* (Cambridge: At the University Press, 1849). The sermon "Of War" is number ix of the Second Decade and is on the commandment "Thou shalt not kill."

Setting the tone for those who would follow, Bullinger begins his treatment of war with just war doctrine. Thus he legitimizes war for Christians first of all by tracing the right of war to God's gift to magistrates of the power of the sword—the twofold power to punish domestic offenders and to repel foreign enemies.[38] Nothing is exceptional in Bullinger's discussion of this point; nor is anything new to be found in his lengthy citation of Augustine to make the point that what is blameworthy in war is what flows from human cupidity: "Desire to hurt, cruelty in revenging, an unappeased stomach, bruteness in rebelling, greediness to rule, and whatsoever else is like to these."[39] The opening to holy war comes at the point of Bullinger's enumeration of causes that lead Christians legitimately to war. Again, the first is familiar: defense. But Bullinger continues in an unorthodox vein:

> [O]r else the magistrate of duty is compelled to make war upon men which are incurable, whom the very judgment of the Lord condemneth and biddeth to kill without pity or mercy. Such were the wars which Moses had with the Midianites, and Josue with the Amalechites. Of that sort are the wars wherein such men are oppressed, as of invincible malice will both perish themselves and draw other to destruction as well as themselves, with those also which, rejecting all justice and equity, do stubbornly go on to persist in their naughtiness. Such were the Benjaminites. . . . Such are at this day those arrogant and seditious rebels which trouble commonweals and kingdoms. . . .
> Hereunto appertain the wars that are taken in hand for the defence of true religion against idolaters and

[38] *Ibid.*, p. 370.   [39] *Ibid.*, p. 371.

111

enemies of the true and catholic faith. They err, that are of opinion that no wars may be made in defense of religion. [For if worldly things may justly be defended, why not "things of greater account"?] But there is nothing of more and greater weight than sincere and true religion is.[40]

In this passage Bullinger diverges from late medieval just war doctrine in four particulars, all of which tend toward a doctrine of holy war. First, he admits that the "magistrate" may make war for religion alone, arguing that if lesser things may be defended, so may the greatest thing man has, true religion. By this reasoning the *state* may initiate religious war. Second, he admits punitive war against the "incurable," claiming that even God has totally rejected them to pitiless death. In such war the state but enforces the judgment of God. This argument is like that for the death of incurable criminals and those who have committed unforgivable crimes; when it is used as a justification for war, however, it requires assumptions to be made that may be valid in domestic law but are invalid in international relations. Most importantly, to use this reasoning requires the assumption that there exists a stable and generally accepted set of values, so that the flagrant offender can be identified and the nature of his crime determined objectively in terms set by the value system. But this is emphatically not the case in the international conflicts that ravaged Europe in the late sixteenth and early seventeenth centuries. There the warring parties brought two standards of right, two opposing sets of fundamental values, two mutually exclusive religious ideologies. To apply Bullinger's argument for punitive

[40] *Ibid.*, pp. 376–77.

warfare in such a context is to call for holy war. Moreover, the claim that even God has rejected those who
are to be punished by such war includes implicitly a
dichotomy between the righteous, who execute God's
wrath, and the unrighteous, on whom the punishment
falls. This is the third departure from just war doctrine,
which makes no such distinctions. Fourth, those whom
God condemns are to be killed "without pity or mercy"
by the servants of righteousness. Besides implying the
removal of the limits of the *jus in bello*, this provision
takes away the need for penance on the part of soldiers
for the evils they have committed in wartime. In such
war as Bullinger is describing here, the sinners are all
on one side, and at the end of the war they will all be
dead. The survivors, all servants of righteousness, are
to utter prayers not of penitence but of glorification of
God and thankfulness for his giving this victory over
sin.

Each of Bullinger's points modifying Christian doctrine on war in the direction of holy war is taken up
and amplified by English proponents of holy war during the next eighty years. These particulars alone mark
him as a key figure in the movement being analyzed
here. But Bullinger served the proponents of holy war
in England in yet another important respect: he referred them to Old Testament examples of war and
warlike men. Here God's commandment of war and
even participation in war are central themes. The great
leaders of Israel are also warriors, represented as having
special guidance and protection from God in all their
ventures. The Old Testament model is essential to the
developing English theory of holy war.

The link Bullinger forged between holy war and
war to put down rebellion must have given comfort to

generations of English monarchs plagued by armed revolt among Irish Catholics and more covert acts of rebellion from irreconcilable English Catholics (a key element in Bainton's argument that the Puritan Revolution was a crusade is, moreover, his contention that Cromwell's expedition against the Irish rebels was pursued mercilessly).[41] Yet there is a certain ironic twist to holy war pretensions that is well illustrated by just this issue of rebellion. For when the *Decades* became required reading for the English clergy Bullinger's was not the voice most stridently calling for warfare for the sake of religion in England. Indeed that voice was not even Protestant; it belonged to William Cardinal Allen, the exiled English Catholic bishop, whose *A True, Sincere, and Modest Defence of English Catholiques*[42] promoted the cause of holy war far more forcefully and explicitly than did Bullinger's comparatively cautious sermon. And Allen turns the tables on those who termed the Catholics rebels; for him those who oppose the authority of the Pope are the true rebels, and it is they who are to be hunted down and punished with the scourge of holy war.

"Ther is no warre in the world so just or honorable be it civil or forraine, as that which is waged for Religion," proclaims Allen, "we say for the true, ancient, Catholique, Romane religion . . . and not for wilde con-

---

[41] Bainton writes, "The conduct of the war was affected by the religious alignment. Catholics received no quarter from the Puritans. The garrison at Drogheda was massacred." *Christian Attitudes toward War and Peace*, pp. 150–51.

[42] William Allen, *A True, Sincere, and Modest Defence of English Catholiques that Suffer for Their Faith both at home and abrode: against a false, seditious and slaunderous libel intituled: The Execution of Justice in England* (London: William Cecil, 1583).

demned heresies, against most lawful Christian Catholiques, Kinges & Priests. . . ."[43] Here the holy cause is
expressly reserved for the Catholic side and denied to
the Protestant. Bacon's cast of characters should again
be recalled. In general, however, this restriction of
Allen's is no surprise; it is integral to holy war doctrine
that one's own side be defined as totally righteous and
the other as totally reprobate. The Cardinal continues:
"[N]o crime in the world deserveth more sharpe and
zealous pursuite of extreme revenge, then revoulting
from the Faith to strange religions. Who-soever seeketh
not after the Lord God of Israel, let him be slaine (said
King Asa admonished by Azariah the Prophet) from the
highest to the lowest without exception."[44] Allen conveniently overlooks what from a more tolerant perspective appears blatantly obvious: that Protestants and
Catholics alike sought the same God. Yet this blindness,
if it is such, afflicted both sides, and the close juxtaposition of Bullinger and Allen on holy war against "rebels"
serves to demonstrate this fact. Like Bullinger, Allen
would prosecute such war to the limit. If all the unfaithful are to be slain "without exception," then that
most powerful restraint present in the just war doctrine on *jus in bello*—noncombatant immunity—is irre-
trievably lost. Women, children, clerics, the aged, the
infirm—all these and other classes as well who according to just war doctrine and accepted practice of war
up to this time are to be spared the ravages of war—
all are now to be subjected to a "sharpe and zealous
pursuite of extreme revenge," as Allen puts it.

In war fought against heresy, argues Allen, the supreme commander can be no other than the Pope.
Moreover, since all temporal power and authority de-

[43] *Ibid.*, p. 103.   [44] *Ibid.*

rive from the spiritual, any temporal ruler who opposes the Pope is a rebel and deserves to be treated as one. On the other hand, if any subjects of an apostate prince rise up in war against him in the cause of the true Catholic religion, they must not be regarded as rebels, for they are obeying a law higher than that imposed by their earthly prince. In this manner Allen excuses what had become a cause of extreme resentment among English Protestants: the Pope's giving to the Irish rebels not only priests but money, arms, and a Spanish army.[45] Allen attempts to deal with the problem of rebellion by redefining it so as to tar the other side. The Irish are not, as he sees the matter, rebels; rather, the English Crown and its supporters are the true rebels—against Papal authority. The holy cause of the Irish excuses their contention against their earthly prince, and they are assured of triumph because Christ's vicar on earth is their supreme commander.

It is instructive that the most authoritative direct response to Allen, prepared by Thomas Bilson, Anglican Bishop of Winchester, counters his claims by an explicit repudiation of the attempt to shift the argument to new grounds by redefining rebellion. Sidestepping the issue of holy war altogether, Bilson argues that the Pope has no temporal authority and cannot command in war, so that the Irish are in fact rebels.[46] That rebellion excuses extreme measures in punishment is accepted by both Allen and his Anglican critic, but Allen transmutes this into an apologetic for holy war, war in which extremities are excused because of the

[45] *Ibid.*, pp. 136–41.

[46] Thomas Bilson, *The True Difference betweene Christian Subjection and Unchristian Rebellion* (Oxford: Joseph Barnes, Printer to the University, 1585), pp. 379–81.

overwhelming righteousness of the Catholic cause. This confusion in categories suggests one reason why advocacy of holy war in the English context does not always carry with it the abrogation of *jus in bello* limitations. If modification of the *jus in bello* in holy war doctrine requires the presence of the issue of rebellion, including the long-standing tradition of harsh punishment of rebels, a correct characterization of holy war doctrine might justifiably be limited to points concerning the *jus ad bellum*. Fuller consideration of this possibility must be deferred until the Appendix to this chapter.

One final point: though Allen and all Catholic advocates of war for religion can look to the Pope as their supreme commander, the Protestants have no Pope. They are thus driven to look elsewhere for the certitude of righteousness that alone can lead them to battle for the Lord. Ultimately this "elsewhere" is their own consciences, informed by Scripture. This perhaps is one reason those Puritans who advocated war for cause of religion insisted so stridently that the soldiers of righteousness must themselves be righteous men.

PURITAN HOLY WAR ADVOCACY

The most fervent propagandists for holy war, surpassing even Cardinal Allen, were Puritans, a fact illustrated by the three works now to be examined. Moreover, if "complete" holy war doctrine is anywhere to be found—defined, one must suppose, by the presence of all recognizable characteristics of holy war thought—it is perhaps in the treatise of William Gouge, a discussion of which follows. Certainly the Bainton typology, framed with Puritan examples in mind, fits best here. And yet, as this chapter has argued throughout, holy war thought

is to be found in the writings of a diverse lot of Englishmen during the late 1500's and early 1600's, so that
Puritan propagandists demonstrably have no monopoly.
Giving crusade-minded Puritans their proper perspective requires also the recognition of such influential divines of this party as William Perkins and his pupil William Ames, who oppose the drift in the direction of holy
war—Perkins by his denunciation of popular apocalypticism in more than one treatise, Ames by his detailed
updating of just war theory in *Conscience, with the
Power and Cases thereof.*[47] The holy war movement in
English thought in the sixteenth and seventeenth centuries is thus not merely a Puritan expression; nor are
all members of the Puritan party advocates of holy war.
Treating Puritan writers of a crusading mind after the
other writers discussed in this chapter is not the result
of saving the best for the last, as it would be if I were
trying to illustrate Bainton's theory; it is rather the result of an attempt to put the three men now to be discussed into proper perspective in a much larger movement of thought among Englishmen for whom the
received just war theory had become, in greater or
lesser degree, a doctrine of holy war.

William Gouge's "The Churches Conquest Over the
Sword," one of three treatises in a book called *Gods
Three Arrowes*, published in 1631, is a kind of climax
in English attempts to rewrite the Christian doctrine of
war. This treatise is in the form of a commentary on
Exodus 17:8–16, which describes the birth of the conflict between Israel and Amalek. Throughout this work
Gouge demonstrates that his concern is not to place
limits on Christian participation in war, which is the
fundamental aim of just war doctrine, but rather to

[47] See Chap. III, second and third sections, below.

118

prove to his readers that Christians may not in duty avoid certain wars. This is, of course, a theme not uncommon among proponents of holy war.

> Warre is a kind of execution of publique justice: and a means of maintaining right. . . . [The iniquity of men] causeth a necessity of warre: and the benefit that thence ariseth causes pious and righteous men to use it. By it a free and quiet profession of the true Faith is maintained: peace is setled: kingdomes and common-wealths are secured: lands and inheritances quietly possessed: all manner of callings freely exercised: good lawes put in execution: due justice executed: ill minded persons kept under: and many evils prevented.[48]

With such benefits arising from war, "pious and righteous men" ought—far from deeming it a scourge—to praise God for giving it to mankind! This is Gouge's tone throughout the present treatise.

As the above passage indicates, justice is a reason for war to which Gouge wishes to hold firm. But, as in the case of Gosson and others, use of the word "justice" does not imply the presence of just-war thinking. On the contrary, when Gouge sets out to define "what warres may be counted just and lawfull," at the top of his list is all those wars "extraordinarily made by expresse charge from God."[49] "No question must be made of them," he continues, "because they had the best warrant that could be, Gods command."[50] Still, such wars

---

[48] William Gouge, *Gods Three Arrowes: Plague, Famine, Sword, In three Treatises. I. A Plaister for the Plague, II. Dearths Death. III. The Churches Conquest over the Sword* (London: George Miller for Edward Brewster, 1631), p. 214.
[49] *Ibid.*   [50] *Ibid.*, p. 215.

are unusual, and "ordinary warres" need discussion also. These Gouge divides into two types: defensive and offensive.

"Defensive warre is that which is undertaken to defend our selves or friends from such wrongs as enemies *intend, or attempt* against us. . . . No question can be made of the lawfulnesse of such wars as these are. Necessity forces men thereto."[51] Like Bacon and like Gosson, Gouge would not have a potential prey wait until an actual attack has been launched for defense to be legitimate. Of course, just war doctrine also allows for defense against evil intention, but there the model is a hostile army massing on one's frontiers; in Bacon and Gosson all that is required is a hostile mentality, recognizable in profession of a different religion, or in twentieth-century terms, a different national ideology. At this point Gouge is ambiguous in the meaning he attaches to "intent." In the overall context provided by his paean to holy war, however, the second meaning would seem more likely.

Gouge clearly stretches just war limits in allowing offensive war for certain ends. Of the seven justifications he lists for offensive war, four of them come from just war doctrine, where they are treated as cases of legitimate defense (recovery of property unjustly seized, revenge, subduing rebels, helping allies), and two are plainly "politicke" (drawing enemies away from some dangerous plot, weakening enemy power). But the uppermost cause for offensive war is, in Gouge's words, "Maintenance of Truth, and purity of Religion." "This moved the Israelites in Canaan to think of making warre against their brethren on the other side of Jordan," he explains. "In this respect the

[51] *Ibid.*, emphasis added.

warres of the Kings of the earth against Anti-Christ are commended. . . ."[52]

There are thus two definite openings to holy war in Gouge's position: the extraordinary war commanded by God, and the offensive war to maintain truth and purity of religion. Though Gouge relies verbally on the received doctrine of just warfare, his meaning clearly supports a theory advocating holy war. For example, in his arguments for the lawfulness of war for Christians, Gouge is concerned not with depicting war as the lesser of evils, the conclusion toward which just war doctrine tends, but rather with showing that, far from forbidding war, God actually urges his people into battle. The legitimizing reasons for war number a redundant thirteen, all derived from Scripture.

1. "Saints" such as Abraham and Joshua, some of the Judges and "the best of the Kings" have waged war with God's approval.
2. They have prayed to God for direction and received it.
3. They have prayed for God's assistance and received it.
4. Their wars are "waged in faith, Heb. 11. 33. 34." (Notably this is the *only* New Testament reference in this listing.)
5. God has commanded certain wars.
6. God has visibly participated in certain wars and "is stiled a Captaine of his peoples host."
7. God has given directions for "well waging warre" in general.
8. God received from Israel part of the spoils of war.

[52] *Ibid.*

9. Priests of God went to war among the Israelites.
10. "Victory in warre is promised as a blessing."
11. "God is said to teach mens hands to warre, and fingers to fight."
12. "Battels are stiled warres of God, and the Lords Battels."
13. "God himselfe is stiled A man of warre, and the Lord of hosts."[53]

In all this lengthy and repetitive listing of reasons proving war lawful for Christians, Gouge looks only once to the New Testament, and then only for a supporting reference to Israelite experiences in war. Though the just war doctrine has its base in Augustine's concern for the showing of Christian charity to enemies as well as neighbors, Gouge nowhere includes even a reference to charity; yet he is deeply concerned with righteousness. This is best illustrated by the following passage, in which his rhetorical eloquence favoring Christian holy war reaches a peak in zealousness. Gouge writes that individual soldiers may

. . . go in faith, with much confidence, cheerfully, and courageously. If there be peace betwixt God and their owne soules, if they have truly repented of all their sinnes, if their persons be justified as well as their cause warranted, they may not onely call upon God, . . . but also undauntedly meet death in the mid-way, and comfortably commend their soules into Gods handes. . . . *For a souldier to die in the field in a good cause, it is as for a preacher to die in a pulpit.*[54]

It is not the manifestation of God's love in limiting the cruelties of war with which Gouge concerns him-

---

[53] *Ibid.*, pp. 209–10.   [54] *Ibid.*, p. 217, emphasis added.

self; it is rather the upholding of a narrowly conceived
personal righteousness on the part of the soldiers on his
own side. These are the only ones to whom God's love
extends, and to them only so long as they keep free
from sin. Gouge concludes the above exhortation by
calling the sort of war of which he speaks "the worke
of the Lord, . . . his warre" and by terming soldiers who
die in battle "martyrs." Of course not all wars are of this
type, and not all soldiers fight for righteousness. But
any war in which true Christians participate *must* be
the work of God, Gouge argues, by definition.

> True it is, that when Heathen with Heathen, Idolaters
> with Idolaters, wicked men with wicked men make
> warre, the issue of warre is uncertain: For, God en-
> gageth himselfe on neither side. . . . But in his peo-
> ples wars the case is otherwise, in case they go along
> with him, and fight not without good warrant from
> him, nor swerve from the directions which he pre-
> scribeth to them. Such warres are Gods warres, the
> battels of the Lord, which he can and will prosper.
> . . . The Lord is the chiefe Captaine and generall in
> them.[55]

[55] *Ibid.*, p. 290. The great distance that Gouge had departed
from late medieval just war doctrine can fairly be judged by this
passage. While Suarez, Ames, and Grotius, all roughly contemporaries of Gouge, were each in his own way developing just
war doctrine away from the trial-by-combat model, Gouge unequivocally adopts just this model. Just war theory in Suarez,
Ames, and Grotius—especially in Suarez and Grotius—develops
by assuming nothing about the religious state of the nations
concerned, but only whether they are sovereign powers; Gouge
dismisses from his theory all wars that are fought for reason of
state only, which are wars between "wicked men." For Gouge a
Christian may not engage in warfare at all unless it is in a holy
cause, and then he may not swerve from God's way for him.

In this passage the distinction earlier made between extraordinary commanded wars and ordinary offensive wars for religion has totally disappeared, and the kind of war described by Gouge has all the characteristics of the commanded wars of the Israelites. Nor may we expect that Gouge would at this point seriously maintain the "extraordinary" nature of such war. God's direction of the affairs of his saints is, after all, a regular feature of Puritan doctrine.

"The Churches Conquest Over the Sword" is an unequivocal assertion of a Christian duty to go to war for purposes of religion. Though Gouge represents this position as belonging in the just war tradition, keeping some of the distinctions made in that tradition (though changing the context in which they are presented) and scrupulously using the term "just warre" for the type of war of which he is writing, he is in fact presenting a full-blown concept of holy war as the only kind of war legitimate for Christian participation. Against whom is Gouge's crusading zeal directed, against what "Anti-Christ"? Does he speak of the Turks, Christendom's traditional enemy? Are the "Heathen" he mentions the Indians of the New World? Indeed not; Gouge is far more concerned with stirring up the truly faithful against those who falsely call themselves Christians: "Some that outwardly professe the Christian Faith may be as great enemies to the true Faith, as plaine Infidels. . . . *Papists* profess the Christian Faith, yet are Anti-Christians, the directest and deadliest enemies that Christs true Church ever had."[56] Or, in another place, "papists are to Protestantes as Amalekites to Israelites."[57] Gouge is none other than a "Protestant

[56] *Ibid.*, p. 213, emphasis added.
[57] *Ibid.*, p. 188.

124

Zelant" such as Bacon introduces in his Advertisement.
The Puritan holy war is to be against the forces of the
Church of Rome.

Gouge represents an extreme among Puritan writers,
but he is by no means altogether lonely in his stand.
Alexander Leighton, in his *Looking-Glasse of the Holy
War*[58] also evokes the memory of the war of the Israelites against the Amalekites, and he too argues from a
distinction between commanded wars and others. Defensive war is allowed by the law of nature and nations,
he asserts, and is "not repugnant to the law of God."
"Or [war] is grounded upon the absolute command of
God, for the revenging him upon his enemies, or the
delivery of his friends. . . . The like warrent is given to
warr against the Whore and her confederates."[59] Both
defensive and offensive wars are permitted to Christians, but offensive wars, in Leighton's mind, must be
commanded by God. This is not far different from
Gouge's conception. Another similarity is in Leighton's
argument for Christian participation in war. Three of
his points sum up all of Gouge's: 1) God commands
some wars recorded in scripture; 2) God has set down
laws for war; 3) God is called a man of war. Leighton's
final point, however, comes directly from the just war
tradition: John the Baptist approved of a soldier's
calling.

In other respects too Leighton pays considerable attention to the received doctrine; yet he modifies it in
subtle though significant ways into a doctrine of holy
war. He requires the presence of both *jus ad bellum* and
jus in bello, explaining both in a superficially traditional

[58] Alexander Leighton, *Speculum Belli Sacri: or the Looking
Glasse of the Holy War* (n.p.: 1624).
[59] *Ibid.*, p. 6.

manner, but introducing modifications that make of just war holy war. For example, Leighton writes, "[T]here must be a just cause, which may be briefly exprest, *under the maintenance of religion*, or civill right, either for our selves, or our Christian confederates."[60] The italicized phrase changes the meaning of the idea entirely. The explanatory remarks that follow clarify Leighton's meaning: "In the war injoyned by God to his people against the nations, and in other warrs permitted occasionally, they were alwayes to looke to the equitie of the cause, as the main ground whereupon they were to go. *For God himselfe injoyneth nothing without a good ground*."[61] An equitable cause here becomes a "good Ground," and permitted wars are assimilated to enjoined wars. Again, the holy war here appears in just war guise. Only a few pages further on, Leighton has abandoned all pretense: "Oh then that wee would make a holy Warre indeed," he prays, ". . . and then neither Gog nor Magog should prevaile against us. To this end, the Lord biddeth us sanctifie a war."[62]

Leighton differs from Gouge in giving serious attention to the problems of *jus in bello* (Gouge glosses over the issue, concerning himself almost exclusively with *jus ad bellum*). But here, Leighton's source is not so much just war doctrine as contemporary books on military discipline. Spoliation, drunkenness, rapine, murder, and "cruell oppression" are all condemned, but for no other reason than prudence.[63] His closest approach to religious concern in this connection is to counsel that soldiers should hate their captives with a "perfect hatred" and not with an "irreconcilable hatred."[64] But

[60] *Ibid.*, pp. 9–10, emphasis added.
[61] *Ibid.*, emphasis added.   [62] *Ibid.*, p. 27.
[63] *Ibid.*, pp. 227, 245–47.   [64] *Ibid.*, p. 248.

on close inspection this is not simply a restatement of Augustine's dictum against irreconcilable hatred; it is chiefly an evocation of the holy war concept of the morally perfect soldier. Again he intones the litany: "Oh then that wee would make a holy Warre indeed; that is, to be holy in our selves. . . ." Once again Leighton closes ranks with Gouge.

Leighton's treatise is explicitly directed toward convincing England to enter the Thirty Years' War on the Protestant side.[65] Another treatise with like aim is Thomas Barnes' *Vox Belli, or An Alarm to Warre*. Here too a peculiar warping of just war tradition results in a doctrine of holy war. Barnes takes seriously the intent of the just war doctrine to limit Christian participation in war. In fact, as he understands the doctrine, no Christian may participate in war at all except on the *command* of God! Once commanded the Christian may not refuse to make war. As Barnes writes, "[T]he sword may not be stretched out to bloud without a call. . . . [T]o bid the sword keepe scabbard, when God calls it forth, exposeth it to the Curse."[66] Barnes' point is that God does not merely *permit* war for just cause, he actually *commands* it. But upon what causes does God command war? Barnes lists five sins "such as for which Moab was to be wasted by the Chaldean sword": "1. Monstrous pride. 2. Insolence against God. 3. Insulting over the Church. 4. Tumultousnesse and rebellion. 5. False-heartednesse. Which vices . . . have been Gods warrant to his owne Worthies, to fight his battels in the Old Testament."[67] It is a page later before he mentions

[65] *Ibid.*, p. 12.
[66] Thomas Barnes, *Vox Belli, or An Alarme to Warre* (London: H. L. for Nathaniel Newberry, 1626), p. 9.
[67] *Ibid.*, pp. 29–30.

the most fundamentally just cause allowed in just war doctrine, defense. And here this cause is mentioned only in passing.

Unlike Leighton, Barnes places no restrictions on cruelty in war. Once war is commanded, cruelty, wickedness, and inhumanity follow inexorably. The only restraint possible is in the decision whether to begin war; yet even here the decision rests with God. Barnes' rather bloodthirsty stance is concisely expressed in this statement: "The stretching out of the sword to bloud, *requires the putting on of a kinde of cruelty*; as wee see in Samuell, who hewed Agag in pieces without any shew of compassion; as wee see in Joshua, who hanged up the five heathenish kings without any compassion."[68] This sentiment is as far as possible from the spirit of Augustine's mournful warrior who kills only because it is the more just choice. Of course, Barnes continues, we know that Scripture calls on Christians to be merciful. But this means only that as Christians we must always take special care that the call to war be a true one, so that we will not be merely indulging our blood-lust and the sinful desire to treat others cruelly.[69] His implication is inescapable: blood-lust and cruelty remain in a holy war but are sanctified by the cause and by God's command. Having a godly call to war is for Barnes essential, for once in a war there can be no limits to its ravages.[70]

[68] *Ibid.*, p. 20, emphasis added.

[69] *Ibid.*, p. 21.

[70] In this, though in nothing else, Barnes would have agreed with Erasmus' anguished pacifism in his widely circulated treatise of condemnation of war, known by its beginning words: *Dulce bellum inexpertis*—"War is sweet to them that know it not," as a contemporary English translation renders it. Erasmus

To one familiar with just war doctrine, two departures from the late medieval form of that doctrine are especially notable in English holy war theorizing: the introduction of a concept of "commanded" war, replacing war that is only "permitted"; and almost exclusive reliance on the Old Testament in place of the just war doctrine's heavy reliance on New Testament teachings. Neither the Calvinist tradition generally nor the Puritans in particular were so exclusively preoccupied with the Old Testament as popular opinion today has it. Yet in Puritan teaching on holy war it is obvious that the New Testament has little or no place. The three men discussed here might almost be said to have a Hebrew, and not a Christian, doctrine on war—a dichotomy they most certainly would not accept.[71]

---

too discards just war doctrine, arguing that misery, famine, destruction, plague, and all possible kinds of evil are necessary accompaniments to war. But for Erasmus, unlike Barnes, this observation led to the conclusion that war should be avoided at all costs. An interesting parallel in the American attitude toward war has been noted by Ralph B. Potter in *War and Moral Discourse* (Richmond, Va.: John Knox, 1969). Americans, Potter writes, have historically displayed almost a pacifist's reluctance to enter war; yet "once drawn into war in response to the wickedness of enemies, we have shown a disinclination to be bound by the fine distinctions of the *jus in bello*" (p. 51). This raises the intriguing question—which cannot find an answer here—of a possible psychological link between the pacifist and the crusader, and a mutual aversion of them both to the just war compromiser.

[71] That such a judgment may be proper, however, is suggested by the widely used biblical commentary of Henry Ainsworth, leader of the Separatist congregation at Amsterdam. Ainsworth's *Annotations upon the Five Books of Moses* (London: John Bellamie, 1627; commentaries on individual books were published earlier: Genesis in 1616, Exodus in 1617) makes reliance on Jewish theology explicit. To explain certain passages on war

CONCLUSION

Given the diversity of types of Englishmen advocating holy war, it is impossible to speak of characteristics of English holy war thought as if this were a unified, coherent body of thought—a "type" to be set alongside others all defined by discrete marks. I have repeatedly emphasized that holy war thought in the post-Reformation period is very much a kind of just war thought, whichever measure is applied—that of language, of

---

Ainsworth leans heavily on Maimonides, and admits it; he also cites the *Targum* and the *Pirkei R. Eliezer.* Since his own comments are generally limited to matters concerning variant texts, these Jewish sources stand as virtually the whole of theological commentary in his work. The similarity between Ainsworth's position and the holy war theorizing of Gouge, Leighton, and Barnes can be judged by the following excerpt from the *Annotations*, where reliance on Maimonides is considerable. The subject is Deut. 20:1, in Ainsworth's translation, "When thou goest out to battell aginst thine enemies, and seest horses and chariots, a people more than thou, be not afraid of them, for Jehovah thy God is with thee, which brought thee up out of the land of Egypt."

> When thou goest out] This is meant of all lawfull warres, offensive or defensive, that is, begun by Israel, or by other nations against Israel. And the Hebrewes hold, that Israel might never begin first to warre, but in the warres commanded of God; and those were the warres with the seven nations in Canaan, (Deut. 2.24. and 7.1.) and the war against Amalek, (Deut. 25.17,19.) and to help Israel out of the hand of the adversary which is come upon them, (as Judg. 3.12.–28. &c.) Warres permitted, were with other peoples that oppugned Israel, as Judg. 11.4.12.–27. 2 Sam. 10.2,6,7, &c. "For warres commanded, it is not necessary to have leave of the high Councell (or Synedrion;) but the King may goe out of himselfe at any time, and compell the people to goe out: but in the warre permitted, he leadeth not the people out, but at the

130

categories employed, of sources cited, of conclusions sought. This probably is the most fundamental thing to be said about the advocacy of war for religion that appeared in the sixteenth and seventeenth centuries. Without recognizing the relationship it is impossible to comprehend what happens with those who follow the other branch of classic just war doctrine, naturalizing its value base and turning it ultimately into the somewhat different war doctrine of secular international law. It is the attempt by holy war theorists to make the classic allowance of war for religion into an ideological support for the cause of one or another prince or nation that makes it necessary for the naturalists to root out religion from among the just causes for war.

If the most fundamental thing to say about post-Reformation holy war doctrine is that it is a kind of just war doctrine, the next thing that must be said is that the fluidity of holy war advocacy makes it more proper to speak of it as a movement within the just war tradition, not as a form into which classic just war doctrine is poured and recast. I have above identified six

---

mouth of the Senate of 71, Magistrates. Maimony in Mishnah, tom. 4. treat. of Kings, chap. 5. sect. 1, 2.

The distinction here made between permitted and commanded wars is drawn from Maimonides explicitly, though a similar one is found in Augustine. In any case this distinction overrides any that might be attempted between offensive and defensive war. I do not suggest that Gouge, Leighton, or Barnes had necessarily read Ainsworth's *Annotations*; nor do I know whether any of them knew Maimonides. The similarity of ideas is striking, however. Though the three Puritan holy war advocates ostensibly speak from the Christian just war tradition, their concepts and even their language tend toward the position enunciated in the *Treatise of Kings* and abstracted by Ainsworth in the *Annotations*. For Gouge, Leighton, and Barnes the road to Maimonides might well be straighter than that to Augustine.

characteristics of English holy war thought as they appeared in the writings of the various figures discussed in this chapter. Modified to be as general (hence as inclusive) as possible and put in order of frequency of appearance, the six are as follows:

1. Religious purpose (a phrase I have found more generally apt than Bainton's "holy cause"—though perhaps they convey the same meaning)
2. Expansion of classic just war doctrine to include defensive war by the state as warranted for defense of religion
3. Introduction of a concept of offensive war for religion, usually enunciated as a concept of war "commanded" by God
4. Assertion of the necessity that soldiers for the right be personally godly, usually accompanied with the assumption that those on the other side are personally sinful
5. A change in meaning of the term "just" war from "justifiable" to "justified" war, implying a thoroughly righteous cause and thoroughly righteous or godly ("justified") champions for it
6. *Occasionally* the requirement or suggestion that holy war must be prosecuted more scrupulously according to the dictates of charity, in tension with an equally occasional insistence that holy war be fought without restraint (*cf.* Gosson and Leighton, Allen and Barnes respectively)

Again, these characteristics should not be understood to define an ideal type but should rather be used as clues to possible positions within the general English movement from classic just war doctrine to the most radical holy war thought. Such a dynamic use of this list is most in keeping with the fundamentally dynamic quality in English holy war thinking. Used this way, moreover, this list can also be demonstrated to characterize continental holy war advocacy throughout the period of the religious wars.

Finally, since holy war is a kind of ideological war, and since we today have been conditioned to think of ideological war as being without restraints, the fact that the *jus in bello* (then only present in the Christian tradition on war for about a century) is abridged by but a few post-Reformation holy war advocates suggests that warfare for ideology can under some circumstances be conceived and fought with the same limits as are recognized in warfare for reasons of state. To discover what these circumstances are would require a careful comparison of post-Reformation war for religion and twentieth-century ideological war, a work outside the scope of this present study. But there is another possibility suggested by the alternatives given in characteristic 6 above. I return to it in the Epilogue of this book, where I argue that ideological concerns can act as a brake as well as an incentive to war. This suggests one way in which future study of ideological war should move.

One further matter demands attention in any serious study of English holy war thought: Roland Bainton's attempt to understand and typologize it, and Michael Walzer's recent application of Bainton's thesis in his own investigation of Puritanism as a revolutionary ideology. Since what I have come to call the "Bainton-Walzer thesis" is basically out of agreement with the interpretation offered in this chapter, I have discussed it with some care and at some length in the Appendix to this chapter.

The Puritan Revolution as Crusade

WHEN in the course of his 1942 paper, "Congregationalism: From the Just War to the Crusade in the Puritan Revolution,"[72] Roland Bainton defined "the crusading idea," he set the pattern for his own thought as well as that of countless others during a considerable future. Bainton wrote at that time, "The crusading idea requires that the cause shall be holy, and no cause is more holy than religion, that the war shall be fought under God and with His help, that the crusaders shall be godly and their enemies ungodly, that the war shall be prosecuted unsparingly."[73] These same four characteristics are enunciated in almost the same words in *Christian Attitudes toward War and Peace* more than twenty years later. In the earlier article as well as in the later book Bainton's reasoning is formed by his judgment that the Puritans—specifically the Congregationalists or Independents—were crusaders, the prime movers in the transformation of just war ideas into ideas of holy war. The influence this judgment has had on a generation of scholarship is too pervasive to catalogue; an illustration of its extent, however, is offered by

[72] Roland Bainton, "Congregationalism: From the Just War to the Crusade in the Puritan Revolution," pt. 1 of the 1942 Southworth Lectures, *Andover Newton Theological School Bulletin*, 35, no. 3 (April 1943), pp. 1–20. Hereafter "Congregationalism."

[73] *Ibid.*, p. 15. The same four characteristics appear in only slightly different language in *Christian Attitudes toward War and Peace*, p. 148 (or see note 23, above).

134

Michael Walzer's recent book, *The Revolution of the Saints*.[74] Beginning with Bainton's characterization of holy war, Walzer adds impressive evidence to support the Bainton thesis that the Puritans were crusaders, their Revolution a holy war.

Walzer stresses the martial imagery employed by Puritan preachers, discerning two ways in which it is expressed: by the description of God as the warlike Lord of the universe and by the identification of man's moral struggle with the struggles of a soldier in battle.[75] The rigorous moral self-discipline required of a saint is linked here with the growth of disciplined armies, easily distinguished from the disorganized, motley bands who, Walzer asserts, had previously fought wars.[76]

Surveying the "hundred years of Protestant militancy that stretched roughly from the 1550's to the 1650's," he believes he has found the *terminus ad quem*:

> The culminating point was reached in Cromwell's England. For if the political analogue of the just war was the limited act of legal resistance, then the analogue of the crusade—once the nation had replaced the world of Christendom—was revolution. Behind both crusade and revolution lay the idea of contention for a cause. It was at revolution that Calvinist thinkers finally arrived, by imposing their conscientious purposes upon the medieval notions of warfare.[77]

Walzer's analogy—just war is to crusade as limited, legal resistance is to revolution—goes beyond Bainton's

---

[74] Michael Walzer, *The Revolution of the Saints* (Cambridge, Mass.: Harvard University Press, 1965).

[75] *Ibid.*, chap. 8; see especially p. 278.

[76] *Ibid.*, pp. 286–88.   [77] *Ibid.*, p. 270.

argument but agrees with it in identifying the Puritan
Revolution as a crusade. Walzer is surely building upon
Bainton's foundation when he identifies the bond between crusade and revolution: "Behind both . . . lay the
idea of contention for a cause." Though Bainton gives
revolution only a glance in *Christian Attitudes toward
War and Peace,* in his 1942 paper he too links the
themes of revolution and crusade,[78] though he does not
develop this connection in any systematic way. But
Walzer's book is an attempt to interpret Calvinism as
a revolutionary ideology, and in the context of the book
something more seems to be claimed. For Walzer crusade and revolution are analogous because both are
ideological warfare, a term for which "contention for a
cause" is a euphemism. Behind Walzer's analysis may
be discerned a point of view formed by contemporary
concerns—without, I think, warping the analysis itself.
That the Puritan Revolution is analogous to a twentieth-
century ideologically inspired revolution is a creative
insight and one with which I am in substantial agreement. But one must be extremely careful in exploring
the analogy Walzer makes between just war and crusade, legal resistance and revolution, for within it is
another implicit comparison—one between crusade and
revolution. I do not know whether Walzer intended this
comparison or not; these two ideas are no more alike
than are just war between nations and legal resistance
within a nation to its rulers. The comparison Walzer
makes is true of all possible pairs of comparable terms
only in a context like that which he is addressing: a
revolution that is also a crusade. Leaving aside for now
the important question whether the Puritan Revolution

[78] Bainton, "Congregationalism," p. 3.

was in fact a crusade, as Walzer (and Bainton before him) contends, I wish to suggest a more generally correct relationship between the ideas of crusade and revolution. I suggest that the real comparison, obscured in Walzer's analysis by the historical context he is addressing, is between the crusade motif and ideology, while revolution—I should prefer to say revolutionary war—is a type definitionally distinct from either of these two ideas. That is, a crusading revolution—we might coin the term "holy revolution," signifying one fought for purposes like those that define holy war—is analogous to an ideological revolution. A similar analogy might be laid alongside: holy war is like ideological war. The only difference between these two sets of compared terms is that between the signification of "revolution" and "war," the former denoting an intranational, the latter an international conflict.

This is not the place for further consideration of the general relation between ideology and warfare, revolutionary or otherwise. I wish instead to focus on evidence provided in this chapter regarding the relation, in the context of English thought during the sixteenth and seventeenth centuries, between holy war and revolution; specifically, on how to define holy war in this context. Doing so will involve a final decision on a matter already broached: whether removal of the limits of the *jus in bello* forms a necessary part of the holy war theme.

Again, Bainton's four defining characteristics for the crusading idea are a holy cause, God's direction and help, godly crusaders and ungodly enemies, and unsparing prosecution. I have already suggested several times that this list is inadequate to characterize the entire phenomenon of English holy war thought.

First, the derivation of the list is inadequate. Bainton correctly speaks of a movement in English thought from just war to holy war doctrine, but he locates the Independent Puritans at the center of this movement, placing it in the early seventeenth century.[79] As this chapter has shown, however, holy war thought can be traced back at least to Allen and Bullinger, and many diverse types of Englishmen can be identified as holy war thinkers, not just Independents. The entire phenomenon, not just the small segment that Bainton chooses, must be the source of defining characteristics for holy war.

Second, the use of the list is improper. Bainton speaks of a *movement* in thought; yet the crusading idea that he defines is an ideal type, characteristic only of those who, to his mind, have moved all the way to the end: the Independents in the Puritan Revolution. This requires all four characteristics to be present in order to define a given figure as crusader. More, however, can be comprehended about the *movement* of holy war advocacy by not insisting on the presence of all defining characteristics. As I have shown, a spectrum of advocacy of holy war appears in English writings in the period being examined; that spectrum is the product of a flow of ideas as well as of a divergence in temperaments and occupations. But Bainton's preoccupation with the crusading idea as an ideal type prevents his discerning any but Independents as would-be crusaders. Assuming that it is possible, through an investigation that is circular—or rather spiral—to list characteristics of holy war thought, the proper application is to identify more colorations within the spectrum, not

[79] *Ibid.*, especially pp. 3–6.

simply to identify those persons who are closest to the "ideal."

Third, Bainton's list of characteristics is incomplete, and fourth, his last characteristic does not belong in such a list. I shall discuss these points in showing how my own characterization of English holy war thought is constructed on the basis of the figures examined in this chapter.

Systematically, one beginning in a vacuum might best proceed to define holy war as war fought for religious purposes, then attach other elements to that nucleus, using the work of theorizers and practicians of holy war over time. But such a vacuum does not exist in the interpretation of history: both the influences on those being examined and the interpretations of previous analysts combine to provide the atmosphere in which every new attempt is made to understand and describe a particular historical moment.

Rather than to begin with one single defining mark, then, let us begin with Bainton's four and study them in connection with the positions advanced by the eight theorists examined above (La Noue, who is important only in regard to the question of limits on the prosecution of holy war, is not counted in this group). All eight of these men accept the idea of war for a godly cause, *i.e.*, for the sake of true religion. This is true whether the religion is Roman Catholic, Calvinist, or that of the established Church of England. But surely some further distinctions should be made and are indeed possible. All eight men join in enlarging the classic just war doctrine's allowance of defensive war to include defense of religion—not unusual when religion and nationalism were inseparable concepts, when no one thought to challenge the idea of one people, one religion, and when the Lutheran-Catholic compromise—*cuius regio, eius religio*—still seemed a sensible principle. But five of the figures treated above add a concept of war commanded by God, an idea present in Augustine but as likely, in the English context, drawn from a new look at the wars of the Israelites. Those who do not assert that God himself declares some wars for religion are diverse: the "Politicke" Bacon, the "Moderate Divine" Gosson, and the "Catholic Zelant" Allen. Bacon and Gosson both allow preemptive defensive war for religion, a position that comes perilously close to permitting offensive war for this cause, but they do not anywhere advance the idea that God commands Christians into some wars. Allen, finally, allows war for religion at the *Pope's* command; yet this is not formally different, in his conception, from allowing it at the command of any sovereign prince, and it is in direct line with the late medieval separation of churchly from secular authority for waging just war.

As for Bainton's second characteristic, the presence of God's direction and help, only four of the writings we have examined state explicitly that God directs his chosen ones or actively fights himself for their cause. Bullinger, who goes quite far in most respects, does not claim that God actively participates in a holy war; and Gosson, who alone among these four has no concept of divinely commanded wars, asserts that God does help the godly to win victory.

Only Bacon, perhaps exercising a prudent restraint in his judgment of English moral qualities, does not claim godliness for the soldiers on his side and ungodliness for the enemies. The idea of personal godliness or righteousness is of course what is at issue here, not the rightness of one's own brand of religion. Bacon alone, among the holy war proponents discussed above, would admit the possibility of impure warriors fighting in a pure cause. And we must ask further just what is implied in the godliness advocated by the other seven of the above figures; rather than agreeing on what constitutes godliness, they reveal a spread of meanings ranging from Barnes' statement that war "requires putting on a kinde of cruelty"—a position that suggests strongly that there is a special variety of godliness peculiar to the soldier of righteousness—to Gosson's argument that godliness means the charitable impulse not to take any more life than necessary to win the war. In the one case godliness implies the removal of the just war limits on the prosecution of war; in the other it implies more scrupulous observation of these limits because they are inspired by charity.

Finally, concerning the question whether any limits must be observed in the conduct of a holy war, only three of the positions discussed above advocate unsparing prosecution: those of Bullinger, Allen, and Barnes. And even these may be discounted. In Bullinger and Allen the context is that of the punishment of rebels— action that in their day was generally expected to be unrestricted. Luther's anger against the German peasants' rebellion might be recalled. Perhaps more immediately to the point is the admiration Thomas Churchyard expressed in 1579 toward the method by which the most recent Irish rebellion of his time had been suppressed. He speaks of Sir Humphrey Gilbert, the commander of the Government's forces:

> He further tooke this order infringeable, that when soever he made any ostyng, or inrode, into the enemies Countrey, he killed manne, woman, and child,

141

and spoiled, wasted, and burned, by the grounde all that he might: leavyng nothing of the enemies in saffetie, whiche he could possiblie waste, or consume. . . . [T]he men of warre could not be maintained, without their Churles, and Calliackes, or women, who milked their Creates, and provided their victualles, and other necessaries. So that the killing of them by the sworde, was the waie to kill the menne of warre by famine, who by flight oftentymes saved them selves from the dinte of the sworde.[80]

Churchyard is not in the least concerned in his treatise as a whole or in the passage just cited with making a case for holy war against the Irish because they are Catholics. His venom against them flows entirely from the fact that they are rebels. Moreover, he argues implicitly in the above passage for a counterrevolutionary strategy given new form in our own day: if revolutionaries live among the people like fish in water, the way to kill the fish is to dry up the water. This is in opposition to the accepted practice of warfare between states in Churchyard's day, according to which supply trains and peasants on the land were to be accorded immunity against the ravages of war.[81] It is clearly the fact of rebellion that for Churchyard, as for his age generally, excuses extreme measures in warfare. Since Churchyard, Bullinger, and Allen are contemporaries, it is seri-

[80] Thomas Churchyard, *A Generall Rehearsall of Warres, called Churchyardes Choice* (London: Edward White, 1579), Sig. Q. ii.
[81] See my argument in "The Meaning of Non-Combatant Immunity in the Just War/Limited War Tradition," *Journal of the American Academy of Religion*, xxxix, no. 2 (June 1971), pp. 151–70.

ously questionable whether the advocacy of unlimited war put forward by the latter two comes from considerations of the implications of holy war or those of revolution. The evidence, however, argues for the latter.

The strong witness of the two Huguenot partisans, La Noue and Saillans/Loque, further challenges the association of unlimited prosecution with war for religion. Both French writers explicitly indicate the importance of the customary limits on war, those given in just war doctrine and those hallowed by long practice among armies at war. For these men war for religion in no way removes these limits.

On the other hand again, Barnes would have holy war fought unsparingly. But his reasons derive from considerations that, on closer examination, are suspect. His argument is that war necessarily requires cruelty and induces human blood-lust. The only restraints on war are those on the entry into war; once fighting is begun, it must be unrestrained. God's command to war, then, sanctifies acts that in time of peace would be profoundly sinful. For Barnes it is not *holy* war that requires unlimited prosecution; it is *war itself*. I will not here challenge this interpretation of the requirements of war, either in general or in the seventeenth-century context; I wish only to indicate that the call for unrestrained cruelty made by Barnes comes out of his judgment as to the nature of *war*, not out of his perception of the requirements of God's command to *holy* war.

Finally, though there is no space here to go into this matter at length, the execution of the Puritan Revolution does not support the judgment that the Puritans were crusaders, their revolution a holy war. David Little has argued against Bainton on this point through the

analysis of certain key Puritan figures writing during
and after the first civil war.[82] Little concludes that
though holy war appeals play an important part in the
literature of the revolution, just war arguments are also
present, so that it is incorrect to speak, as do Bainton
and Walzer, of an irreversible shift from just war to
holy war in Puritan thought. Even in Cromwell (whom
he terms one of "the most obvious crusaders") Little
discovers "an appeal to the very standards of legitimacy
and just cause, based on the principle of free consent
and commonly available right reason," such as is expressed more explicitly in Milton, Cromwell's contemporary, and later figures like Locke—and, we might
add, in just war thought present in Christian doctrine
in the seventeenth century. Little's analysis bears out
the judgment that there was a spectrum of opinion
favoring holy war, that the movement away from just
war doctrine proper was in a sense never fully completed, which I have argued implicitly throughout this
chapter. Two further points in connection with the
Puritan Revolution must be made, concerning the lack
of limitations in wars for religion. First, the battles on
English soil were not marked with especial cruelties,
even though they might have been expected to be since
the Parliamentarians and the Royalists mutually regarded each other as rebels against the source of true
authority in the English nation. Second, Cromwell's expedition to Ireland was, in the context of the times,
remarkably restrained: Cromwell attempted to fight

[82] Little makes this argument in an unpublished paper, "Some
Justifications for Violence in the Puritan Revolution," read at
the 12th annual meeting of the American Society of Christian
Ethics, Wesley Theological Seminary, Washington, D.C., on January 23, 1971.

against armies, not against the populace; his terms when besieging towns were, though firm, not unusual for wars of the period, and even the massacre at Drogheda upon which Bainton places so much weight was the result of a loss of communication between commander and troops. Whatever he might have thought of them, Cromwell treated the Irish rebels as honorable opponents in war, not in the manner of a Sir Humphrey Gilbert suppressing the rebels of Munster. Even granting Bainton's (and Walzer's) point that the Puritans (the Independents especially, who were at the core of the New Model Army) were convinced crusaders in a holy cause, they did not practice war without restraints. Indeed, one of Walzer's points appears to contradict another in this connection. Wherever, in this period, lack of restraint was to be found in the acts of soldiers, it was usually associated with lack of discipline. This can be seen in the depredations of the Thirty Years' War, the cruelties on both sides in the French wars of religion, and in Cromwell's loss of control of his ordinarily superbly disciplined forces at Drogheda. It is indeed curious to discover Walzer arguing, then, on the one hand for Bainton's definition of holy war as requiring unlimited prosecution, and on the other hand for war for religion as the context of a significant increase in military discipline deriving from the need for careful discipline in the Christian life.

In sum, it does not appear that unrestrained prosecution, or removal of the limits required by the just war doctrine on *jus in bello,* is an essential part of holy war doctrine as it developed in English thought in the sixteenth and seventeenth centuries. Where holy war advocacy is accompanied by a removal of limits *in bello,* this latter characteristic is the result of some extraneous

145

factor—a judgment as to the nature of war in general, as in Barnes, or a wedding of holy war and counter-revolutionary interests, as in Bullinger and Allen. Even in the latter case, elements of moderation may impose restraints on those fighting the rebels, if the witness of Gosson, Leighton, La Noue, and Saillans is taken seriously, and if the example of the Puritan Revolution is examined closely.

To return to Walzer's implicit comparison, crusade and revolution are not similar concepts. Though a crusade is indeed "contention for a cause," revolution is not such except in the case of what I have above termed "holy revolution" by analogy with holy war.[83] The proper analogy is not between crusade and revolution, but between revolution for religious purposes and revolution for purposes implied by, say, Marxist/Leninist ideology. What should be compared are the functions of the purposes in coloring the conduct of the revolution, and the comparison should involve an understanding of both the religion and the ideology, as well as scrupulous observation of the actual conduct of revolutionary wars fought for both these causes. The problem is obscured by Walzer's treatment of the ideas of crusade and revolution in the context of Puritanism during the first civil war, a confusion of ideas to which he was led by Bainton's characterization of holy war. As the argument of this chapter has shown, this characterization is inadequate taken as a whole, and its last provision, that holy war be prosecuted unsparingly, is generally false.

[83] At least revolution is not "contention for a cause" in the same sense as is holy war, unless Walzer is referring to that minimal and totally general sense in which *any* human action is controlled by some "cause."

Biographical Data

Of the men discussed in this chapter *Francis Bacon*, Lord Verulam (1561–1626), is least likely to need any introduction. But a brief statement will place him in the context of this chapter. Bacon studied at Trinity College, Cambridge, and at Gray's Inn, where he was a friend of William Fulbecke (see Chapter III) and collaborated on a masque with him and six other students. Bacon's uncle, William Cecil, Lord Burghley, using his influence at court early launched the young Francis upon a diplomatic career. Bacon rose quickly and became an adviser to Queen Elizabeth, with his relation to Burghley helping to assure him ready access to the Queen. Bacon retained his position at court after Elizabeth's death, but he never became as close to James as he had been to Elizabeth, and his influence suffered accordingly. The two writings considered in this chapter are from late in Bacon's life and are generally directed to the supposed Spanish design for a universal monarchy with the Spanish King at its head and the Catholic religion as its faith.

Stephen Gosson (1554–1624) was educated at Corpus Christi College, Oxford (B.A., 1576). He preached twice at St. Paul's Cross Church while serving as Rector of Great Wigborough, Essex; *A Trumpet of Warre*, the sermon treated in this chapter, was the second of these sermons, and its popularity led to its subsequent printing.

The Swiss reformer *Henry* (or Heinrich) *Bullinger* (1504–75) was an immensely popular figure among the reformist wing of the English church during the reign of Edward VI, when the aid and presence of continental reformers were being actively courted by those around the King. During the subsequent reign of Mary, Bullinger played host to many of the English Protestant exiles, and upon Elizabeth's accession to the throne they carried Bullinger's influence back to England with them. Bullinger was in many respects a moderate among the reformers; this characteristic allowed Elizabeth to use his prestige as a counter to the more rigid Calvinists among the Puritan party. Bullinger's great degree of favor in England is illustrated by the fact of his *Decades* being made required reading for the English clergy during Whitgift's tenure as Archbishop of Canterbury.

William Cardinal Allen (1532–94) was the foremost spokesman for English Catholics during the reign of Elizabeth. Educated at Oriel College, Oxford (B.A., 1550), and a fellow there, Allen did not resolve to become a priest until Mary became Queen of England. Most of his life—all of that for which he is well known—was spent abroad, after his removal to Flanders in 1561. He taught first at the University of Louvain, and he also began to write there. In 1567 he was ordained a priest. Through his efforts the English College of the University of Douay was founded; Allen became Regius Professor of Divinity there in 1570. After 1579 he was involved in various political intrigues in the Low Countries, where politics were largely defined by adherence to Catholic or Protestant religion. His reward for service to the Catholic cause came in 1587, when Sixtus V broke his own rule by elevating Allen to cardinal at a time other than a church festival. The treatise discussed in this chapter dates from the latter part of Allen's life, when he had become a well-known antagonist of the Elizabethan compromise on religion.

William Gouge, Alexander Leighton, and *Thomas Barnes* all fall under that somewhat hard-to-define rubric, Puritanism. Gouge (1578–1673) is by far the best known of these three. This divine was educated at King's College, Cambridge (B.A., 1598; M.A., 1602), where he later taught. His specialties were logic and Hebrew, but he wrote prolifically on a wide range of theological subjects, displaying a strict Calvinism and an equally rigid social conservatism. A member of the Westminster Assembly, he sat on the committees on the examination of ministers and on the confession of faith. Gouge was a popular preacher; many of his sermons (including the one discussed in this chapter) were later published. Leighton and Barnes, contemporaries of Gouge, are less well known and were in their time less influential. Leighton is the more colorful of the two. A Scot, educated at St. Andrew's (M.A.) and Leyden (M.D.), he practiced medicine in London and wrote tracts expounding his preferences in religion. Besides his *Speculum Belli Sacri* (treated in this chapter), he wrote a treatise called *An Appeal to the Parliament, or Sion's Plea against the Prelacie* (1628), which grew out of a petition he had earlier presented to Parliament against bishops and for presbyterianism. The subtitle of this work gives its flavor: "an appeal to political presbyterianism to take sword in hand." A holy cause thus extended, for him, even to justifying revolution to establish the right form of church government.

149

CHAPTER III

The Beginnings of a Secular
Just War Doctrine

THE JUST war doctrine bequeathed by the late Middle Ages to the modern period was an amalgam of elements supported by two quite distinct rationales: the theological, derived principally from Augustine through Thomas Aquinas and the canon law; and the legal, drawn from Roman law, the chivalric code, and common practice among men. Though the doctrine manifested considerable unity on the practical level—exemplified as early as Bonet's *Tree of Battles*—no specific attempt was made on the theoretical level to reconcile the disparate rationales that informed it. Unity on the theoretical level was provided rather by the general relation between nature and grace as conceived in Scholastic theology, whereby nature was comprehended within grace and grace was the perfection of nature. By the end of the Middle Ages, however, this synthesis had broken down and was being supplanted by new explanations, which were not always capable of doing justice to everything that the Scholastics had placed within their order. The changes in just war doctrine in the sixteenth and seventeenth centuries may be regarded as two attempts to give new explanations, both of which somewhat truncate the medieval doctrine on war. Thus the movement toward advocacy of holy war may be understood, with some justification, as a simplification of late medieval just war doctrine based on the assumption of all its elements under the single rationale of the theological; and the contrary movement toward what was to become international law may similarly be understood as an attempt to subsume everything under the rationale of a secularized law of nature—and in particular under the *jus gentium*—cut off from its relation to supernature.

This description of the movements in thought does, however, somewhat oversimplify what is in essence a most complex phenomenon. Even the most radical proponents of holy war did not entirely forsake guidance they deemed worthwhile, even though they could not trace it directly to God. Alexander Leighton's position on *jus in bello* is an example; it derives principally from works on military discipline. Conversely, removing just war doctrine from natural law did not mean, in the sixteenth and seventeenth centuries, laying aside something of value that belonged to the realm of the supernatural as defined in the Middle Ages; there was a common reliance on Christian charity, for example, as providing wisdom not accessible to unbelievers. In the context being explored here just war doctrine remained a mixture of elements not altogether compatible on the level of theory. Historical judgments are always relative, and it is only from the viewpoint of a later age, after movements begun in the sixteenth century have run their course, that it can be said that the men examined here were engaged in reducing just war theory to either of two rationales, the theological or that of natural law. They would themselves not yet have understood this dichotomy. For all the differences between the positions explored in this and the previous chap-

151

ter—which it is to our purpose to set in stark relief—
there is also a great deal in common, a fact deriving
not only from their growth in the same historical period.
In sum, then, two opposing facts must be held in tension for correct understanding of just war doctrine in
the sixteenth and seventeenth centuries: first, holy war
doctrine and a secularizing just war doctrine come into
being, largely in opposition to each other, as attempts
to subsume late medieval just war doctrine under either
the theological rationale or that of natural law; second,
these doctrines have much in common due to their
common rootage in the medieval theory and to their
common genesis in the historical context of the post-
Reformation period.

England provides a unique crucible within which to
examine the growth of holy war advocacy in the sixteenth and seventeenth centuries, but there is no similar
crucible within which to place the increasingly secularized just war doctrine that was to grow into the modern science of international law. Not only in England
but in France, Germany, and Spain holy war theses
were raised in practical and theoretical works on war;
yet in England the entire range of holy war advocacy
is uniquely present. Thought from all over Europe
focuses there during the period of relative calm that
marks the English Reformation as opposed to the religious wars of the Continent. Considerable attention has
in the past been directed to the Spanish theorists Victoria, Soto, Molina, and Suarez as providing the foundation for modern international law.[1] These men—espe-

[1] See, e.g., James Brown Scott, *The Spanish Origin of International Law* (Oxford: at the Clarendon Press; London: Humphrey Milford, 1934), and Bernice Hamilton, *Political Thought in
Sixteenth-century Spain* (cited Chap. I, n. 33, above).

cially Victoria and Suarez—have indeed left a strong impression in this movement of thought. But a more accurate picture of the movement toward a secularized just war doctrine results from taking into account representatives from the Netherlands and England as well as from Spain. Examining this type of thought as advanced by Englishmen will also help to preclude the erroneous idea that while Englishmen busied themselves with crusading thoughts, Spaniards were building up the foundations of a new international order. Had only Spaniards been thinking along these lines, the new order would never have emerged; its genesis and growth derive not only from changed historical conditions but also from fairly widespread attempts to think out the implications of these changed conditions with the help of natural law considerations. Accordingly, in this chapter we shall examine not only the positions of Victoria and Suarez on war but also those of the Englishmen Matthew Sutcliffe, an adviser to Queen Elizabeth; William Fulbecke, a jurist; and William Ames, Puritan theologian and student of William Perkins. Ames was, moreover, resident in Holland when he prepared his position on war, which is included in his highly influential *Conscience, with the Power and Cases Thereof.*[2] Grotius, Locke, and Vattel will be treated in the next chapter.

What unites the theorists now to be examined is their common reliance on natural, as opposed to supernatural, sanction for the guidelines they advance for just war. We must explore the implications of this reliance on their definitions of just war, particularly their

[2] William Ames, *Conscience, with the Power and Cases Thereof* (n.p.: 1639). This is often called by its Latin title, *De Conscientia.*

attitudes toward war for religion, their use of the inherited tradition on the *jus ad bellum*, and their use of the newly emerged *jus in bello*.

THE REJECTION OF WAR FOR RELIGION

FRANCISCUS DE VICTORIA

To ground war in nature seems implicitly to require rejection of warfare for the sake of religion; at least that is the common opinion of the writers treated here. Victoria bluntly sets the tone: "Difference of religion is not a cause of just war."[3] Nor is extension of empire[4] or glory or advantage to the prince.[5] "There is a single and only just cause for commencing a war, namely, wrong received."[6] The question of what sorts of wrong can be cause of just war will be taken up later; the point here is that Victoria does not make the easy assimilation that even Bacon makes: that difference in religion is *implicitly* wrong done. Both in this *locus* and in the relectio *De Indis*, where he develops more fully his prohibition of war for religion, it is the case of offensive war that is at issue: war for propagation of religious faith. Indubitably defensive war is in order against those who are making war against one to impose an alien religion. Yet according to Victoria even such foes may be resisted—and, in the end, punished—for the natural and political disorders that follow from their invasion, not for their intent to settle an unwelcome

---

[3] Franciscus de Victoria, *De Indis et De Jure Belli Relectiones*, ed. Ernest Nys, in *The Classics of International Law*, ed. James Brown Scott (Washington: Carnegie Institute, 1917): *De Jure Belli*, sect. 10.

[4] *Ibid.*, sect. 11.   [5] *Ibid.*, sect. 12.   [6] *Ibid.*, sect. 13.

religion upon the land. Victoria's only treatment of this matter in *De Jure Belli* comes in connection with the question whether a war can be just on both sides simultaneously. Such a possibility might arise, he suggests, if war were to be waged merely as the result of the prince's belief that he is in the right. Such is the case when Turks and Saracens attack Christians to propagate Islam, believing this to be a just cause. The Christians, in such a case, have the obvious right of defending themselves, and thus they fight in a just cause. But if both sides are fighting justly, a paradox arises: "In this way all belligerents would be innocent and it would not be lawful to kill them."[7] In this case the paradox is easily resolved, for the Turks and Saracens only *believe* themselves to have a just cause, while the Christians actually *have* one. Offensive war for religion is thus repudiated for infidels, but the Christians' self-defense is grounded in natural causes—the right to oppose pillage, rape, killing, and everything else war brings—and not religious causes.[8]

But does the lesson thus taught apply when the tables are turned? May Christians make war against infidels to convert them? This question receives considerable attention in *De Indis*, section II, where the specific problem is whether the Spanish in the New World may convert the Indians by force. Again, Victoria's basic point is the same: if the Christians may attack for this reason, the Indians have the natural right to defend themselves; therefore if it is just to make war for religion, the paradoxical conclusion must be that such war is just on both sides, so that no one may kill anyone.

[7] *Ibid.*, sect. 20.   [8] *Ibid.*, sects. 18–19.

What is most interesting in Victoria's discussion is his demolition of various sorts of claims for the justice of the Christian cause against the Indians—an argument which applies equally to all who would make war to propagate religion, whether Spaniards, Turks, or Englishmen. His reasoning, compressed considerably for our purposes here, runs as follows: if the Indians have had Christianity announced to them, this is not ground for war, because they must have its truth proved to them; if they have had its truth proved by rational argument, example, and miracle, this is not ground for war since coercion of the will only produces feigned belief; finally, even the mortal sin of the Indians in refusing to accept the faith once its truth is set forth sufficiently is not ground for war, since the Spanish have no authority over them to punish their sins, not even through the Pope.[9] In connection with the second point Victoria invokes Aquinas, "where he says that unbelievers who have never received the faith, like Gentiles and Jews, are in no wise to be compelled to do so."[10] But his point is fundamentally that in natural law belief cannot be forced, and therefore war to force belief can never be just. Similarly, in connection with the third point, Victoria cites the Old Testament, not to make a theological point, but to give a concrete example to illustrate the natural-law argument he has advanced:

> [E]ven in the Old Testament, where much was done by force of arms, the people of Israel never seized the land of unbelievers either because they were unbelievers or idolaters or because they were guilty of

[9] *De Indis*, sect. II, 10–16.
[10] *Ibid.*, 15. Victoria cites Thomas' *Summa Theologica*, II/II, Quest. 10, Art 8.

other sins against nature (and there were people guilty of many such sins, in that they were idolaters and committed many other sins against nature, as by sacrificing their sons and daughters to devils), but because of either a special gift from God or because their enemies had hindered their passage or had attacked them.[11]

If the Indians attack the Spanish or interfere with their peaceful passage for trading purposes, the Spanish may justly respond in kind, since the injustice of the Indians' actions is known from natural law;[12] yet the Spanish have no sway over the Indians for any other reason. What of the possibility of some "special gift from God" such as the Israelites received? This, indeed, is what holy war advocates often claim to have received, as the previous chapter shows. But this possibility does not exist, as Victoria sees the matter. God's lordship, so far as it is exercised through men and not directly, flows through legitimate channels—the Pope in matters spiritual and the Emperor and other princes in matters temporal. But these have no authority over the Indians, who have not submitted themselves to them.[13] Thus they cannot justly authorize war against the Indians to punish their sins, so long as these sins hurt no one except the Indians themselves.

Victoria's argument returns always to the same fundamental proposition: *a just war may not be waged except for causes provided for in natural law.* Only these bind all men equally. To allow war for religion opens up the paradoxical possibility of a war seemingly just on both sides; that possibility presents difficulties, though they

[11] *De Indis*, sect. ii, 16.   [12] *Ibid.*, sect. iii, 8.
[13] *Ibid.*, sect. ii, 3–7.

are not insurmountable. Victoria's main point seems to be that belief cannot be forced, and it is therefore illegitimate to try to do so. This argument against war for the propagation of religion thus cuts equally against all who advocate holy war, whatever be their faith. It is in fact only a supplementary point that Christianity is to be spread through preaching the Gospel, not through the sword;[14] but to say so heaps coals of fire upon the head of any Christian who would promote holy war against unbelievers. Just war may be waged only for wrong received, as Victoria states the doctrine he has received; yet for him "wrong received" must always be defined in terms of natural rights violated, never solely in terms of spiritual offense given.

Victoria's influence was considerable, and his example was widely followed. The "New Laws of the Indies" of Charles V (promulgated in 1542) depended heavily on the relectios *De Indis* and *De Jure Belli*. Of the writers treated below, Suarez and Fulbecke cite Victoria, and Sutcliffe and Ames show unmistakable signs of having read him. Grotius, of course, draws much from him. Echoes of his position thus are to be expected in the arguments of all these men, and yet each adds something of his own.

MATTHEW SUTCLIFFE

Sutcliffe's major contribution, which places the *jus in bello* in connection with a dissertation on military discipline, is developed below. As regards war for religion, he, like Victoria, admits it only for defense, and even then it is natural law that provides the justification: "First it is lawfull to use force, and take armes in de-

[14] *Ibid.*, 8, 15; sect. III, 9.

fence of our country, true religion, our goodes or liberty. Reason teaches the learned, and custome instructeth all nations thus much. . . ."[15] Still, he maintains something of the medieval attitude that war is a trial by arms, with God sitting as judge and, moreover, aiding his favorite. He cites Bernard, "If the cause of him that warreth be good, the issue cannot be evil"; yet uncertainty requires that this bald statement be qualified. What Bernard means, Sutcliffe comments, is that having a good cause makes soldiers more courageous, and *vice versa*, since they "*hope* to receive favour of God in the issue, and triall."[16] His tentative tone continues: "[T]he event *oftentimes* is according to the justice, and qualitie of the cause; *seldome* do they return in safety, that go forth to draw their swords in evill quarrels."[17] This is a far cry from the certainty of God's favor and even his help announced by the proponents of holy war among Sutcliffe's contemporaries, and moreover it does not even echo the faith of the Middle Ages in the right outcome of just war. Sutcliffe avoids the pitfall of "might makes right," the result of secularizing just war doctrine while continuing to uphold the belief that the side that is in the right always wins; he moves rather in an opposite direction. Not yet so secularized that he wishes to set aside the watchfulness of God over human activities (including war), he nevertheless refuses to ground victory unequivocally in God's help. It is the courage of soldiers who believe their cause to be just that, other things being equal, provides the margin of

[15] Matthew Sutcliffe, *The Practice, Proceedings, and Lawes of Armes* (London: Christopher Barker, 1593), p. 3.

[16] *Ibid.*, p. 2.

[17] *Ibid.*, emphasis added.

victory. Victory is thus grounded in the natural. This, with Sutcliffe's implication that the wrong side sometimes wins, is the road taken by the main line of international law in opposition to Machiavellian doctrine.

WILLIAM FULBECKE

Augustine had permitted war commanded by God; this provision, repeated by Gratian and Thomas Aquinas, is an inescapable element in the just war doctrine bequeathed by the Middle Ages and forms the core around which holy war doctrine crystallized. But though the theorists of the sixteenth and seventeenth centuries could not escape this provision, they could, and did, modify it by endless qualifications. The carefully wrought twisting and turning of the thought of the scholarly jurist William Fulbecke, a contemporary of Gosson and Bacon, affords an example. Following the lead of late medieval thinkers, he separates this possible just cause for war from those given by nature. Augustine's provision is, moreover, left shredded and empty by the end of Fulbecke's treatment of it.

It is instructive to follow Fulbecke's argument. To his own question of what causes of war are just, he replies:

Just cause of warre is the defence of our countrie, our selves, our friends, our fellowes, & goods. A defensive warre is grounded upon the lawe of Nature, therefore C. Pontius the Captaine of the Samnites said well, That warre was just unto them, to whom it was necessarie, and that their armes are honest which have no hope of safetie but in weapons. Likewise it is a just warre which is taken in hand for the recoverie of thinges wrongfully, and by force taken from us by our enemies. . . . And the revenge of an injurie . . . is likewise a good cause of warre . . . and that prince hath just cause of warre, who pursueth by armes rebelles and such as swarve from obedience. . . .[18]

Two pages later, after exploration of the above causes and considerable explication of the definition of rebels and what may be done against them, Fulbecke finally returns to the remaining just cause of war: Augustine's provision that God may command some wars directly. Of course, Fulbecke avers, this is a just cause; witness the example of certain wars of Israel. But in his own time this cause is abused by the unrighteous. The Turks "doe alwaies pretend this cause of their warre";[19] and "the late King of Spaine Phillip, did pretende this defence of his warres. . . ."[20] Is it possible that a man of Fulbecke's own time could wage war on God's command without pretense? The *possibility* remains, but no examples can be found. When this subject arises again somewhat later Fulbecke's pessimism has not departed. He cites those who reject holy war: Victoria, Covarruvia, Baldus; yet he also knows of some who approve it: Thomas Aquinas, according to Covarruvia; "the fathers of the councell of Toletum"; Bernard; the Lacedemonians when they warred against the Athenians, and *vice versa*. "But surely," he concludes, "such pretences are but colours of avarice and crueltie, for there is no religion so barbarous, which moveth us to slay men of a contrarie religion." Examples follow: "King Ferdinand entitled the Catholike, did cover all his dishonest desires with the vaile of religion. . . . And Charles the Emperor the nephew of Ferdinād did not

[18] William Fulbecke, *The Pandectes of the Law of Nations* (London: Thomas Wight, 1602), p. 38b.
[19] *Ibid.*, p. 40a.　　　　　[20] *Ibid.*, p. 40b.

garnish his ambitious enterprises with any other colour." Fulbecke concludes by rejecting war for the "pretence of religion," since it is always moved under false colors and since "the cause of religiō is not betwixt man & man, but betwixt man and God."[21]

There is, however, still one circumstance in which religion plays a part in providing just cause for war: that of rebellion by people who profess a faith contrary to that of the nation. Even here difference of religion only is not a sufficient cause for the prince to rise in arms. So long as the nonconformists live peacefully, they are to be tolerated. "Surely such religion as destroyeth the government of common weales and Monarchies, is not to be suffered: But if the religion be good and do not hurt Princes, they that withstand it are like the stubberne Persians which resisted Daniell."[22] That is, such matters should be left to God. Unity of religion is a good thing, but it is to be understood as only one of the elements contributing to the unity of a nation. This latter unity, which is the greater, must be preserved first. "I would not have weapons and armes to stir up warre for Religion onelie, if rebellion or disloialtie be not mixed with it."[23]

Fulbecke's position, though influenced by Victoria's, is nevertheless his own. He goes much further than Victoria—and most other men of his day—in advocating toleration of peaceful dissent, though he was himself a conformist. In his thought war is made entirely a matter of reason of state. It is a political enterprise to the exclusion of all else. Just wars are those fought out of necessity for the defense and preservation of the state. If the nation's religion is attacked as a means of bring-

[21] *Ibid.*, p. 86a.   [22] *Ibid.*, p. 88a.   [23] *Ibid.*, p. 88b.

ing down the established government, the attackers are to be repelled and punished; but if, within the borders of the state, some men wish to follow a religion other than the one supported by the prince and the majority of the people, so long as they do so in peace, it is a matter between them and God alone. The final conclusion of Fulbecke's argument is the unequivocal rejection of war for the sake of religion.

FRANCISCO SUAREZ

Suarez likewise rejects the possibility that religion may offer just cause for war. His position follows Victoria's closely, though Suarez does not simply repeat his predecessor's arguments. Nor does he go so far as Fulbecke does and argue for toleration of peaceful religious dissent within a nation. Indeed, internal divergence of religion provides the one possibility of legitimately taking arms in the cause of religion. The state may, Suarez affirms, coerce unbelievers in matters of the faith. It may, in the first place, require them to hear the faith expounded; and if this is permissible, he argues, then so is much more. Those who remain unbelievers may continue to be required to hear the gospel preached and rationally explicated; indeed, the state may even insist that all citizens practice the forms of Christian worship, since doing so contributes to the understanding that leads to true belief. Suarez is thus far from favoring religious dissent within a nation.[24]

The right of a prince or commonwealth to coerce belief among its own citizens does not, however, imply a similar right to force religion upon non-citizens.[25] The

[24] Suarez, *On Faith*, Disp. XVIII, sect. 5 (for full citation see Chap. I, n. 54, above).

[25] *Ibid.*, sect. 6.

163

only important distinction between the two cases has nothing to do with unbelief; it is purely a matter of the extent of the state's authority. Suarez' argument does not appear to have a different foundation than does Victoria's, and it is likewise similar in certain respects to Fulbecke's, though there is no likelihood of influence in the latter case. A state may coerce its own citizens because of the authority it has over them by reason of their submission to it, an authority given in natural law. Suarez and Fulbecke take separate paths in their respective decisions about the extent to which religious dissent damages the nation. Both appear willing to grant the reasonableness and even truth of established religion, especially since both are speaking of Christianity, but Fulbecke, a true Elizabethan, is willing to suffer peaceful fools, though perhaps not gladly, if they abide by the civil laws. Suarez is more concerned with making sure that unbelievers have the chance to become Christians; yet there is more to his position. By allowing coercion to the point of forcing all citizens to abide by the forms of the established religion, he insures external conformity to all the laws of the state. The tiny crack Fulbecke opens to possible sedition is closed by Suarez.

Over citizens of another state, however, one's own government has no authority. Foreigners have submitted to another authority, which alone has the right to make laws for them and to enforce those laws. A Christian prince may insist that an unbelieving state admit Christian missionaries to his domains—in this Suarez allows more than does Victoria—but this right is strictly limited. Three cases are defined. First, if the unbelieving king wishes to exclude missionaries and his subjects wish to hear them, he is doing them harm and is not validly exercising the right of government they have

164

given him, and so he may be coerced. In the opposite case, if the king would have missionaries and the people would not, the king may justly coerce them—following the reasoning given for domestic religious dissent—accepting the aid of Christian princes in his action. Third, even if both king and people would not admit missionaries, Suarez writes, "I think that they may be forced to permit the preachers of the Gospel to live in their territories; for this tolerance is obligatory under the *jus gentium* and cannot be impeded without just cause."[26] What precisely Suarez has in mind as coming from the *jus gentium* in this last case is unexpressed; however, the right of free peaceful passage would possibly apply here, requiring that peaceful preachers be allowed to travel within foreign lands. One must wonder, though, whether Suarez would equally freely allow non-Christian missionaries the same rights in Christian lands. This argument for imposing Christian missionaries where they are not wanted poses a direct challenge to domestic law. Victoria's paradox would surely apply: would not an unbelieving nation be just in defending itself against the attacks of a Christian state, even though these attacks are justly intended? Ironically, even Fulbecke's argument for toleration would appear to fit Suarez' third case better than does his own insistence on domestic conformity in religion. For Christian missionaries in a non-Christian land, together with those whom they convert, would form just such a peaceful dissenting minority as Fulbecke describes. Suarez appears guilty of special pleading.

The above argument appears in Suarez' treatise *On Faith*; a similar though briefer version is offered in *On Charity* as part of a general discussion of the morality

[26] *Ibid.*, sect. 8.

of war. Here Suarez discounts the claim made by some authorities that when "it happens that a state worshipping the one God inclines toward idolatry through the wickedness of its prince; . . . it is allowable to make war upon that prince."[27] Here the case is not precisely the same as that considered above; it concerns a Christian nation being led astray, not a nation of unbelievers. One might thus think of England rather than of the Indians in the New World. But the reasoning Suarez employs is the same as that used in the earlier case. Invasion may take place only on behalf of the people who are being coerced. "Their [the authorities'] contention would be valid if the prince forcibly compelled his subjects to practice idolatry; but under any other circumstances, [such a ground] would not be sufficient cause for war, unless the whole state should demand assistance against its sovereign. For where compulsion does not intervene, defence has no place."[28]

Though Suarez does not so definitively rule out offensive war for the propagation of the faith, and though he is guilty of special pleading, consistently favoring Christianity in his arguments, he does not assert an unequivocal right to propagate religion by war. Even the allowance he does make is limited: a Christian state may intervene to guarantee free right of passage to peaceful missionaries, and it may act to protect a people from their ruler when he wrongs them or to help a ruler keep order among disobedient subjects. But these are not specifically *religious* grounds for war; Suarez throughout carefully bases justifying causes for war in natural law. He considers two questions: "What is a

[27] Suarez, *On Charity*, Disp. xiii, *On War*, sect. v, 3 (full citation same as above). Hereafter *On War*.
[28] *Ibid.*

166

just cause of war, on the basis of natural reason?"[29] and "Can Christian Princes have any just cause for war beyond that which natural reason dictates?"[30] In the end the answer Suarez gives to this second question is "No." Certain rights exist with regard to nations of unbelievers and nations that are in danger of falling from Christianity into idolatry, but these rights are derived from natural law (or specifically the *jus gentium*) and known by natural reason. Were he more consistent in applying his argument so that Christian nations are not always favored, his position would be virtually the same as Victoria's, and it would be much stronger.

That Suarez did not intend to open the Pandora's box of holy war is apparent from his systematic demolition of all other reasons that authorities before him had advanced favoring war for the cause of religion. May man wreak vengeance for dishonor done to God? No, for God has not given this power, since he is perfectly able to avenge himself, if he wishes.[31] May Christian states advance the claim that they have received special warrant from God like that which was given to the Israelites? No, for such claims cannot be proved, and moreover the Israelites' wars can be justified by natural reasons.[32] Do Christians have dominion over all the world? No, "all such claims are vain inventions." It would be impossible to demonstrate such title to infidels, and so they would be justified in resisting. "Finally, upon that same ground, the Pope or the Emperor could make war [even] upon all Christian princes."[33] What if the barbarians are incapable of governing themselves? "[S]uch a contention cannot have a general application; for it is evident that there are many unbeliev-

[29] *Ibid.*, sect. IV.   [30] *Ibid.*, sect. V.   [31] *Ibid.*, 1.
[32] *Ibid.*, 2.   [33] *Ibid.*, 4.

ers more gifted by nature than are the faithful, and better adapted to political life." To make war for such causes would require that the unbelievers are "so wretched as to live in general more like wild beasts than like men. . . . However, this ground for war should rarely or never be approved, except in circumstances in which the slaughter of innocent people and similar wrongs take place; and therefore, the ground in question is more properly included under defensive than under offensive wars."[34] The general conclusion reached by Suarez follows: "Therefore, the assertion must be made that there is no ground for war so exclusively reserved to Christian princes that it has not some basis in, or at least some due relation to, natural law, being therefore also applicable to princes who are unbelievers."[35]

RELIGION *VS.* NATURE: THE REJECTION OF
RELIGIOUS CAUSE FOR WAR

To a medieval man the distinction made by those who develop just war theory in the sixteenth and seventeenth centuries between natural and religious causes for war would seem artificial at least and at most would never have occurred. But this distinction is central to the thought both of the writers treated in the previous chapter and of those treated here. As different as are their positions on war, both holy war advocates and secularizers of just war doctrine are more like each other— and like our own age—than they are like men of the Middle Ages. This is true, moreover, in spite of the tendency that all of the men treated here reveal to use forms handed down from the medieval period—specifically, to frame their own approaches to war in terms

---

[34] *Ibid.*, 5.   [35] *Ibid.*, 6.

bequeathed by the Middle Ages. But mere use of language that is similar covers a fundamental change: the men of the early modern period no longer assume the unity of nature and grace that informed the thinking of medieval man. The break between the theological and the natural in the specific case of war doctrine occurred, as the first chapter argues, as part of a more general cultural change, and the two branches of just war thought that began to grow in the sixteenth century are the result of complex developments not easily capsulized. Yet it is clear that representatives of both the branches of just war thought set religion and nature against each other, one branch exalting the role of religious causes for war, and the other largely disallowing these while attempting to subsume all possible justifications for war under natural law. The beginnings of our own age are visible here. The role of religion in justifying war has become what we would call ideological; this is the point of Michael Walzer's book on the Puritan revolution, but it is no more true of the Puritan use of religion than of Victoria's two generations earlier. For surely Victoria's discounting of belief as a just cause of war—because it could be proven correct, because the attacked would justly defend himself, making the war just on both sides—treats even Christian religion as the belief structure of a class of people isolated from other possible classes possessing their own belief; and this is precisely what ideology is.

But the conception of natural law had also, by Victoria's time, moved away from the medieval in the direction of the modern age. Medieval theorists of natural law framed their ideas with the study of Roman law and the Scriptures; the increasing role of custom in defining *jus gentium* helped to break the hold of the

169

past in the late Middle Ages. The conventional notion of natural law was still European; though it claimed to contain norms applicable—and knowable—to all men, it was the product of an insular European culture. But with Victoria this had begun to change. Though his principal intent in the two relectios on the Indians is to apply the received natural law to this new case, he is aware of the inhabitants of the New World as subjects who themselves contribute to the making of natural law. For so far as *jus gentium* is defined by customary relations among men, it, as natural law, is modified when new groups of men, previously unknown to each other, come together. Victoria's refusal to treat the Indians as savages little better than animals, and his insistence that they are men and to be treated as such even in the face of a conflict of cultures as severe as any in history, are manifestations of the spirit of modern international law that were only just possibly conceivable to medieval man, who knew of alien cultures only by fantasy and hearsay.

What has just been asserted of Victoria can also be said, *mutatis mutandis*, of the other writers discussed here. They breathe the air of a new age while they themselves help to fashion that age. The realization that religious pretense can cover aggressive war with a cloud of apparent justice drives them to disallow religion as a possible just cause for offensive war. The interpretation of the traditional criterion of harm done to require that it be *material harm against the state or its citizens* removes the remaining possibility that religion might be cause for defensive war; simultaneously this interpretation begins the movement toward complete repudiation of offensive war that reaches a climax in the

170

twentieth century. It is not to the point to question just yet whether these changes have been entirely beneficial, but this question must be asked in the course of this study. Specifically, we must inquire whether we are not ourselves at the edge of a new age, one in which just war theory must again be rethought to provide wisdom for the future.

THE MODERN *Jus ad Bellum*

To fill out the secularized just war doctrine taking shape in the sixteenth and seventeenth centuries it is necessary to explore not only its repudiation of religious causes for war but also what it says positively about the *jus ad bellum* in general. How is it defined? What is its relation to the doctrine of the Middle Ages, of the holy war advocates, of the later modern period? Here too the question whether a war can be just on both sides needs to be investigated, along with possible implications of an affirmative answer.

Thomas Aquinas had declared three things necessary to a just war: right authority, just cause, right intention. As we have seen, these three characteristics apply chiefly to the *jus ad bellum*, with the third providing the beginnings of the *jus in bello*. We shall explore the secularization of the *jus ad bellum* with Aquinas' characteristics as central focus, beginning with the Puritan divine William Ames.

WILLIAM AMES

Ames' *Conscience, with the Power and Cases Thereof* is at once a triumph of Puritan theological method and an indicator of the profound influence Catholic tradition had on even radical Protestant theology. His discussion of war[36] leans heavily on the *Decretals* and Thomas Aquinas and reveals an acquaintance with the Neo-Scholastic interpretation of both, even as it moves in a direction uniquely his own. Thus he questions, "What conditions are requisite to make a War lawfull?" answering with four criteria: just cause, just authority, right intention, just manner of waging.[37] The first three are those of Thomas; the fourth is the *jus in bello* in capsule form, set by Ames into equality with the medieval criteria (this fourth requirement will be treated in the following section). In the first three criteria Ames generally follows Thomas, though close reading reveals important modifications:

> In the second place is required just authority. Now such an authority though in respect of a defensive Warre is to bee found in every Common-wealth although imperfect; because all men have authority by the Law of nature, to defend themselves and to repell force by force, yet in respect of an assaulting Warre, it is not, but in the power of a perfect Commonwealth, which does not depend nor hath any recourse to a superiour, but is in all things sufficient it selfe and entire in every point, which is requisite to a due Government.[38]

[36] Ames, bk. v, chap. xxxiii.

[37] *Ibid.*, Quest. 2. Ames utilizes a precise but somewhat confusing numbering system in *Conscience*, with each paragraph denoted by two numbers, as 4.A.3. or 11.A.5. The first number gives the paragraph its place in the chapter, the second its place in the question. Thus 4.A.3. is the 4th paragraph in this chapter and the 3rd answer (A. means answer) to the previous question, which is in this case Question 1. Questions are not given paragraph numbers.

[38] *Ibid.*, 12.A.2.

This is not a summary of Thomas' statement in the *Summa Theologica* but of Victoria's argument in *De Jure Belli*, 4–9, where the same distinctions are made between perfect and imperfect states and between the right to offensive war and that to defensive war only.

But there are more clues to the immediate source of much of Ames' position on war. He insists that only a "supreame Judge" can make offensive war, but he means by this term not God but the secular prince who has no earthly superior.[39] Such a prince

> . . . and those Souldiers of the higher ranke, who are admitted to Councels of Warre, are bound most diligently to weigh with themselves, and enquire of other prudent and religious men, whether or no they have just cause to make Warre. For, hee who maketh Warre, beares the place of a Judge in all the highest matter. Now a Judge is bound to use all dilligence in the examination of causes, that so hee may give sentence out of right judgment. It doth not therefore suffice to the Justice of a Warre, that a Prince doe beleeve he hath a just cause, but hee must bee very certain upon triall of knowledge. And hence, the adverse parties reasons, are alwayes to bee heard, if they will discusse about, what is fit and good.[40]
>
> If after sufficient examination and deliberation, the Justice of the warre doe still remaine doubtfull, whether the one part bee in possession or not, there ought to bee no Warre made. . . .[41]

This too repeats Victoria (*De Jure Belli*, 20–24), where he rejects the possibility that a prince's belief in the justice of his cause is enough for a just war: "It is essential for a just war that an exceedingly careful examina-

[39] *Ibid.*   [40] *Ibid.*, 15.A.1.   [41] *Ibid.*, 16.A.2.

173

tion be made of the justice and causes of the war and that the reasons of those who on grounds of equity oppose it be listened to."

Other examples of the dependence of Ames' thought on Victoria's could be given, but the foregoing serves as an illustration. The most striking evidence of the dependence is perhaps not even specific passages but the parallelism of the first half of Ames' treatment of war (that directed to the *jus ad bellum*) and the first part of the relectio *De Jure Belli*: the whole manner of treatment is so similar that Ames appears merely to be summarizing the position set forth by Victoria. Here is ample evidence of the influence of the Spanish Dominican on even Puritan thought on war. Ames' assertion of natural right alone as providing just cause for war—in marked contrast to the positions of his contemporaries and fellow-religionists Gouge, Leighton, Barnes, and the authors cited by Bainton—must be recognized for what it is: part of a broad process of secularization that has parallels in economics ("the Protestant ethic") and in government (Lockean social contract theory).

MATTHEW SUTCLIFFE

Sutcliffe, like Ames, lists four requisites for a just war; his listing, however, differs from Ames', and from that of Aquinas as well: "[T]o make just warres, it is not sufficient only that the cause be just; but that they be enterprised first, by those that have soveraigne authority; secondly, that they be not begun especially by those that invade others, without demand of restitution or satisfaction, or denunciation; and last of all, that they be not prosecuted with barbarous crueltie."[42]

Sutcliffe's last point more nearly anticipates Ames'

[42] Sutcliffe, *Lawes of Armes*, p. 9.

final point (a "just manner of waging") than recalls the Augustinian prohibition of wrong motive that forms Aquinas' third characteristic, and it is best taken up in connection with the *jus in bello*. But what of the other three? They are all defined by natural law, and it is perhaps in this light that Sutcliffe discards the requirement of right intent; intentions cannot in principle be verified. This is not, however, true of the three points pertinent to the *jus ad bellum* as listed by Sutcliffe. There are but four just causes for war—defense, retribution, breach of agreements, and dissuasion of those who aid one's enemies—all of which are grounded in natural law and which can be discovered by empirical observation.[43] Similarly, Sutcliffe defines sovereign authority, with the help of Roman and canon law, by its external features, which are in principle verifiable by any man's observation.[44] Finally, the requirement that just wars may be begun by invasion only if preceded by public demand for satisfaction and, if no satisfaction is forthcoming, by public declaration of war—points that Sutcliffe takes from Cicero—places the judgment whether a given war is just in the conscience of all mankind.[45] In sum, Matthew Sutcliffe means to make of the just war a war that abides by certain forms, all rooted in natural law and natural reason, all of which can be verified by empirical methods. The justice of war here is not something that is to be decided by God; it is rather to be declared by the community of all mankind on the basis of whether all requirements are present. Here the justice of a war is emphatically removed from the theological arena and placed into that of natural law, specifically the law of nations.

[43] *Ibid.*, pp. 3–8.   [44] *Ibid.*, p. 9.
[45] *Ibid.*, p. 10.

175

WILLIAM FULBECKE

Fulbecke, like Sutcliffe, does not treat of right intent as a possible criterion for just wars. Nor does he, as a jurist, turn to Thomas Aquinas for a summary of what makes a war just. But these criteria emerge in his discussion of war: just cause, sovereign authority, solemn declaration ("denunciation").[46] The causes for war that Fulbecke deems just have already been discussed in the preceding section; in sum, he requires that a just war be waged out of necessity as defined by reason of state. The natural-law basis of this requisite has also already been noted, and it is in any case obvious. Fulbecke's judgment on sovereign authority is considerably influenced by the law of arms, the remnant of the chivalric code left to the early modern period. The requirement that there be sovereign authority for a just war turns out, furthermore, to determine Fulbecke's conception that such a war must be necessary.

Warre was first brought in by necessitie, for in that decisions of Courtes of Law, and the determining of controversies by their rules, could not be betwixt two straunge Princes of aequall power, unlesse they should willingly agree to such an order, because they have no superior nor ordinarie Judge, but are supreme, and publike persons: therefore the judgement of armes is necessarie because such warre (saith Demosthenes) is against them which can not be brideled by Law. . . : For as there be two kindes of contention; one by triall of Law; the other by triall of Armes: so we may not use the later, if we may have helpe by the former.[47]

[46] Fulbecke, *Pandectes*, pp. 34b–38b.
[47] *Ibid.*, p. 34b.

Fulbecke takes the surprising step of assimilating duels to war linguistically, though he makes the usual distinction between public and private war. War (*bellum*) is also called *duellum* "because it is the contention of two equal persons," namely the kings of the opposing countries.[48] This contention allows Fulbecke to undergird his argument that war must be between two equal sovereigns; a duel cannot be fought, according to the law of arms, except between those of equal rank. Thus the chivalric code is turned into unusual channels.

That a just war must be necessary therefore has two meanings for Fulbecke: it must be necessary in the sense that defense of country, goods, and justice is necessary; and it must be necessary in the sense that there is no higher tribunal to which those who make war can take their suits. Both of these meanings are defined by natural law: the first, as an extension of the right of self-defense; the second, by Fulbecke's decision not to introduce the concept of God as heavenly judge giving victory to the right—the concept that informs the medieval notion of trial by arms. For Fulbecke it is the absence of any other law that requires sovereigns to go to war, and he holds out no guarantee that the one with right on his side will win. His concern, like Sutcliffe's, is that proper forms be followed and the law be scrupulously applied; if this is done, then the outcome must be accepted. This particular version of the idea of war as a court of law leads Fulbecke to accept the possibility that war may be just on both sides at once. It is necessary for Fulbecke's analogy to hold that both belligerents be accorded equal rights and required to take equal responsibilities until the contest is over and justice has been manifested. That both sides must be assumed to

[48] *Ibid.*, p. 34a.

177

possess a *jus ad bellum* and required to act according to the *jus in bello* is here the result of thinking through war on the model of adversary trials in the English legal tradition, whereby innocence is assumed until guilt is proved.

VICTORIA AND SUAREZ: TWO PROBLEMS
IN THE *Jus ad Bellum*

In addition to the attention already given in this section to Victoria, it is necessary to inquire more closely into his position and that of Suarez on the *jus ad bellum*. Both Spanish theologians depend heavily enough on Thomas Aquinas to deserve the name of Neo-Scholastic, which has been applied to them. For this reason it would advance the present discussion very little to give complete accounts of the doctrines of the two men. Rather we shall focus on two points that clearly go beyond Aquinas' position: the entire question of dispelling doubt as to the justice of a war, and the possibility of a war's being just on both sides simultaneously. These points are also of importance for later development of secularized just war doctrine. It makes sense, moreover, to treat the points together, as they have a certain relation to each other in the thought of Victoria and Suarez.[49]

The Problem of Doubt as to Just Cause. The first question has two aspects, one concerning the need for a prince to be certain before making war and the other concerning the need of his subjects to examine the causes of a war before taking part.

We have already had an introduction to the first aspect of this question through the position of Ames, who

[49] Cf. Hamilton, *Political Thought*, chap. VII.

178

essentially summarizes Victoria on this point. For Victoria the central issue is that a prince must dispel all doubt about the justice of his cause before he may take the step of declaring war.[50] The prince is not *required* to consult anyone other than himself in making his decision; yet his conclusion about his cause may be in error, and if he would act wisely he "ought to consult the good and wise and those who speak with freedom and without anger or bitterness or greed."[51] Suarez appears to go further: "I hold, first, that the sovereign ruler is *bound* to make a diligent examination of the cause and its justice, and that after making this examination, he ought to act in accordance with the knowledge thus obtained."[52] For him the distinction is important between *getting* advice and *taking* it; the prince *must* do the former, but he only *ought* to do the latter. Thus Suarez maintains the power of decision that accompanies a sovereign's supreme responsibility for his nation, a power that Victoria ensures at an earlier stage by only *counseling* the prince to seek advice from others. But the difference between these two goes deeper. Victoria requires the prince to be certain—without doubt—before he acts,[53] and Suarez requires only that he have a cause more probably just than that of his opponent.[54] For Victoria the emphasis on certainty dispels the specter of a war seemingly just on both sides; but Suarez finds this to be no problem in cases in which right reason can discern greater probability of justice on one

[50] Victoria, *De Jure Belli*, sect. 27.
[51] *Ibid.*, sect. 21.
[52] Suarez, *On War*, sect. VI, 1; emphasis added.
[53] Victoria, *De Jure Belli*, sect. 27.
[54] Suarez, *On War*, sect. VI, 2.

side. For cases in which reason rightly used can discern only equal probabilities of justice on the two sides, he would have the matter submitted to arbitration.[55]

Neither of these men allows a prince to seek out the advice of just anyone. For Victoria more than Suarez the emphasis is on objectivity, judging from the description of the counselors cited above. But ordinarily the prince should find such men within his realm, and he should at all times include such men among his counselors. At the very least, then, when deliberating about war the prince ought to seek out the advice of those normally admitted to his council. Such men, moreover, because of their position in the state, are bound themselves to consider the justice of a prospective war to be prepared to give advice. But Victoria goes further than Suarez. For the latter, "generals and other chief men of the kingdom, whenever they are summoned for consultation to give their opinion on beginning a war, are bound to inquire diligently into the truth of the matter; but if they are not called, they are under no greater obligation to do so than others who are common soldiers."[56] But for Victoria,

> Senators and petty rulers and all in general who are admitted on summons or voluntarily to the public council or the prince's council ought, and are bound, to examine into the cause of an unjust war. This is clear; for whoever can save his neighbor from danger and harm is bound to do so, especially when the danger is that of death and greater ills, as in the case of war. But the persons referred to can avert the war,

[55] *Ibid.*, 5; *cf.* Vanderpol, *La Doctrine scholastique*, pp. 124–30; Hamilton, *Political Thought*, pp. 147–49.

[56] Suarez, *On War*, sect. vi, 6.

supposing it to be unjust, if they lend their wisdom and weight to an examination into its causes. Therefore they are bound to do so.[57]

If they do not tell the prince when they have doubts, then they become consenting parties in the case that doubts are well-founded and the war is unjust; they share the blame. The prince is but a man and "is not by himself capable of examining into the causes of a war and the possibility of a mistake on his part is not unlikely. . . . Therefore war ought not to be made on the sole judgment of the king, nor, indeed, on the judgment of a few, but on that of many, and they wise and upright men."[58]

Though Suarez is stricter than Victoria in the language he uses to describe the prince's obligation to seek counsel of others (Suarez says he "must"; Victoria says he "ought"), Victoria goes far beyond the point to which Suarez can follow in describing the obligation of the prince's counselors. Suarez' doctrine presupposes a more absolute kind of monarchy than does Victoria's, which simultaneously recalls the Middle Ages, when powers of kings were limited by their nobles, and presages modern constitutional monarchies and democratic forms of government. Ironically, then, the earlier of these two theologians produces the more modern doctrine as regards rights and responsibilities of ruler and counselors.

The positions of Victoria and Suarez converge again, however, in regard to the question of an ordinary subject's responsibility to weigh the justice of a war. Both agree that he is in no way required to do so. He may in

[57] Victoria, *De Jure Belli*, sect. 24.
[58] *Ibid.*

181

good conscience rest on the judgment of his prince and the latter's counselors. Suarez' summary stands for Victoria as well: "[This conclusion] is based upon the best of reasons, namely, the fact that in cases of doubt the safer course should be chosen; therefore, since the prince possesses rightful authority, the [morally] safer course is to obey him."[59] Victoria adds a further reason: common men have no chance to influence the prince should they discover the war to be unjust; so they have no obligation to inquire into the matter.[60] Still, the case is different when the war is *manifestly* unjust. As Victoria puts it, "[T]he proofs and tokens of the injustice of the war may be such that ignorance would be no excuse even to subjects of this [lower] sort who serve in it."[61] In such a case they may refuse to serve, for to serve would endanger their souls more than refusing to obey their rightful sovereign. Similarly with Suarez: common soldiers "may go to war when summoned to do so, provided it is not clear to them that the war is unjust."[62]

The position that both of these theologians take places heaviest responsibility on the prince, who in effect decides for all his subjects whether a given cause for war is just. This undoubtedly is the reason for insisting that the prince seek the counsel of other men before engaging his nation in war. But it is important to note that neither Victoria nor Suarez removes all responsibility from the common people as regards war. When their prince's cause is manifestly unjust, subjects may not serve in his war. Suarez even pushes the issue back

[59] Suarez, *On War*, sect. VI, 8; *cf.* Victoria, *De Jure Belli*, sects. 25, 31. See also Ames, Quest. 3, 17.A.3.

[60] Victoria, *De Jure Belli*, sect. 25.

[61] *Ibid.*, sect. 26.   [62] Suarez, *On War*, sect. VI, 8.

one step: when arguments have been advanced that raise some doubt in the consciences of the subjects, they must inquire into their prince's cause so as to dispel this doubt. If they discover that the cause is unjust, they may not serve.[63] Two implications may be drawn from these arguments.

First, Suarez and Victoria offer a clear justification for individual conscientious objection to particular wars. The Catholic just war doctrine is generally interpreted today to mean that the Church must declare a war unjust in order for Catholics to refuse to serve in it; this is *not* the position of these two men. The moral authority of the Church over Catholic Christians is nowhere mentioned in discussion of this point in either *De Jure Belli* or *On War*. It is emphatically the *subject's* responsibility to dispel any doubt that may confront him regarding the war in which he is commanded to take part, and if doing so results in certainty on his part that the war is unjust, he must in conscience refuse to abide by his prince's call. Neither Victoria nor Suarez makes any statement concerning whether a conscientiously objecting subject must submit to punishment by his prince for his disobedience. This is a question that must be faced for a full position on conscientious objection, and it would appear that, without the presence of the tolerant spirit of a Fulbecke, only three options would be open: to require that the subject submit to his prince for punishment, to require that the subject leave his prince's jurisdiction, or to require that the subject become a rebel against his prince. All three options were in fact practiced during the sixteenth and seventeenth centuries, and this, together with the silence of the two Spanish theologians on the matter, leaves unanswered

[63] *Ibid.*, 9.

the question of what follows upon the subject's refusal to take part in an unjust war. There is not, therefore, in Victoria and Suarez a fully developed position on conscientious objection. Yet there is a significant beginning in their insistence that each subject retains his moral responsibility for refusing to participate in war when convincing evidence exists that the war is unjust. A modern Catholic must find even more significance in the reservation of this responsibility, and the right and duty it implies, to the individual as opposed to the teaching authority of the Church in moral matters. Victoria and Suarez both assume that the Pope has authority to declare a cause of war unjust in particular cases; that he can do so is not at issue. The individual's authority is independent; he need not wait for the Pope to speak but is bound to refuse to go to war if he discerns the war to be unjust. This position is precisely the opposite of that which informs the treatment of Catholic draftees under present United States law, according to which that Church's just war doctrine is read to mean that no individual conscientious objection to particular wars is allowed.[64]

The second implication that may be drawn from Victoria's and Suarez' arguments concerning responsibility to examine the causes of a prospective war has reference to the role of the citizen in a modern democracy. As noted above, Victoria's position is more directly applicable than that of Suarez, but each makes a contribution. In the context of their own times both assume a division among citizens according to rank. The prince is not by either of these theologians obligated to seek

[64] Cf. John Rohr, *Prophets without Honor: Public Policy and the Selective Conscientious Objector* (Nashville and New York: Abingdon, 1971), chap. VI.

184

the opinion of men of the common rank, though he is to counsel with wise and good men who can use reason rightly, judge objectively, and so help him to avoid mistakes that he might make owing to his own narrow perspective. In the sixteenth and seventeenth centuries the latter were assumed to be men of high rank in society, whether that rank be defined by noble birth, by holy orders, or by academic achievement. There is still often today a *de facto* separation of citizens by rank, though the counselors of, say, a president of the United States or a prime minister of Great Britain are defined by their achievements in politics, business, or (again) academics. But the polity of these democracies does not allow for a theoretical separation to grow from this *de facto* separation between kinds of citizens. If Victoria is to be taken seriously in our time, what he says about the responsibility of the prince's counselors must be extended to the whole citizenry, where there are undoubtedly wise and good men, men able to judge objectively according to right reason. And even following Suarez, it would appear that the entire citizenry must today be included among those who ought to render advice to the chief of state when asked for it. The historical conditioning of the thought of these two Spaniards must not be allowed to cover over the general relevance of their perceptions regarding the responsibilities of rulers and citizens facing the question whether to go to war.

The Problem of Simultaneous Ostensible Justice. It is now necessary to investigate the second aspect of Victoria's and Suarez' thought on the *jus ad bellum*: the question whether a war can be simultaneously just on both sides.

Taking into account the positions of these men and others, Vanderpol argues that the Neo-Scholastic doctrine of war must not be read as allowing the possibility of a war just on both sides. The requirement of St. Thomas must, after all, be maintained: a just war is one fought in response to some fault. This eliminates by definition the possibility of right on both sides. In the case of each prospective belligerent's having a claim on something in dispute, there must be no war, and if one occurs it is not just but *unjust* on both sides at once.[65]

This argument must be read with the realization that Vanderpol wishes above all to maintain the criterion of fault as the essence of just war doctrine. As was shown in Chapter I above, however, this theme is not always present in medieval doctrine on war, and so its influence on the Neo-Scholastics must not be overstated, nor must its presence be assumed or read into their positions. The Pauline statement that the prince is "minister of God to execute his wrath on those who do evil," repeated by Thomas Aquinas and emphasized greatly by Vanderpol, must also not be overworked. Paul's conception of the prince and the requirement that one side be at fault are two naturally reinforcing aspects of a single doctrine, as Vanderpol's extensive reliance on them demonstrates. But even as the theme of fault is not present everywhere in the development of just war doctrine, so the concept of the prince as "minister of God" loses ground as sovereign authority becomes increasingly secularized, tied to natural law and responsibility to the community, in the late Middle Ages. Vanderpol's reading of Victoria and Suarez on the question at hand is not, therefore, to be accepted uncritically. It is faulty by reason of over-

[65] Vanderpol, *La Doctrine scholastique*, pp. 41–50.

emphasis of those tendencies that seem to recall Thomas Aquinas and underemphasis of other tendencies in an opposite direction.

Victoria's position especially is exceedingly complex. In the references we have already made to this question, he appears to regard the possibility of justice on both sides as presenting a dilemma: if each side is just, neither side may kill anyone from the other, and therefore such a war at once both may and may not be fought. Vanderpol's solution to this dilemma is to require that there be no war, that instead the matter be submitted to arbitration. This does indeed appear to be the position Victoria takes in *De Jure Belli*, in which the discussion revolves about a disputed piece of property. In the case of one of the disputants having possession, Victoria argues, the other may not take arms to try to turn him out: "[I]t is never permissible in a doubtful matter to dispossess a lawful possessor."[66] In the case of their being no possessor, however, each disputant has a right to an equal part of the property and "it seems that, if one party wants to settle and make a division or compromise as to part of the claim, the other is bound to accept his proposal, even if that other be the stronger and able to seize the whole by armed force."[67] Third, if a possessor has doubts about his title, he is bound to "examine carefully into the cause and give a quiet hearing to the arguments of the other side."[68] Yet he is not required to give up his property either in whole or in part so long as doubt remains.[69] These cases would seem to support Vanderpol's interpretation of the solution to the dilemma posed by the possibility of justice on both sides in war.

[66] Victoria, *De Jure Belli*, sect. 27.
[67] *Ibid.*, sect. 28.   [68] *Ibid.*, sect. 29.   [69] *Ibid.*, sect. 30.

There is, however, a further problem to consider that qualifies the above cases: that of the existence of invincible ignorance on one or both sides of the dispute. This matter Victoria treats more fully in *De Indis*; again, he uses the example of a disputed piece of property.

> There is no inconsistency, indeed, in holding the war to be a just war on both sides, seeing that on one side there is right and on the other side there is invincible ignorance. For instance, just as the French hold the province of Burgundy with demonstrable ignorance, in the belief that it belongs to them, while our Emperor's right to it is certain, and he may make war to regain it, so it may also befall in the case of the Indians—a point deserving careful attention. For the rights of war which may be invoked against men who are really guilty and lawless differ from those which may be invoked against the innocent and ignorant, just as the scandal of the Pharisees is to be avoided in a different way from that of the self-distrustful and weak.[70]

This passage has great significance. First, it offers a different way out of the dilemma that is posed in *De Jure Belli*; here Victoria seems to say that the dilemma is wrongly posed in the case of invincible ignorance. In such a case it does not follow that neither side may kill men on the other; what follows instead is that the rights of war differ in the case of ignorance from what they are in the case of real fault. This position may be slightly expanded with a result vastly different from that reached in *De Jure Belli*. Let us suppose the case of both sides having invincible ignorance; each side,

[70] Victoria, *De Indis*, sect. III, 7.

"knowing" itself to be in the right, would be obligated to prosecute war against the enemy as persons innocent through ignorance that they could do nothing about. The ignorance of the opponents would mean at the very least scrupulous observance of the *jus in bello*, but it would also have a definite effect on the extent of indemnity that could be exacted and punishment that could be enforced at the end of the war. The English jurist Fulbecke seems to take exactly this position; echoing Victoria, he asserts that a war "may bee truely and verily just on the one side, & on the other by ignorance." He assigns this opinion to "both Divines and Civilians" (persons working in civil law).[71] His examples also echo the case of the French *versus* the emperor, cited by Victoria. Fulbecke concludes that "the Civil law doth attribute the rightes of war unto both parties."[72] But what are these rights of war? For Fulbecke the civil law assumes what the theologians at this point in history are still debating: that a war can be just on both sides at once. But this assumption carries with it the corollary that both sides are required to treat their opponents honorably and according to the *jus in bello*. The ability to reason in this manner follows in part at least, as noted above, from Fulbecke's use of the model of the adversary trial. Here each side is convinced of its rightness, and the decision of the judge following the "combat" that is the trial declares the true possessor of justice in the matter. While the trial continues each adversary is to regard the other as innocent and deserving of respect. In the case of war this perspective requires, as Victoria puts it, matching the punishment to the offense.[73] The

[71] Fulbecke, *Pandectes*, p. 36b.
[72] *Ibid.*, p. 37b.
[73] *Cf.*, for example, Victoria, *De Jure Belli*, sects. 42, 57, 58.

189

jus in bello applies even to those who are truly at fault;
the difference in application in the case of invincible
ignorance is one of degree. Throughout the war and
after it the just side should proceed with measures pro-
portionate to the offense done. But the offense is not so
great when invincible ignorance has caused it. Therefore the war should be prosecuted as mildly as possible,
and rewards rather than punishments should be employed after the war to convince the erring side of what
is right.[74] Finally, allowing the possibility of a war just
on both sides reduces the importance of the *jus ad
bellum* and increases the emphasis on the *jus in bello*.
This dual effect has in fact characterized the treatment
of war in international law over the past three centuries,
in which the *limits* to be set on war have been the subject of far more discussion than the *prohibition* of war
for unjust causes.

The second point to be examined from the passage
from *De Indis* cited above is Victoria's assimilation of
the case involving the Indians and the Spanish to that
of the French and the emperor. The two cases are somewhat different, and their assimilation indicates far more
about what Victoria means by "invincible ignorance"
than is apparent on the surface. In regard to the Indians
Victoria writes: "It is, however, to be noted that the
natives being timid by nature and in other respects dull
and stupid, however much the Spaniards may desire to
remove their fears and reassure them with regard to
peaceful dealings with each other, they may very in-
excusably continue afraid at sight of men strange in
garb and armed and much more powerful than themselves."[75] The Indians are thus invincibly ignorant of

[74] *Ibid.*, sect. 58.
[75] Victoria, *De Indis*, sect. III, 6.

the peaceful intentions of the Spanish. The same considerations figure in Victoria's discussion of the ignorance of the Indians with respect to Christian faith and his conclusions about the rights of the Spanish toward them in that matter.[76] Whatever else Victoria may think the French to be, he does not regard them as dull, timid, or stupid; nor are they dressed or armed differently from the emperor's troops; nor is there any great disproportion of power. Obviously invincible ignorance does not derive from the same considerations in the two cases. To discover the hidden similarity that allows Victoria to draw these cases together it is necessary to look more closely into the discussion of the Indians' ignorance regarding Christian faith, which is the only detailed treatment Victoria gives to the matter of the effect of ignorance on justice in war.

Three stages exist in the attitude of the Indians toward Christianity: invincible ignorance, before they have ever heard anything about Christ; vincible ignorance, after they have been told and have seen proofs such as miracles; and acceptance, when their reticence to believe what they have seen and heard has vanished. In none of these cases is there ground for war, as shown above. But most relevant to the present point is the similar treatment to be given the Indians *whether they are invincibly or vincibly ignorant*: the Spanish must in either case limit their attempts at conversion to preaching and doing good works. Victoria leaves the strong implication that if the Indians have not accepted Christ, they have not yet had sufficient proof of Christian doctrine.[77] It is difficult—perhaps impossible—for a man to judge whether another's unbelief proceeds from insufficient proof of the truth (invincible igno-

[76] *Ibid.*, sect. II.   [77] *Ibid.*, 12–14.

rance) or willful rejection of what has been adequately demonstrated to him (vincible ignorance). In his treatment of the Indians Victoria seems to be qualifying the distinction between vincible and invincible ignorance to suggest that, while it is a valid distinction, it is knowable only to God, and man cannot distinguish the one kind of ignorance from the other. Thus, as regards faith, the three stages named above exist as far as God is concerned, but man must in practice act as though there are but two: ignorance and acceptance.

What does this mean for the parallel that Victoria draws between the Indians and the French? If the above reading of Victoria and the implications drawn from it are correct, the French are to be treated as invincibly ignorant by the emperor, just as the Indians are to be so treated by the Spanish. Or, in more readily understandable terms, just as the Spanish do not know which stage the Indians are in as regards faith, so the emperor does not know whether the French king recognizes the validity of the imperial claim and will not accept it, or simply has not received proof of the truth of that claim. Just as the Spanish must continue to treat the Indians as if they have not yet received enough proof, so must the emperor continue to act towards the French. In the case of war this means prosecution with the least damage possible, as we have seen.

This conclusion is not, in fact, a change in Victoria's position, even in *De Jure Belli*, on whether a war can be just on both sides.

The following is my answer: First proposition: Apart from ignorance the case can clearly not occur, for if the right and justice of each side be certain, it is unlawful to fight against it, either in offense or in defense. Second proposition: Assuming a demonstrable ignorance either of fact or of law, it may be that on the side where true justice is the war is just of itself, while on the other side the war is just in the sense of being excused from sin by reason of good faith, because invincible ignorance is a complete excuse.[78]

Central to this conclusion is the admission that the just side in a war may be ignorant as to the extent of the ignorance the other side possesses of its injustice. That is, *both* sides, just and unjust, are invincibly ignorant: the one of the injustice of its cause, the other of the state of mind of the first. This raises the possibility of treating *all* wars as *de facto* just on both sides, while admitting that God knows the truth and sorts out the just claims from the unjust in the final reckoning. This distinction between nature and charity, modifying an earlier rejection of the possibility of a war just on both sides, is also made explicit by Suarez when he considers the case of a war unjust on both sides but nevertheless engaged in voluntarily by both belligerents. Such a war, Suarez argues, is opposed to charity, not to justice. Such a case amounts to a compact between the belligerents to decide matters between them by arms, and this is allowable in nature though not by God.[79] Since both Victoria and Suarez reduce the concept of just cause to those causes known by natural reason to be just, the possibility is admitted of wars in which both sides must be treated as justly fighting.

This conclusion, which is ultimately the same as Fulbecke's, runs entirely counter to Vanderpol's contention

[78] Victoria, *De Jure Belli*, sect. 32.
[79] Suarez, *On War*, sect. VII, 22; for his rejection of wars simultaneously just on both sides see sect. VI, 3–6.

that Victoria and Suarez reject the possibility of a war just on both sides at once. But a distinction must be made. Victoria does not suggest that invincible ignorance excuses one from punishment by God; the existence of invincible ignorance is itself punishment.[80] And Suarez stands by his opinion that when both sides believe themselves to be right, they should submit to arbitration, not fight.[81] For neither of these writers is there such a thing as a war just on both sides *in the sight of God*. But as far as man's knowledge is concerned the case is different. Invincible ignorance can— and often does—intervene, so that both sides may *think* themselves to have a just cause; and indeed wise men may not be able to decide between them, even though one side—or possibly both—is in the wrong. The war must thus be fought as a compact; the limits of the *jus in bello* must be scrupulously followed to avoid damage to either side so far as possible, and after the war the attempt must be made to convince the losers of the justness of their opponents' cause by rewards, not punishments.

It should be noted that this doctrine, emphasizing the *jus in bello* over the *jus ad bellum*, is well suited to a complex world such as existed at the dawn of the modern period, when lines of authority and power came from many sources, so that often they were in conflict and a decision had to be made arbitrarily for one and against others. It would appear well suited also for *any* period in which facts are in principle or in practice unavailable to even those who would wish to decide international disputes by objective peaceful judgment. This doctrine, in the end, dictates that if a war must be

[80] Victoria, *De Indis*, sect. II, 8.
[81] Suarez, *On War*, sect. VI, 5.

fought, with both sides sincerely believing in the rightness of their cause, it should be as limited as possible, followed by a peace as amicable as can be humanly created.

DEVELOPMENTS IN THE *Jus in Bello*

If the effect of the treatment of the *jus ad bellum* in the writers considered above is to give it less prominence and to raise the significance of the *jus in bello*, it is most important to examine what the writers conceive to be the content of the *jus in bello*. Its sources, as already pointed out, are the Augustinian prohibition of evil intent, and the limits given in canon law and the law of arms on those against whom war may be prosecuted. Two principles are involved, that of proportionality, concerning the relation of means to ends, and that of discrimination, concerning the level of undesirable secondary effects associated with a given act against the enemy. Finally, at this stage in its development the *jus in bello* is almost entirely a statement in regard to noncombatants—who they are, and the rights belligerents possess toward them and their property. A related question has to do with what the victor may do to the defeated nation, whether soldiers or noncombatants, after the war is over. This question will be addressed only tangentially in this section, since it is not precisely a question of what may be done *in bello*, though in general it is possible to move directly from the rights and responsibilities of belligerents during the war toward the innocent among the enemy's populace, to what may be done by the victor after the war, when all are noncombatants but some may be regarded as innocent and others guilty.

195

In addressing the *jus in bello*, then, the writers we are concerned with are mainly addressing the question of noncombatant immunity, and they are doing so on the basis of a distinction between (relative) guilt and innocence among the people present in the area where the war is being fought. This distinction, in accord with what has already been argued in Chapter I, itself derives from consideration of the function of various sorts of people with regard to the prosecution of war. It is important to grasp the concept of innocence as used by these writers, especially since the history of international law on the subject of war has tended to erase the distinction between guilt and innocence.[82] For these writers "innocence" means lack of any direct contribution to the war effort, and it disregards the fact of citizenship in the nation with which one's own is at war. Guilt means just the opposite: direct involvement in the war, whether one is a citizen of the enemy state or not.

To define the concept of noncombatant immunity, then, Victoria first prohibits the killing of the innocent, arguing, "[T]he basis of a just war is a wrong done. . . . But wrong is not done by an innocent person. Therefore war may not be employed against him."[83] Such innocent persons are, he reasons, children, women (except for individual cases of guilt), clerics, religious, foreigners, guests of the enemy country, "harmless agricultural folk, and also . . . the rest of the peaceable civilian population."[84] It is sometimes permissible to kill innocent people, however, "in virtue of collateral

[82] One example of this phenomenon is that of Vattel, *Law of Nations*, bk. II, chaps. V, VIII, IX.

[83] Victoria, *De Jure Belli*, sect. 35.

[84] *Ibid.*, sect. 36.

circumstances," such as the storming of a city in a just war. In such a case use of normal seige weapons would not be possible unless the accidental killing of noncombatants were allowed. A cannon shot does not discriminate between guilt and innocence. The evil of such practice remains, though it is unavoidable in such cases if towns are to be taken and advantages secured. But the right to use such means as result in the death of the innocent is limited by the principle of proportionality: it is necessary "to see that greater evils do not arise out of the war than the war would avert." Victoria concludes that even the unintended, indirect killing of the innocent is not to be allowed except when there is no other way to carry on a just war.[85]

Suarez restates in its essentials the doctrine of Victoria, though he defines the innocent a bit more broadly: not only the sorts of people listed specifically in canon law are to be treated as noncombatants, but also "those who are able to bear arms, if it is evident that, in other respects, they have not shared in the crime nor in the unjust war."[86] Again, their killing is to be permitted only when there is no other way to prosecute a war otherwise just.

Certain implications are contained in such an argument. It presupposes weapons of a nondiscriminating character as in general use and does not condemn them. One might well question how far this acceptance could go. Might it include, for example, the thermonuclear bombing of a city or cities of the enemy if the cause of the war were just? Provided that the end result would not be disproportionate to the good received, the answer would seem to be affirmative. But how are matters

[85] *Ibid.*, sect. 37.
[86] Suarez, *On War*, sect. vii, 15.

of proportion to be resolved? Considering what has been said on the issue of invincible ignorance in regard to the *jus ad bellum*, the belligerents might in many cases be unable to judge the amount of good associated with their end, and so the principle of proportionality would be impossible to apply accurately. Here it would seem that a better application of that principle would follow from consideration of the *jus in bello* itself: is the use of such weapons consistent with the mandate to pursue war in as mild a way as possible? The answers to these questions are beyond the scope of this book. Here it is sufficient to note that the position taken by Victoria and Suarez, though it embodies restraining factors, opens the way for erosion of restraints in the name of military necessity. In wars not known certainly to be just, such erosion is extremely dangerous.

This possibility is reduced in the position enunciated by William Ames. His position, developed under the rubric of just manner of waging (his fourth criterion for a just war), is particularly significant because it makes explicit the separation of noncombatant immunity from the Augustinian prohibition of cruelty and implacable animosity, a topic Ames treats in connection with his third criterion. This separation has already begun in the canon law, in the regulation concerning noncombatants in *De Treuga et Pace*, but Ames goes considerably beyond canon law in enumerating the classes of persons normally to be regarded as innocent: "Among the guilty, neither Children nor ordinarily Women, nor indeed any other quiet men, who disagreeing are forced to stay with the enemies, ought to be numbered."[87] Moreover, the ground for judging whether

[87] Ames, Quest. 6, 31.A.2.

198

someone is a noncombatant is plainly functional—whether he is directly involved in prosecuting the war. Finally, it is *justice*, not charity, that requires that such persons not directly involved be allowed to live in peace. The term *just war*, which in its origins can often be rendered *justifiable war*, is here plainly associated with the justice of a war's prosecution: "Every just Warre is waged properly and directly against the Offendours and those that are guilty, that is against those, whose cause and fault it is, that the Warre was begunne. Therefore those onely in true vindicative Justice ought directly and of purpose be punished. . . . So that the Israelites seeme to have sinned grievously, by slaying the Sonnes of Benjamin without choyce, Jud. 20."[88]

Ames is not unrealistic; like Victoria and Suarez he realizes that in some cases it is difficult to avoid giving harm to the innocent, but even in such cases "Charity and Aequity doth require, that the Warre be so managed as the innocent may bee as little damnified as possible."[89] He continues by disallowing one of the most common military practices of his day, the spoliation of conquered towns by the victorious forces. This, he reasons, "cannot lawfully bee maintained, because among many other horrid things, which thence follow in such a pillage, *there is no distinction set betweene the guilty and the innocent.*"[90] He further condemns as "robbery [rather] than a just Warre, where the oppression of innocent husbandmen is intended, and such a kind of Warre is that, which Ferdinand the Emperor now wageth in Germany."[91] This reference to the actual conduct of the imperial forces during the Thirty Years'

[88] *Ibid.*, 30.A.1. [89] *Ibid.*, 33.A.4.
[90] *Ibid.*, 34.A.5; emphasis added.
[91] *Ibid.*, 35.A.6.

199

War serves as a reminder that the practice of war in the sixteenth and seventeenth centuries did not always conform to standards of morality—a discrepancy that must always be dealt with in attempts to frame limits to war. Still, Ames is adamant that noncombatants, whatever sort of persons they may be, are not to be deprived of life, goods, or liberty if justice is to be done.

This absolute prohibition is somewhat stronger than the provisions of Victoria and Suarez. Both Spaniards are willing to allow spoliation of the innocent in certain circumstances, and Ames' case of a town that is sacked in the course of being taken is covered partially as one of these cases and partially by the allowance to kill the innocent during a siege. Victoria argues that it is always permissible to "despoil the innocent of goods and things which the enemy would use against us, such as arms, ships, and engines of war."[92] He continues by allowing the spoliation of "the agricultural and other innocent folk" if the war cannot otherwise be carried on "effectively enough."[93] Addressing similar questions, Suarez permits spoliation of the innocent if, after everything possible has been gotten from the guilty, sufficient satisfaction has not been received from the enemy state.[94]

The arguments of Suarez and Victoria tend to erode the rights of the innocent whenever necessity—whether military necessity or that of vindicative justice—requires treating them as one with the guilty. This is true both in war, when noncombatants may sometimes be despoiled to keep the enemy from making use of their property, may sometimes be killed, as when they are in a city that must be taken, and may be made to support

[92] Victoria, *De Jure Belli*, sect. 39.
[93] *Ibid.*, sect. 40.
[94] Suarez, *On War*, sect. vii, 12.

one's own soldiers against their will and with no remuneration; and after the war is over, when those who took no part in the war may be forced, merely because they are citizens of the conquered state, to pay the victors if the goods of the guilty do not provide sufficient restitution. In short, the two Spanish theologians are inclined to accept what had become common practice in war; they follow the generally growing tendency to define *jus gentium* as customary practice among nations. They do not wish to allow killing and spoliation of the innocent, which they consider contrary to justice. But in certain cases—as unintended side effects or in order to secure restitution for wrong done by the enemy forces—Victoria and Suarez find no injustice in permitting the innocent to be deprived of life and property. The only theoretical limitation that remains to be placed upon the victorious forces is the one we have invoked before: when one's cause is not *certainly* just, the war should be waged as mildly as possible and rewards, not payments, should characterize the treatment of the conquered foes. This restraint does not have much power for these writers, and it is not one developed in the present connection.

It is thus very much to the point to take seriously Ames' argument that justice requires *no prosecution of war* against noncombatant citizens of the enemy nation. In singling out the practices of the imperial forces against the German peasant population he isolates a case precisely like those that the two Spanish theologians discuss. Prosecution of the war against the peasants was justified on the grounds that they aided the enemy because they were of the same stock, that the enemy used their goods in any case, that the imperial forces were suffering so much they had to be allowed

201

to plunder, and so on. The doctrine put forward by Victoria and seconded by Suarez provides insufficient safeguards against such abuse of the noncombatant population. Ames' absolute prohibition treats such cases far more adequately.

This rejection of the position taken by the Spaniards must not, however, be pursued too far. Their arguments are formally—that is, theoretically—correct according to their premises. The difference between them and Ames is not in fact on a theoretical point but on the *application* of what justice theoretically requires to a particular set of circumstances. The correct reading of Victoria and Suarez requires prefacing their conclusions with one of two conditions: either there must be certain justice on one side, or both sides must be searching for justice in good faith. In the first case the just side, in the second case both sides may move in justice against innocents as Victoria and Suarez provide. Ames' judgment likewise must be prefaced with a condition: it is too dangerous to assume the presence of either of the above requirements in particular wars. Thus the safest way to ensure that justice is done by all is to prohibit all harm to the noncombatants in the enemy population. In making this provision Ames moved beyond the Spaniards in the direction that international law was to take. Further specification of the exact nature of noncombatancy would provide the other side of a general prohibition of harm to persons so defined. This Ames begins to do (but so do Victoria and Suarez) in providing that there may be exceptional cases in which women, clerics, and religious persons ought not to be treated as noncombatants. Presumably similar reasoning might also apply to the other classes, maintaining in all events the *exceptional* character of such provi-

202

sions. This too is the subject of further development in international law. Finally, prohibition of harm to noncombatants in war has its analogue in prohibition of harm to the general populace of a conquered nation after the war is ended. Neither Ames nor the Spaniards will go so far; for all of them justice seems to demand adequate restitution (except as provided in cases of ignorance on the part of the vanquished). Development of this point may also be traced in subsequent theory.

In sum, the doctrine on *jus in bello* in the sixteenth and seventeenth centuries was in transition. Although the *jus in bello* was already implicitly set above the question of *jus ad bellum*, its development had not yet proceeded far enough for it to take over adequately the role of limiting warfare. But at the same time the wars of the hundred years following the Reformation so seriously cast into doubt the very possibility that a just cause could be known to exist that the *jus ad bellum* as explicated in traditional doctrine was no longer able to operate as an effective brake on warfare. This problem was not adequately faced by the theologians who prepared the foundations for early theorists of international law; it remained for these secular theorists, as heirs to the just war tradition, to fashion a doctrine on limiting war that employed the *jus in bello* almost exclusively.

Biographical Data

FOR most of the life of *Franciscus de Victoria* (1492–1546) Charles V ruled in Spain and as Holy Roman Emperor. This was the "golden age" of Spanish hegemony in Europe and the New World, a period in which Spanish political and military might and Catholic religion joined together in directing an empire that extended from central Europe to Mexico and Peru. Victoria, a Dominican, was educated in Burgos and Paris; he taught theology in Valladolid and Salamanca. Victoria, like Suarez after him, was a Neo-Scholastic; he sought to apply scholastic methods and particularly the theology of Thomas Aquinas to the issues of his day. The two works discussed in this chapter were delivered in relectio form: the relectio was nominally a recapitulation, at the end of a course of lectures, of the material treated in the lectures; in practice relectios often applied the lecture material to some particular topic. In both *De Indis* and *De Jure Belli*, Victoria takes up the political subjects that made him so widely respected. Victoria opposed ill-treatment of the Indians, and he set his opposition into a theoretical framework with broad implications for international law. Together with his recasting of the just war tradition for his own historical context, the work on the Indians has led to his being regarded as one of the fathers of modern international law. Victoria's personal influence reached all the way to the emperor, who consulted him four times on matters of state, twice in 1539 and twice again in 1541. In 1545 he was invited to attend the Council of Trent, but he declined because of ill health. Many of Victoria's students (numbering some 5,000 in all) became bishops or professors in Spain and the New World, further disseminating the influence that he had on Spanish religious and political life.

Francisco Suarez, S.J. (1548–1617), remembered with Victoria as one of the theologians who recast medieval political theory into the beginnings of modern international law, studied at Salamanca; he later taught there, at various Jesuit colleges including the one in Rome, at Alcala in Spain, and at Coimbra in Portugal. During the life of Suarez, King Philip II was actively seeking to reverse the tide of the Reformation. Suarez' work should be seen against the backdrop of Philip's attempts to suppress heresy in the Netherlands (through the armies of the Duke of Alva and others) and in Spain itself (through the Inquisition), as well as to undermine Protestant supremacy elsewhere. The English fear of Spanish motives that was so widespread in the late sixteenth and early seventeenth centuries traces to the activities of Philip II and his successor, Philip III. Philip II repeatedly sought the advice of Suarez on domestic and foreign matters, and the appointment of Suarez as prima professor of theology at Coimbra, the most important Portuguese university, was in part a political reward for Suarez' advice to the King on the question of annexing Portugal. After the death of Philip II, Suarez continued to exercise great influence at court, particularly through his close friend the Duke of Lerma, the powerful foreign minister of Philip III. The work of Suarez is more careful and conservative than that of Victoria, which radiates a fresh, vital inquisitiveness and a fearlessness in opinion absent from Suarez' writings. Yet this difference in tone does not extend to the content of their positions, which are in many respects quite similar. The very different sociopolitical conditions confronting these two theorists doubtless helped to flavor their writings.

Matthew Sutcliffe (1550–1629) occupied the ecclesiastical positions of Dean of Exeter and royal chaplain under Elizabeth and James; yet it is not his position as a churchman that makes him interesting to us but his success as a courtier. It was principally the latter that led to his comfortable ecclesiastical appointments and to the establishment of one of his special projects, King James' College at Chelsea, to which he was named the first provost. Sutcliffe strongly promoted the settlement of New England and encouraged the efforts of John Smith in Virginia. He wrote on a variety of topics, including military discipline (in which his theory of just war appears), a concern that was sure to be popular among the nobles at court. In short, Sutcliffe should be understood for what he was in life: a courtier and intimate of two monarchs first, and a churchman second and almost incidentally. His influence divided accordingly.

William Fulbecke (1560–1603) was a friend of Francis Bacon at Gray's Inn, where they both studied. Fulbecke, however, remained close to the profession of law and became a well-known and highly respected legal writer. His studies at Oxford (B.A., 1581; M.A., 1584) produced degrees and learning unusual for lawyers in this time. Fulbecke's *Pandectes of the Law of Nations*, discussed here, his introduction to legal study (reprinted as late as 1820), and numerous histories testify to the use to which he put his broad Oxford education in the classics. His knowledge and use of classical precedents is similar to that of Grotius (see Chapter IV below).

William Ames (1576–1633) studied at Christ's College, Cambridge, where his tutor was the eminent Puritan divine William Perkins. The influence of Perkins, who was at once an open, liberal thinker and an extremely disciplined scholar, is apparent in Ames' writings, including his most famous work, *Conscience* (*De Conscientia*), discussed in this chapter. Ames' style is close to the scholastic (a fact that antagonized certain Protestant critics), but his theology is scrupulously Calvinist. Ames spent his entire working life in Holland, where he took part in the controversy over Arminianism, attended the Synod of Dort, and taught (at Franeker, where he became Rector in 1626, and at Rotterdam, where he died). He was an enormously influential theologian among Calvinists, both Dutch and English. His works (including *Conscience* and his other major work, *Medulla Theologiae*) were considered essential to Puritan libraries both in England and in New England.

CHAPTER IV

Secularized Just War Doctrine:
Grotius, Locke, and Vattel

THE two preceding chapters have analyzed the results of a bifurcation of medieval just war doctrine into two thematically different theories with radically divergent conceptions of what constitutes a "just" war. The first of these progeny of the medieval doctrine, holy war theory, flourished only during the approximately one hundred years of religious wars following the Reformation and ceased to exist as a unified body of thought when wars were no longer fought for religion; the second became the basis of writings on war by theorists of the new science of international politics and law as it developed in the seventeenth and eighteenth centuries. I have argued that the second form is characterized by an increasing reliance on natural-law foundations and a de-emphasis of the uniquely Christian elements in the idea of the just war. It is precisely this character of the doctrine developed by theologians such as Victoria, Suarez, and Ames, jurists such as Fulbecke, political advisors such as Sutcliffe, and others during the late sixteenth and early seventeenth centuries that makes it so amenable to incorporation within theoretical works on international law based on the study of natural law and agreements among nations. The similar elements in contemporary international law and contemporary Christian just war theory may be traced to their common rooting in the just war doctrine that was not yet completely secularized, and was promulgated by sixteenth- and seventeenth-century theorists such as those treated in the previous chapter.

Victoria, Suarez, Ames, Sutcliffe, and Fulbecke represent a transitional stage in the development of a secular theory of just war. This chapter will show how, in the more advanced stages, the theory took shape. In the thought of Grotius, who was roughly a contemporary of both Suarez and Ames—slightly younger than the former and slightly older than the latter—the doctrine is still in transition, though primary reliance is definitely placed on natural law and the *jus gentium*, not on religious sanctions. In Locke and Vattel, writing respectively toward the end of the seventeenth century and about the middle of the eighteenth, the transitional stage has decidedly been left behind. Though a just war doctrine much like that of a century earlier is present in their thought, it is developed without reference to the theological base that informed Augustine, Aquinas, and even to some extent the men treated in the previous chapter. It should not be assumed that secularization of just war doctrine meant adulteration and loss of moral intensity; Locke and Vattel both propose more stringent limits on the power to make war than their theological predecessors had conceived. This alone would make them worth scrutiny. In addition Locke's influence on the United States in its foundation gives his thought a particular relevance within the context of war doctrine as it has developed in this country.

HUGO GROTIUS

OVERVIEW: GROTIUS' INTENT AND METHOD

Grotius' *De Jure Belli ac Pacis* has exerted from its very first appearance a profound influence on the development of international law in the modern period. Grotius drew together the thought of the preceding age, reworked it in light of changed assumptions about men and their interactions, and produced a new conception of the relations among nations for the age on whose threshold he stood. To a degree this is also true, for example, of Victoria, on whom Grotius often relies; yet the commitment of Victoria remains strongest to the Middle Ages, and that of Grotius is directed forward in time. Their different orientations are manifested in their professions—Victoria the Dominican friar, Grotius the secular jurist—but perhaps most of all in their use of material from the past. Victoria is motivated by a desire to update the thought of Thomas Aquinas, and he uses Thomas for an anchor for his own position as he attempts to deal with other theorists. Grotius, on the other hand, presents what he writes as his own theory; and though he uses his predecessors (including both Thomas and Victoria) copiously, he does not intend to argue from their positions to his. Typically figures from the past serve him as examples only, whether they represent ancient Greece or Rome, medieval Christendom, or the New World. His attitude toward his sources enables him to join past and present into a program for the future, and this, in turn, provides Grotius' significance.

One of the most notable features of Grotius' treatment of the subject of war is the distinction he attempts to maintain between what is allowed by nature and what is permitted to Christians. This distinction is a residue of that which was drawn during the Middle Ages, but it is *only* a residue, since the synthetic union of the two categories, nature and grace, wrought by Thomas Aquinas has long since evaporated. Like his predecessors Grotius closely identifies the natural with

210

what obtained in the classical world; nevertheless, his natural-law doctrine on war applies to all men since it is knowable by reason. Christians, by faith, possess some additional knowledge, which in part supplements and in part replaces that which natural reason provides. If warring nations are Christian, then, they are bound by limits that are unknown to other nations and therefore do not bind them. In wars between non-Christian nations natural law alone provides the rules by which war should be fought. Grotius never adequately resolves the question of war between two nations, one Christian and one not. To what extent are Christians bound by their own moral knowledge in such circumstances? Grotius' answer is somewhat ambiguous, but it points the way to the unequivocal assertion by Vattel that war is to be fought by rules provided in nature—though Vattel resolves this question by utilizing a conceptual device that reduces Christian morality to an element within the natural. In Grotius the distinction between natural law and Christian morality persists, along with the ambiguity it engenders. The following discussion of Grotius' position on war attempts to deal both with this distinction and with its implications.

The first problem is to understand Grotius' conception of war. He posits two sorts of war, public and private, depending on the authority that makes the war.[1] This distinction is an old one, noted here simply for the sake of definition. Grotius' main concern is with public war, which he again treats by dichotomy, dividing it into "solemn" (just) and "not solemn" (unjust) types.[2]

[1] Grotius, *Rights of War & Peace*, bk. i, chap. iii, pp. 31–52 (for full citation see Chap. II, n. 5, above).
[2] *Ibid.*, p. 34.

211

Now that a war be solemn according to the Law of Nations, two things are requisite: First, that it be on both sides made by the Authority of those who in their respective cities have the soveraign power: And next, That it be waged with such Rites and Formalities as the Law of Nations requires. . . . And because these are jointly requisite, therefore the one without the other is not sufficient: That publick war which we call less solemn, may be both defective in these rites, and also be made against private men, and that by the Authority of any Magistrate.[3]

At the very least, in this passage Grotius treats just war as war that, when internal to a nation, is defined by sovereign authority, and, when between nations, is defined by adherence to forms mutually agreed upon. Since sovereign authority derives from below (signifying a natural rather than a divine source),[4] this passage seems to define just wars as those that are fought by mutual consent. Grotius does not in fact quite argue for such a conception (mutual consent is a necessary but not sufficient condition), but to understand this it is necessary to inquire what is his conception of the "Rites and Formalities" that are included in the law of nations and specify the contents of the *jus ad bellum* and the *jus in bello* in Grotius' theory.

Before we proceed, however, another question posed by the above passage should be noted. The passage may be read to indicate that war internal to a nation—war

[3] *Ibid.*

[4] See especially Chap. I, fourth section above for the birth of this understanding of the source of sovereign authority; *cf.* Hamilton, *Political Thought*, chap. II.

against rebels—is not limited by international "Rites and Formalities" and so may be prosecuted unlimitedly. This conclusion is not a *necessary* one; Grotius consistently attempts to construct a moral floor, not to set up medial norms for action. Thus even war against rebels is limited by what the natural law allows, and moreover the sovereign and his rebellious subjects may mutually agree, whether tacitly or by formal covenant, to further limitations. These restrictions are analogous to the bounds provided in the *jus gentium* by custom or common consent. Thus in spite of the dichotomy between "solemn" wars and those "less solemn," with the latter category including revolutions, Grotius' main point persists: war is a human enterprise capable of being limited by human decision. This aspect of his theory most clearly carries the stamp of the modern age.

Grotius' methodology reveals something of his intent. In classic just war doctrine the *jus ad bellum* includes three principal criteria: right authority, just cause, and right intention. In Grotius' discussion of the *jus ad bellum*, though, which comprises book II of *De Jure Belli ac Pacis*, the criterion of just cause is treated almost exclusively. The nature of right authority is not discussed here but is subsumed in the treatment given the concept of sovereignty in connection with Grotius' definition of war in book I. The third criterion, right intention, is treated only incidentally during the development of the concept of just cause; it is again treated in passing during Grotius' discussion of the *jus in bello* in book III. Ames' treatment of right intention offers a kind of precedent to this latter discussion, but Grotius goes far beyond Ames in de-emphasizing the third criterion bequeathed by the classic *jus ad bellum*. Grotius' method allows justice in war to be measured by externals: sovereignty replaces the criterion of right authority; just causes, as we shall see, are limited to those that can be discerned by an objective observer; and right intention, the most clearly subjective of the classic criteria, is treated only scantily and in connection with other topics. This emphasis on externals is a mark of secularized just war doctrine already noted in the previous chapter.

GROTIUS' MODIFICATION OF THE *Jus ad Bellum*

Grotius asserts that the causes for a just war are analogous to the causes for civil actions; they are, moreover, connected with injury done or offered. War may thus be waged "for prevention of Injuries not yet done, . . . that no acts of violence shall be offered, nor any damages done us" and "for injuries already done as namely that they may be recompenced, or the injuring person punished."[5] Here two points need explication: the broadening of the category of self-defense to include offensive war against those whose intent is certainly to make war against one's own nation, and the limitation of self-defense, a right guaranteed by nature, by the law of charity (as defined by Grotius). First, Grotius insists that just wars are all defensive. The Romans, he notes, took care never to go to war unless they had been injured by a neighbor.[6] But what is permitted by nature appears to go beyond this practice of the Romans, for it is not necessary, Grotius argues, to wait for a blow to be struck before striking in self-defense. But to employ such preemptive self-defense it is absolutely required that the other's intent be certain. Uncertain fear of a neighboring country whose power

[5] Grotius, *Rights of War & Peace*, bk. II, chap. I, p. 70.
[6] *Ibid.*

214

is swelling is explicitly named as an unjust cause for war.[7] The causes of a war should be made public, so that everyone may decide as to their justice.[8] If any doubt remains, it is necessary to wait, meanwhile seeking to avoid war.[9] It is thus obvious that the intent of an enemy must be manifested overtly: "It is . . . required, that the danger be present and ready instantly to fall upon us"—he gives the examples of a drawn sword or a weapon snatched up—and not simply a matter of opinion based on no obvious signs.[10] When Grotius allows preemptive self-defense he is not granting license to princes to go to war simply on the basis of their reading of the state of another's mind. Still, by allowing the first blow actually struck to be that of self-defense, he is broadening the meaning of self-defense beyond simply justifying a strong frontier and is moving toward a concept of war by general consent. All that is required is that the signs be read as hostile. Though this reasoning justified, for example, English attacks on Spanish shipping in order to hinder the formation of the Armada, it also provided the justification used by Germany against Russia in World War II, and it was invoked by American advocates of "preemptive retaliation" (nuclear first strike) against the USSR in the 1950's. The limit Grotius imposes is thus not absolute; it depends to a certain degree upon the state of mind of those who judge themselves to be threatened. Grotius does not allow for national paranoia. His broadening of the category of self-defense to include preemptive strikes would thus appear to be inherently dan-

[7] Ibid., pp. 76–77; cf. ibid., chap. xxii, p. 404.
[8] Ibid., chap. xxvi, p. 430.
[9] Ibid., chap. xxiii, pp. 410–12.
[10] Ibid., chap. i, p. 71.

gerous. But his examples of dangers "present and ready instantly to fall upon us" suggest that, even where there is some measure of paranoia, the fear must be grounded in a threat observable by any third party to be imminent. Preemptive strikes are not to be launched out of psychological or ideological motives only. Because of this limitation Grotius does not find it necessary to prohibit all first resort to force as inherently unjust (though in the twentieth century, international law was to make just such a prohibition).[11]

The concept of self-defense is, moreover, limited in another way. Though the right of self-defense extends in nature to the death of the assailant, this full right should not be exercised if the danger or harm is relatively minor.[12] Again, charity limits resort to this full right in the case of Christians.

> It was . . . very well said of Aquinas, if it be rightly understood, that in a true defensive war, we do not intentionally kill others; not but that it may sometimes be lawful, if all other means of safety fail to do that purposely whereby the Aggressor may die. But that this death was not our choice, nor intended primarily (as in capital punishments) but our last and only refuge, there being no other visible means then left to preserve our own lives, but by killing him that seeks to kill us; nay, and even then, he that is violently assaulted ought to wish rather that some other

[11] The *jus ad bellum* according to the Kellogg-Briand Pact and the United Nations Charter generally prohibits first use of force as aggression and permits second use of force as defense. For a fuller account of the twentieth-century *jus ad bellum* see my article "Toward Reconstructing the *Jus ad Bellum*," *The Monist*, 57, no. 4 (Oct. 1973).

[12] Grotius, *Rights of War & Peace*, bk. ii, chap. i, pp. 72–73.

thing would happen, whereby the Aggressor might be either affrighted, or some ways disabled, than he should be killed.[13]

In sum, both proportionality, a consideration deriving from nature, and good wishes, which derive from charity, limit use of the full right of self-defense. But this second restriction does not apply to non-Christians. This distinction illustrates Grotius' use of categories provided by nature and grace separately in developing his concept of just war.[14]

In certain cases, however, the lessons taught by nature and by Christianity are the same; proportionality and charity may be inextricable one from the other. Under the heading "War, though Just, not to be undertaken rashly," Grotius notes that in some cases it is better to forego our own rights rather than to engage in a war, even if the war would be just, because of the carnage that would ensue. This sacrifice is taught by Christianity, which counsels men to lay down their lives for the sake of others; but the same policy is also counseled by Polybius and Aristotle, who are taken to be

[13] *Ibid.*, p. 71.

[14] Grotius defines two other natural limitations on self-defense that do not properly apply to the case of war between nations. In the case of a threat from some person "useful to others" in the state, one may not go so far as to kill him. Thus one has no right to kill his prince or agents sent by him, even though one's own death may result from such restraint (*ibid.*, p. 73). Second, in cases of "private war" between citizens of a state, the belligerents may not try to kill each other but are bound to bring their quarrel before a judge (*ibid.*, p. 76). These limits on use of force *within* a nation (as opposed to force between nations) show that Grotius is still bemused by a comparison between *duellum* and *bellum* dating from the age of chivalry and not yet dead in the early modern period.

217

spokesmen for natural law. Such restraint, Grotius notes, is particularly to be attempted when the issue is punishment of a nation that has done harm to one's own or when the safety of one's own citizenry will be jeopardized.[15]

In setting these limits Grotius does not go beyond provisions already in just war doctrine much earlier. Two differences between his position and earlier doctrine are, nevertheless, worth noting. Grotius takes great pains to ground just war in the natural category of self-defense. In restricting the right to punish another nation for harm done and in extending the right to make preemptive strikes against prospective enemies to keep harm from being done, Grotius is not uttering the justification that Vanderpol finds to be the essence of Scholastic just war doctrine: "The prince is minister of God to work his wrath against the wrongdoer." It may be argued, as I have done already, that this conception of the prince is not even in medieval times so central a justification as Vanderpol holds it to be; beyond any doubt this justification does not figure in Grotius. The prince's prime concern, for Grotius, is to protect his nation. For *this* reason he may make the first strike against one who is arming against him, though the wrong has not actually yet been done; for *this* reason he may refrain from pursuit and punishment if his subjects' weal will be endangered. The prince here is not "minister of God"; he is the guardian of his people's lives, property, and prosperity. Thus it is possible, if a wrong judgment is made as to a neighbor's intent, for one's own nation to be the actual wrongdoer, though the intent was to *avert* harm. Thus also it is possible for one who intentionally does evil to profit from his

[15] *Ibid.*, chap. xxiv, p. 416.

action, if it would cost more to punish him than it would be worth to his victim.

Grotius also differs from earlier just war doctrine in distinguishing between what is known by nature, which binds all men, and what is known by charity, which though good is binding only upon Christians. This concern tends to produce a winnowing of the category of justice, which as Grotius uses the term is a purely natural category. The result in his thought is a minimal concept of just war, a moral floor on the right of man in nature to make war as he likes, with another set of standards superimposed, which define what Christians may do. This separation has an ironic result. Since European nations were by definition "Christian," and since the customs and mutual agreements in the *jus gentium* were also products of interactions among European nations, it was difficult during the early modern period to distinguish between standards drawn from Christianity and those drawn from the *jus gentium*. Thus, as we shall see, much of what Grotius separates off as deriving from charity reappears in secular form in Vattel's category of "voluntary law of nations." This is directly counter to what appears to be Grotius' intention, but it is also a direct result of his treatment of justice *versus* charity.

The final point to be discussed in connection with the *jus ad bellum* has to do with Grotius' treatment of the possibility of selective conscientious objection.[16] It is helpful to contrast his position to that of Victoria set forth in the preceding chapter. For Victoria a subject is under no compulsion to inquire into the causes of a war in order to ascertain their justice, for he must trust his superiors as part of his submission to them, and

[16] *Ibid.*, chap. xxvi, pp. 428–31.

furthermore, unless he is among their counselors, he could in no way influence their decision. Nevertheless, if the injustice of the war is clearly manifested to him so that he has no doubt that his prince is acting unjustly, he must refuse to fight in the war.

Grotius proceeds somewhat differently. For him the just causes of the war ought to be made public by the sovereign so that all may view them and be (or not be) convinced by them. Subjects and citizens have deliberative authority and are not required to trust blindly. As Grotius puts it, "Prudence, indeed, as Aristotle notes, is a Vertue proper to Princes; but Justice belongs to men as they are men."[17] Therefore, he argues, while princes' counsels are not to be published abroad, ". . . the reasons of their actions as men may be proclaimed. These things considered, we conclude with the Pope Adrian, That where the subject doth not only doubt the lawfulness of the War, but by very probable Arguments is induced to believe that it is unjust, especially if that War be offensive, and not defensive; *he is bound to abstain.*"[18] For a subject to disobey his sovereign's call to war is very grave, for Grotius as well as for Victoria. But Grotius requires only that "very probable Arguments" be given to induce certainty of injustice in the minds of the subjects, and moreover he provides that the prince submit his cause symbolically for all to see and judge. This is far removed from the position taken by Victoria and even farther from that of Suarez. His agreement with Adrian, furthermore, stands in sharp contrast to the rejection of Adrian's opinion by both Spanish theologians.[19]

[17] *Ibid.*, p. 430.　　　　[18] *Ibid.*, emphasis in original.
[19] Victoria, *De Jure Belli*, sects. 30–31; Suarez, *On War*, sect. VI, 9.

Only one case exists in which, according to Grotius, it is lawful for subjects to engage in a war they know to be unjust: when they are being threatened by the opposing force, which though acting in a just cause is about to do harm to them, their property, others or their property. In this case they may by the law of nature fight in self-defense, and thus they are not properly engaged in the public war that their sovereign is fighting unjustly.[20] This point is of considerable significance, though Grotius makes very little of it. When Victoria approaches the question of possible war for religion he rejects it because, among other reasons, to admit war for religion would lead to wars just on both sides. This follows from the right of those attacked to defend themselves, itself a just cause. Grotius is as uncomfortable—and just about as ambiguous—as is Victoria on the subject of wars just on both sides, and he rejects unequivocally the justice of religious war. But the distinction Grotius makes between two possible ways of conceiving the actions of those who fight in self-defense raises problems with Victoria's argument about war for religion. If Grotius' distinction is allowed, there is no way of reasoning from the justice of self defense to the injustice of war for religion. Subjects fighting in self-defense, according to Grotius, are always in the right, regardless of whether the cause motivating their sovereign is just or not. Thus, if we for a moment grant that a war for religion would be just, an infidel *prince* would be unjust to oppose it; yet his *subjects*, acting as individual men, would not. Conversely, if war for religion is unjust, a prince may justly oppose it, and his subjects should support his cause. In either case the

[20] Grotius, *Rights of War & Peace*, chap. XXVI, p. 431.

subjects may do the same thing, but only in the second case, according to Grotius' distinction, is the *war* truly just on their side. Applying Grotius' distinction to Victoria's argument, then, produces a result somewhat different from Victoria's: if war for religion is just, opposition is unjust, and the war is just on one side; if war for religion is unjust, opposition is just, and the war is just on the other side. In either case the *war* is just but on one side; yet in either case citizens of the attacked country may do precisely the same things—acting in the former case in their private capacity to defend themselves and their property, acting in the latter case in their public capacity as called forth to war by their sovereign. Grotius in fact rejects war for religion, since its cause is irreducible to the realm of the natural.[21] I shall return later in this section to his treatment of the possibility of a war just on both sides.

THE *Jus in Bello*: LIMITATION BY "MODESTY"

Grotius approaches the subject of the *jus in bello* indirectly by a general statement: "[T]hose things that conduce to the End, do receive their true intrinsick value from the End; wherefore whatsoever is necessary to the End, that is to receive or recover his own Right, (taking the word Necessary not physically but morally,) that we are understood to have a power unto."[22] The entire treatment of the *jus in bello* in book III of *De Jure Belli ac Pacis* derives from an exploration of what is truly necessary, in the moral sense, in given situations. Thus in fact Grotius' position is considerably more restrictive than the general statement above suggests. As in the case of the *jus ad bellum*, some restric-

[21] *Ibid.*, chap. I, pp. 70–71; chap. XXII, pp. 406–10.
[22] *Ibid.*, bk. III, chap. I, p. 434.

tions derive from nature and apply to all, and others come from charity and apply only to Christians. In general Grotius' procedure is first to set wide boundaries to what may be done in war, then to narrow them by reference to criteria from nature, *jus gentium*, and charity. This is most apparent in his treatment of noncombatant immunity.

Grotius' argument in some respects represents a backwards step, especially when compared with Ames' position, also expressed in the Dutch context and antedating Grotius'. Grotius seems to find in nature very few restraints on the prosecution of war against noncombatants: "[T]he Right of license or impunity in [prosecuting] War extends it self very far, for it reacheth not only to such as are actually in Arms, nor unto such only as are Subjects to these Princes against whom the War is made; *but unto all such as reside within their territories or dominions. . . .*"[23] Grotius will allow only that foreigners be given some time during which they have leave to depart. Those who come into enemy territory after war is declared and begun may be treated as enemies.[24] Although an enemy may be "persecuted" everywhere, under no circumstances may neutral countries or their populations be despoiled.[25] This immunity does not, however, extend to the noncombatant population of the enemy country or to their possessions. They may all be taken prisoner, and any prisoner, including women and children, may be killed.[26] The only restriction Grotius will admit at this level is one imposed not

[23] *Ibid.*, chap. IV, p. 458; emphasis added.
[24] *Ibid.*   [25] *Ibid.*, p. 459.
[26] *Ibid.*, p. 460. In fact, in the seventeenth century, prisoners were normally exchanged or ransomed. Grotius is speaking of the *worst* that might, by the law of nature, be done to them.

by the law of nature but by the *jus gentium*: prisoners may not be put to death by poison![27] The reasoning behind such a position may be condensed into two points. War is made not only against a prince but against all his subjects and lands; thus any subject of an enemy is himself an enemy. And further, a conquered enemy becomes the slave of the victor, who has power of life and death over him. In fact, however, even the provision that the loser be a slave to his conqueror is a modification in the direction of humanity of the strict dictate of nature that an enemy be put to death.[28]

This does not, however, constitute Grotius' last word on this subject. There remain the boundaries imposed

[27] *Ibid.*, p. 461.

[28] In chapter v Grotius writes: "Cicero in the third of his Offices gives this Rule, . . . It is no whit repugnant to the Law of Nature, to spoil and plunder him, whom it is lawful to kill. It is not then to be wondered at, That the Law of Nations permits the spoil and devastation of an Enemies Land and Goods, seeing that it permits him to be killed" (p. 465). Yet in chapter vii this blanket permission is restricted. Here Grotius argues that *unless the civil law provides otherwise*, the victor's rights extend to the power of life and death over his captives. This implies that all captives taken in solemn war must be slaves to their captors (p. 481). But a more general restriction is set forth a page later: "Now this unlimited Power [to make slaves and to seize property] is by the Law of Nations granted for no other Cause than that the Conqueror being allured by so many advantages might be willing to forbear that utmost cruelty that they may lawfully use by killing their captives, either in the heat of fight, or afterwards in cold blood" (p. 482). The Law of Nations as well as, in some cases, the civil law prohibits what the Law of Nature allows, and the reason is self-interest. But is not self-interest grounded in natural law? I submit that it is, and as I argue later in this chapter, ultimately all Grotius' restrictions on the conduct of war—even those of charity—can ultimately be traced to nature.

by charity. Thus, continuing from the above, Grotius notes that in spite of the comparative license granted in natural law and law of nations, Christian countries proceed more mildly against their enemies because of the force of charity, which keeps Christians from killing wantonly. Because of charity Christian countries do not need permission to enslave conquered peoples, since this permission is instituted only as necessary to keep the victors from wholesale slaughter of the vanquished.[29] That is, charity does for Christians what slavery does for others. Further restrictions on the harshness to be exercised by the victors are also imposed by religion—most perfectly by Christianity, but also by Judaism and Islam.[30]

Charity, then, is not the only source for moderation in war; some elements of moderation are introduced in the law of nature, especially through the *jus gentium*, and others are brought in through various religions. Christianity's uniqueness, as Grotius conceives it, is that it brings to perfection what is present in imperfect form in nature, *jus gentium* and non-Christian religions. In this vein chapter x begins with a declaration:

I am now to look back, and take away from those that make War almost all those Rights which I may be thought to have granted them, *though indeed I have not*. For when I began to explain this part of the Law of Nations, I also declared, That many things were said to be right and lawful, because they were not punishable by Law, partly because they derive their authority from Military Councils, which notwithstanding either swell beyond the Bounds of honesty, whether we confine it to Right

[29] *Ibid.*, chap. vii, p. 484.   [30] *Ibid.*, chap. x, p. 495.

strictly taken, or place it in the Precepts of other Vertues; or else they are such as may more religiously, and amongst good men, more commendably be left undone. [Grotius cites Seneca:] "What law forbids not, Modesty commends."[31]

Not merely what the law would punish but the normative course indicated by "modesty" thus provides for Grotius the basis of the *jus in bello*. And significantly it is not just Christians who can know what is required by this higher standard and act accordingly; the requirements are accessible to all men through conscientious use of right reason. The standards imposed by "modesty"—or, as Grotius usually says, "moderation"—are not those of supernatural love; they are but the purest equity.

Justice, then, and not charity, provides the *jus in bello*; hence all nations must limit their wars by it:[32]

Neither is that generally true that is commonly said, He hazards all, who what is just denies. That of Cicero is much better, There are some good offices to be performed, even to those who have injured us; there is also some moderation to be used even in revenge and punishments. And even in the sharpest War, there ought to be some grains of mildness and clemency, if it be regulated according to Christian Discipline. Nay the very Philosopher hath already pronounc'd them cruel, who though they have cause, yet know no measure in punishing.[33]

But what, in sum, does moderation in war require? At a minimum it requires that certain distinctions be

[31] *Ibid.*, p. 494; emphasis added.
[32] *Ibid.*, pp. 494–95.   [33] *Ibid.*, chap. xi, p. 497.

drawn and acted upon: the authors of an unjust war are to be held more liable than their followers or subjects; and, even among the authors of such a war, those should be treated less harshly who were persuaded by causes more probably just than should those making war for reasons patently unjust (this essentially duplicates Victoria's position). Nevertheless, even these latter may be pardoned, though they deserve death.[34]

More particularly with regard to noncombatant immunity, Grotius borrows from Polybius to state his own general position: a good man should not prosecute a just war any longer than needed to secure satisfaction for harm done, and in any case he is "not to involve the innocent with the nocent in the same punishment."[35] Specifically to be regarded as innocent are women and children, priests and students, husbandmen ("who are also provided for in the canons"), merchants (both subjects and foreigners), and all captives.[36] Grotius' reasoning throughout in marking out these classes is based on their functioning vis-à-vis the war. Husbandmen are mentioned as "benefactors to both parties"; women are exempt unless they have "personally performed such service, as belongs to souldiers only." But in general the reason for immunity is that stated for priests and students: their profession is not to bear arms. In fact, as Grotius notes of the merchants, it is more to their good that there be no war, so they can better go about their business. These classes of people are innocent in both respects regarding war: they have little or no say in the decision that takes the nation to war (though they may, as noted above, personally judge the justice or injustice of the cause), and they do not aid directly

[34] *Ibid.*, p. 502. [35] *Ibid.*, p. 504.
[36] *Ibid.*, pp. 506–509.

in its prosecution. It would thus be contrary to justice to include them in the punishment or to exact retribution from them. The ultimate penalty war may exact is death. "Now that the punishment may be just," declares Grotius, "it is necessary that he that is killed should offend, and that in so high a measure, as that by the sentence of an upright Judge, he may be condemned to death."[37] Lesser punishments follow accordingly.

In succeeding chapters Grotius argues for "Moderation in the spoiling of an Enemies Country" (chapter XII), "Moderation concerning things taken in War" (chapter XIII), "Moderation concerning Captives" (chapter XIV), "Moderation in the acquiring of Empire" (chapter XV), and "Moderation concerning such things as by the Law of Nations want the benefit of Postliminy" (chapter XVI). In each case the argument follows the pattern laid down in the case just discussed, which Grotius treats under the title, "Moderation to be used in killing of men in a Just War." The punishment that may be meted out to an enemy in a just war is limited to that which an "upright Judge" would allow in a civil case, on the basis of equity as known by right reason. Two points need further exploration with respect to this argument.

First, it is notable that in spite of numerous parallels with his theologically oriented predecessors, especially Victoria, whom he in one place enthrones as a "Judicious Divine," Grotius has effected a revolutionary change in the relation between nature and charity from that which they assumed. In spite of their energetic efforts to ground just war doctrine in natural law, both Victoria and Suarez remain bound by the Thomistic

[37] *Ibid.*, p. 498.

conception of charity, according to which charity is a higher morality in two senses: it embodies precepts that do not derive from the law of nature, and it conveys grace to do what these precepts require. In the Thomistic conception, natural law requires less than does the law of charity, for nature derives from grace and is less perfect than grace. But Grotius' treatment of natural law and charity assumes an opposite relation. Nature becomes the fundamental reality; everything required of man is included in the natural. Charity is still grace, and it is still in a certain sense on a higher plane to act according to charity than to act according to nature. But for Grotius the higher morality provided by charity consists in a special sensitivity to the dictates of nature that only those possess who have charity. Victoria and Suarez find greatest support for their idea of charity in the position of Thomas Aquinas; Grotius finds support in a movement that in his lifetime was only beginning, and conceived Christianity to be the perfection of man's natural religion. This is precisely what Grotius is saying when he argues that comparative license is granted in war by the strict dictates of natural law and *jus gentium*, but that philosophy discerns elements of moderation, which are also imposed by religions such as Judaism and Islam and are brought to final perfection by Christianity.[38] Such a reversal in the conception of the relation of charity to nature is of the greatest importance for the development of just war doctrine in international law after Grotius. Though Grotius, as a bridge figure, continues to write of the dictates of nature and those of charity as differing, he has removed the fundamental divider that separates

[38] See *ibid.*, chap. v, p. 465; chap. vii, p. 484; chap. x, p. 495; *et passim.*

natural and supernatural morality in the followers of Thomas Aquinas. Thus for Grotius and his successors to ground just war theory in natural law means considerably more than for Victoria, Suarez, or even Ames. For the theologians it had to imply a kind of truncation of the "top" of the doctrine; some of the limits—namely, those traceable to charity but not to nature—must be required only of Christian nations. In Grotius a residue of this thinking is still present; he too writes of what charity requires as pertaining only to some. But if, as he perceives it, charity is but the perfection of nature, the limits imposed by charity are *in principle* imposed on all men. It thus ceases to be necessary in theory to speak of charity and nature as *separate* sources of morality—which Grotius still does in fact—for there is only *one* morality, that of nature. Both Locke and Vattel take this last step, and Grotius' treatment of charity makes it possible.

The second point to be noted with respect to Grotius' concept of the *jus in bello* is that he sets up absolute standards in opposition to the dictates of necessity. This too contrasts with Victoria's treatment of the *jus in bello*.[39] "[W]hatsoever is necessary to the End, . . . (taking the word Necessary not physically but morally), that we are understood to have a power unto"; this is Grotius' *first* word on the subject of the *jus in bello*.[40] It quite clearly allows the end to determine the means: if the war is just, Grotius argues a few lines later, then the means required to gain victory are also just. Moreover, because the nature of war is to create more injustice, some things are permissible to the just side once in war that were not allowed at the beginning. This

[39] See above, Chap. III, third section.
[40] Grotius, *Rights of War & Peace*, bk. III, chap. I; p. 434.

line of reasoning takes Grotius to the point of allowing prosecution of war not only against princes and their armies, but against their subjects and any others who may be in their territories as well.[41] According to such reasoning there seems to be little that a nation prosecuting a war in a just cause may not do to attain its end. Nevertheless, in his *second* word on the subject of the *jus in bello* Grotius sets himself to qualify these seeming rights to methods determined by necessity. The restrictions that follow are not subject to abrogation by necessity; they are *absolute* limits. All of the counsels of "moderation" that Grotius offers are of this type, and the overall result is a strict limitation on what may be done in war if the war is to remain just. Insofar as Grotius lays down a harder line than does Victoria or Suarez it is because he traces his limits to the law of nature or the *jus gentium*, so that they apply to all men. When restrictions on cruelty are taken to derive from charity the *jus in bello* is weaker than when they are understood as implied by nature or human agreement. In Grotius' position, then, the *jus in bello* is considerably less open to any undermining by arguments from necessity than are those of the Spanish secularizers of just war doctrine.

SIMULTANEOUS OSTENSIBLE JUSTICE

There remains the problem posed by the possibility that a war may be just on both sides. Grotius treats this subject only briefly, yet his argument is significant. Unlike the Spaniards, the Dutch jurist makes "just" war equivalent to "solemn" war; he interprets justice in terms of formal requirements set by natural law or *jus gentium* and adhered to by belligerents. Thus it is pos-

[41] *Ibid.*, chap. IV, p. 458.

sible that both sides could be "just" in this sense; indeed, it is usually the case. This reasoning de-emphasizes the *jus ad bellum* by reducing it to formalities. But simultaneously it places more weight upon the *jus in bello*, which becomes the *locus* for criteria defining justice in a purely moral sense. When a war is solemn, as is the case when declarations have been issued on both sides, the formalities of the *jus ad bellum* have been observed; it is clear that both sides are fighting by mutual consent, and all that remains is that they observe the *jus in bello*.[42] In regard to the emphasis placed on the two parts of the just war doctrine, then, Grotius has left the position taken by Victoria, and he has thereby given direction to the development of international law until well into the twentieth century.

JOHN LOCKE:
NEW LIMITS ON WAR FROM NATURE

John Locke's thought deserves examination here for three reasons: his contribution generally to theory of government, his particular influence on United States governmental theory and forms, and his development of the *jus in bello* according to natural principles beyond the point where it rests with Grotius. This section will focus on the *jus in bello* as conceived by Locke. To set this conception into perspective it is necessary first to look briefly at the *jus ad bellum*.

Richard H. Cox sums up Locke's position on the limits on the right to war in three points. First, he writes, according to Locke "[e]very government is bound, by the law of nature and the conditions of the original com-

[42] *Ibid.*, chap. III, p. 454.

pact, to preserve its subjects and their properties. The individual's right to make war is given up to the commonwealth with the express limitation that it shall be employed 'in the defence of the commonwealth from foreign injury,' which is to say only for 'the public good.' "[43] Accordingly, a ruler making use of the war power for unjust conquest opens himself to being deposed and punished by his subjects. Secondly,

> Nor, to take the matter from the other side, has any government the right arbitrarily to attack its neighbours' lives, liberties, and possessions. Individual men in the state of nature have no power arbitrarily to commit rapine, or attack the life, liberty, health, and possessions of others, and they cannot be understood to have transferred any such powers to the government. Therefore, rulers can never legitimately use the public force in war against the people of another society for the purpose of subjugating them.[44]

And finally, "[T]he public force of the commonwealth can never legitimately be used to instigate a war on religious grounds, such as in an attempt to stamp out heresy and idolatry."[45]

These three points capsulize Locke's position on the *jus ad bellum*. Though he proceeds from somewhat different assumptions from those of the other writers so far treated, his conclusions are substantially the same as those reached by Grotius and the secularizing just war theorists discussed in the previous chapter. Locke goes beyond them, however, in his conception of the *jus in bello*.

[43] Richard H. Cox, *Locke on War and Peace* (Oxford: Clarendon Press, 1960), p. 154.

[44] *Ibid.*, p. 155.   [45] *Ibid.*

Like Grotius, Locke first gives and then takes away. For just defense, he argues, it is not necessary to have an overt act of aggression, since "[t]he state of war is a state of enmity and destruction; and therefore declaring by word or action, not a passionate or hasty, but sedate, settled design upon another man's life puts him in a state of war with him against whom he has declared such an intention. . . ."[46] In this sentence the important phrase is "sedate, settled design." If another nation has evil intentions of this nature, discernible in its official pronouncements ("words") or its actions, then a just defense is warranted. What limits such defense? Locke here seems to draw no bounds; or rather he sets an outer limit so generous as to be the utmost that could be done: it is "reasonable and just [that] I should have a right to destroy that which threatens me with destruction; . . . by the fundamental law of Nature, . . . one may destroy a man who makes war upon him. . . ."[47] Nevertheless, there are other limits that qualify this extreme outer one, or rather specify its meaning so that the right to make war does not become the unmitigated right to do anything and everything in war.

A just defender certainly has the right to punish the guilty and exact reparations from them. But this right extends no further than to those who are actually guilty: "For the people having given to their Governours no Power to do an unjust thing, such as to make an unjust War, (for they never had such a Power in themselves:) They ought not to be charged, as guilty of the Violence

[46] John Locke, *Two Treatises of Civil Government* (London: J. M. Dent and Sons; New York: E. P. Dutton and Co., 1924), bk. ii, *An Essay Concerning the True Original, Extent and End of Civil Government*, sect. 16.
[47] *Ibid.*

and unjustice that is committed in an Unjust War, any farther, than they actually abet it. . . ."[48]

Though use of "force to do or maintain an injustice" gives the offended a power over those who "have concurred in that force," he has no more title over others resident in an enemy's lands than he does over subjects of some third nation or indeed "any other who, without any injuries or provocations, have lived upon fair terms with him."[49] If a victorious defender extends his punishments and reprisals to the innocent, even though they are among his enemy's subjects, he is himself in the wrong, and his just defense thereby becomes unjust conquest. This in principle severely limits the prosecution of war. Since the guilty are defined as those who "actually abet" the war, Locke does not allow a victorious defender to take perpetual control of the enemy's land, nor does he permit any action to be taken against the wives and children of the guilty.[50]

The implications of these limits are drawn out by Locke in far-reaching ways. Not only may those persons not actually guilty of abetting the unjust war not be harmed; they also have positive rights to the lives and property of the guilty that restrict how much punishment and indemnity may be exacted by the just victors. The wife and children of a guilty man have at the very least a claim to a subsistence living; this not only implies that all of his property may not be seized in reparation for damage done, but may also even imply that he may not be imprisoned or killed if doing so would mean that his wife and children would perish from lack of subsistence. Locke argues: "The Fundamental Law of Nature being, that all, as much as may be, should be

[48] *Ibid.*, sect. 179; *cf.* sect. 180.
[49] *Ibid.*   [50] *Ibid.*, sects. 180–83.

preserved, it follows that if there be not enough to *satisfy* both, *viz.*, for the *Conqueror's Losses,* and Children's Maintenance, he that hath, and to spare, must remit something of his full satisfaction, and give way to the pressing and perishable Title of those, who are in danger to perish without it."[51] Or, as he summarizes in another place, "[t]he right . . . of conquest extends only to the lives of those who joined in the war, but not to their estates, but only in order to make reparation for the damages received and the charges of the war, and that, too, with reservation of the right of the innocent wife and children."[52]

It is Locke's concern throughout this discussion that justice be done, and depriving the innocent of their livelihoods is patently unjust. Two implications follow from this. First, no spoliation of the land is to be permitted that would render a country uninhabitable for years after the war, and even the amount of destruction of crops, barns, etc., effective only *during* the war is also restricted. Second, the victor has no right to perpetual dominion over the lands and people of the conquered country. Locke asserts that no amount of destruction in wartime can justify taking all the wealth of a land in perpetuity, for this latter would vastly exceed in value all the damage done.[53] But neither does conquest grant dominion over innocent people in the conquered land. If their governors are imprisoned or put to death for their guilt in perpetrating an unjust war, then the people have a right to choose a new government for themselves—the same right that they had when they first came out of the state of nature and entered upon a social contract.[54] They may, of course,

51 *Ibid.*, sect. 183; emphasis in original.
52 *Ibid.*, sect. 182.   53 *Ibid.*, sect. 184.   54 *Ibid.*, sect. 185.

236

choose to be governed by the victors. But if a government is forced upon them, they have the right to rebel, either immediately or at some future time, against this injustice.[55] This right extends even to the case in which all the grown men in a country are in fact guilty of making unjust war—a most unlikely case. Here the victors have both the right and the responsibility to form an interim government, but when the children of the vanquished are grown to adulthood, they have the right to make for themselves a new government and expel their protectors.[56]

There remains to be considered the case in which the victor does not have "and to spare," with the same being true of the vanquished. In the extremity of this case it would be impossible for all of the innocent to be preserved. In such circumstances, according to Cox, "[I]t follows, as Locke points out, that the children of the vanquished—which is to say those who are most innocent of any violation of the law of nature—may legitimately be left to starve and perish."[57] This is not, however, what Locke says. The full passage cited in part by Cox follows immediately the passage beginning "The Fundamental Law of Nature . . ." quoted in the previous paragraph. Here Locke denies that the victors may despoil the losers to the point at which the innocent will perish from lack of subsistence. Then the section— and the subject—changes, and the passage cited by Cox begins: "But supposing the charge and damages of the war are to be made up to the conqueror to the utmost farthing, and that the children of the vanquished, spoiled of all their father's goods, are to be left to starve

[55] *Ibid.*, sect. 192.　　　　[56] *Ibid.*, sects. 189, 193.
[57] Cox, *Locke on War and Peace*, pp. 170–71; emphasis in original.

237

and perish, yet the satisfying of what shall, on this score, be due to the conqueror will scarce give him a title to any country he shall conquer."[58]

Locke does not say, here or anywhere, that the children of the vanquished "may legitimately be left to starve and perish." His point here is that even *assuming* that the victors may take satisfaction up to the denial of subsistence to the innocent—a right that they do not possess—they are in no way justified in claiming the right of dominion over the conquered country as part of their satisfaction.

It is impossible, then, to conclude with Cox that

[p]ut more generally, . . . the distinction between the "innocent" and the "guilty" disappears when the conditions approach that of the truly natural condition: for if all men have an equal right to be preserved, then it is impossible to say that certain men have a better right to be preserved than others. In effect, then, the distinction of principle which Locke repeatedly makes between "just" and "unjust" conquest disappears whenever the situation of governments and their peoples becomes really desperate.[59]

Locke never says and cannot be read to imply that in straitened circumstances the distinction between guilt and innocence evaporates. In such a case as that described above the guilty may still be punished to the extent that they would have been in less extreme cases. That would leave in *all* cases the innocent to be dealt with—those who fought justly and won, their dependents, and the wives and children of the guilty together with others who did not aid the war effort on the con-

[58] Locke, *Civil Government*, II, sect. 184.
[59] Cox, *Locke on War and Peace*, p. 171.

238

quered side. In circumstances in which there is not enough for all, there are *only innocent* persons who must parcel what is available out among themselves in order with the "Fundamental Law of Nature" that "all, as much as may be, should be preserved."[60] This does not imply, as Cox would have it, "that certain men" *among the innocent* "have a better right to be preserved than others."

Also, the distinction between just and unjust conquest does not disappear as men approach the state of nature. In the case of a truly desperate situation created by war, in which no government could fulfill its proper function of preserving its people's livelihoods, civil society dissolves, and all who were in it return to the state of nature. But in this state no more than in that of civil society does any man have the right to invade others' rights or do harm to another.[61] What every man in fact is authorized to do by the law of nature is to preserve himself and, so far as he is able, help others to preserve themselves as well. But under no circumstances may he regard other men "as if we were made for one another's uses, as the inferior ranks of creatures are for ours."[62] The distinction between just and unjust conquest of one nation by another goes back to this description of what is allowed among men in the state of nature, where no one is allowed to encroach on the rights of the innocent and the only power one can have over another comes from the latter's harming the former in some way.[63] Since the distinction between just and unjust conquest originates in the state of nature, it is an extremely strange—and incorrect— argument that when governments dissolve into the state

[60] Locke, *Civil Government*, II, sect. 183.
[61] *Ibid.*, sect. 7.   [62] *Ibid.*, sect. 6.   [63] *Ibid.*, sect. 8.

of nature as the result of war, the difference between just and unjust power over the losers disappears.

In sum, then, Locke severely restricts what may be done in prosecuting war according to justice as known in the law of nature. Though he adds nothing to the definition of noncombatancy, which by now has become virtually fixed, Locke goes far beyond Grotius and the theologians we have examined in erecting non-transgressible bounds for the *jus in bello*—and this in spite of nowhere considering the possibility of a "higher" morality, such as that of charity, as the source of the more stringent limits on the harshness of war. For Locke natural justice alone requires more than does charity in these earlier writers. Nowhere previously in the just war tradition is Locke's argument advanced that the innocent have a strong counterclaim against the just victors regarding what is to be done to punish the guilty and exact repayment for damage done. The significance of this point grows when it is realized that the claim of the innocent derives from nature itself— the claim of a wife on her husband, a child on his father. Neither is there present anywhere earlier in the tradition such a limit as Locke defines on what may be done with the enemy's land: it may not be despoiled to the point that the innocent will die from want, and it may not be seized in perpetuity for the victors to rule over. Far-reaching limitations on the rights of even a *just* victor are implied in these new stipulations that Locke draws from the tradition on just war.

EMMERICH DE VATTEL

Like Grotius, Vattel seems at first to offer *carte blanche* to the state in regard to war. He argues that a nation, which came together for the common welfare of all, has not only the right but the obligation to preserve itself and its members. This implies the right to "every thing that can secure it from . . . a threatening danger, and to keep at a distance whatever is capable of causing its ruin; and that from the very same reasons that establish its right to the things necessary to its preservation."[64] The license here implied is not, however, allowed to remain unlimited. Vattel elsewhere makes clear that it is primarily the turning away of aggressors that he regards as the proper use of the state's power, and correspondingly a state, to be perfect, must have enough power to "repulse aggressors, secure its rights, and render it every where respectable."[65] And an even further restriction derives from the duty, which comes from nature, to assist others in reaching their own perfection:

> If every man is obliged, even by his very nature, to assist in the perfection of others, he is much more forbid to increase their imperfection and that of their state. . . . This general principle prohibits all nations every evil practice tending to create disturbance in another state, to foment discord, to corrupt its citizens, to alienate its allies, to sully its reputation, and to deprive it of its natural advantages.[66]

Thus a state has rights closely analogous to those Locke ascribes to individuals in the state of nature and, by derivation, to the state those individuals form when they contract to enter civil society. These rights extend to self-preservation, but they require one to live in

[64] Vattel, *Law of Nations*, bk. I, sect. 20 (for full citation see Chap. II, n. 6 above).
[65] *Ibid.*, sect. 177. [66] *Ibid.*, bk. II, sect. 18.

241

peace with his neighbors and whenever possible to help them. For Vattel as for Locke it is the fact that all possess the same rights to self-preservation and self-perfection that limits the extent to which these rights can be invoked. A state or an individual may enjoy the full value of his natural rights insofar as they do not transgress on another's enjoyment of the same rights, and *vice versa*. The attempt of one to usurp the rights of another gives the latter the right to punish the former and secure reparation from him, and even to put him out of condition to make the attempt again.[67] These propositions define the limits of just warfare as conceived by Vattel.

To avoid repetition I shall not here analyze Vattel's entire position but rather restrict discussion to the four areas that do most to further the secularization of just war theory: the concept of sovereignty, the relation between church and state, noncombatant immunity, and limitation of the destructiveness of war. The first two most properly belong to the *jus ad bellum*, specifically the criterion of right authority, and the last two pertain directly to the *jus in bello*.

SOVEREIGNTY

For Vattel the authority possessed by the sovereign derives explicitly from beneath. The right to make war, which every individual possesses by nature, is the right to restore the order of natural justice by force when it has been impaired. But in society this right of individuals has been transferred to the state and is vested in the sovereign. Thus only the sovereign has the authority to decide whether to go to war and to raise the forces necessary to wage war.[68] This makes final the

[67] *Ibid.*, sects. 52, 53.   [68] *Ibid.*, bk. III, sect. 4.

change begun in the late Middle Ages regarding the source of sovereign power. For Vattel this power rests secure on rights conferred on men by the law of nature, and accordingly the idea of the prince as "minister of God" has entirely disappeared. But along with the evaporation of the medieval concept of ruling authority has also gone the limitation on ruling power that it implied. Moreover, Vattel does not replace this restriction by a new one deriving from the people. For him sovereignty has a definitely absolutist cast. So long as the ruler acts justly—and for Vattel this means the same thing as acting in the national self-interest—his power cannot be challenged. His actions, furthermore, must be understood as committing every citizen of his state to his cause. His power over his people obligates them to follow his lead unless it manifestly contradicts their corporate best interests, and his responsibility for his people requires that if he chooses the wrong course of action he alone must pay for it. These provisions have interesting implications.

Taking the second point first, Vattel's conception of sovereign responsibility requires that the ruler must bear all the guilt for an unjust war and pay all its costs.[69] Explicitly contradicting Grotius, but incidentally also reversing the entire just war tradition, Vattel asserts that the citizens and even the military of a nation do not have to pay the debt of an unjust war.[70] Though this logically follows from the position on sovereignty set forth by Vattel, it clearly is contrary to distributive justice except in circumstances in which the harm done by war is small and the personal resources of a sovereign are great. The realization that he will be ruined if he loses might dissuade a bellicose ruler from hastily mak-

[69] *Ibid.*, sects. 183–85.   [70] *Ibid.*, sect. 187.

ing war, but justice is not served if those who unjustly suffer losses in war cannot receive repayment. Moreover, in spite of Vattel's attempt to isolate the sovereign from his subjects, there are in fact always in government men who collaborate with the ruler in making decisions, and under any kind of government the power that must be given to military commanders in the field is often sufficient to allow them to commit unjust acts on their own resolve. In Vattel's theory there is no way of requiring these men to share in the guilt or to help restore the losses of the injured. By giving the sovereign such high power and authority in the state Vattel is led to connect guilt and innocence regarding war solely to the person of the sovereign. In so doing he has removed some of the justice from just war theory.

As to the obligation of the people of a nation to follow the course set by their sovereign, the position of the sovereign as the "real author of war,"[71] which is "carried on in his name, and by his order,"[72] gives him almost unlimited power to call up citizens to serve in the military. "No person," Vattel writes, "is naturally exempt from taking up arms in defence of the state; the obligation of every member of society being the same."[73] The state, however—that is, the sovereign— may choose to grant some exemptions because to do so would be in the common interest: thus old men, women, and children are exempted as "incapable of handling arms, or supporting the fatigues of war," and except in cases of dire necessity all others should be exempted "who are employed in stations useful or necessary to society."[74] As we shall see below, such persons are also to be treated as noncombatants.

[71] *Ibid.*, sect. 2.   [72] *Ibid.*, sect. 6.
[73] *Ibid.*, sect. 10.   [74] *Ibid.*

CHURCH AND STATE

The question of sovereignty also provides an entry into the question of the relation between church and state as regards war. This goes far beyond the mere repudiation of war for religion, though that is certainly included.

Notably missing from Vattel's list of those not required to take arms are clergy and other religious persons. Vattel writes: "The clergy cannot naturally, and by any right, arrogate to themselves a particular exemption. . . . The canon law, by prohibiting ecclesiastics from shedding human blood, is a convenient invention for shielding from danger those who are often so eager in kindling the flame of discord, and exciting bloody wars."[75] Still, for the same reason that magistrates are exempted, so are all clergymen who are "truely useful; those who teach religion, govern the church, and celebrate the public worship."[76] These, Vattel means to say, perform services valuable to society, and they are accordingly to be treated the same as government officials ("magistrates"). The church has no call upon the state; rather the situation is the other way around. Here the church has become a servant of the state, a humanly created institution that, along with everything else necessary for the common good, is given over by individuals to the state upon the creation of society. In another place Vattel makes this point explicitly, calling religion "the will of a nation," that which everyone "considers as divine."[77] In this latter place the issue is whether offensive war for religion is permissible. Vattel answers no, reducing the question to that of coercion of the will

[75] *Ibid.*   [76] *Ibid.*
[77] *Ibid.*, bk. II, sect. 59.

of the individual or of the state. Just as it is wrong to coerce others in property matters, so it is wrong to coerce them in matters of the will, such as belief. The possibility of the church's having special rights because of a claimed supernatural character is here left entirely to one side as Vattel makes religion solely one of the state's functions.

On the question of exemption from military service, the assumption that the church exists for the state and has no end in itself means that those who would serve it as having such an end are not to be allowed to do so. Vattel fumes:

Those immense numbers of useless religious, who, under pretence of dedicating themselves to God, in effect give themselves up to an effeminate idleness, by what right do they proceed to a prerogative pernicious to the state? [By being exempted from military service they put hardship on other men.] It would be more reasonable if, in order to exempt the religious from carrying arms, they were employed in laborious works for the relief of the soldiers.[78]

Even this provision for alternative service once again reduces religion to the service of the state.

NONCOMBATANT IMMUNITY

The high position Vattel accords to the sovereign— as the sole director of all the resources and institutions of the nation functioning in behalf of the common good—has its corollary in regard to noncombatant immunity. In the first place, the duty all citizens owe to their sovereign renders irrelevant one kind of distinction between rulers and subjects: all citizens of an

[78] *Ibid.*, bk. III, sect. 10.

enemy nation are enemies, and all those of one's own or a friendly nation are friends. This would seem to imply no distinction between combatants and noncombatants. Vattel, however, does not proceed to this conclusion but rather moves from another kind of distinction: not all enemies are guilty, because not all function in such a way as to cause direct harm to oneself or one's friends. Here the criterion of function in society as regards war is linked to the concept that the sovereign alone is guilty in unjust war to produce Vattel's position on the definition and immunity of noncombatants. With guilt associated with the sovereign, those who most closely adhere to his unjust designs on others are to bear with him, during the war but not afterwards, the punishment of war. Others in the enemy society, who to be sure are obeying their sovereign but who nevertheless are engaged in just pursuits having to do with the internal good of their society, are to be regarded as entirely innocent and treated accordingly.

As pointed out above, everyone not "incapable of handling arms, or supporting the fatigues of war" or performing services "useful and necessary to society" is subject to becoming a soldier; the other side of this is that all who are too weak or too useful to go to war are by definition of their own society noncombatants. Since Vattel is speaking of the universal case, all such persons are universally defined as noncombatants. Examining the contents of the general definition reveals that certain classes of people are always to be immune from being called to war: for inability to function as soldiers, women, children, and the aged are immune; for useful function in society, magistrates, some clergy, and teachers are excepted. At the very least, these persons should be regarded as noncombatants. Since such types of per-

247

sons exist in every nation, furthermore, it is in the mutual self-interest of nations at war to observe certain limits with regard to them.

Vattel follows through on this principle in considering how harshly war is to be prosecuted. Again, all the citizens of a state with which one's own is at war are enemies, the noncombatant classes included. But still an army should exercise restraint toward noncombatants:

> Women, children, the sick and aged, are in the number of enemies. And there are rights with regard to them, as belonging to the nation with which another is at war, and the rights and pretensions between nation and nation affect the body of the society, together with all its members. But these are members which make no resistance, and consequently give us no right to treat their persons ill, or use any violence against them, much less to take away their lives. . . . However, if women are desirous of being spared, they are to employ themselves in the occupation of their sex, and not play the men in taking arms.[79]

The same holds for clergymen, men of letters, "and other persons, whose callings are very remote from military affairs." These have no character of inviolability from their nature, but "as they do not appear in arms, and oppose no force against the enemy he has no right to use any against them."[80]

In the next section Vattel makes clear that peasants on the land are also included in these exceptions. He notes that in his own time custom exempted the peasantry from harm as long as they did nothing hostile, and he comments further: "A laudable custom, and truly worthy of those who pretend to humanity . . . ; by

[79] *Ibid.*, sect. 145.   [80] *Ibid.*, sect. 146.

protecting the peaceable inhabitants, keeping the soldiers in strict discipline, and preserving a country, the general procures an easy substance to his army, and saves it many losses and dangers."[81]

Thus self-interest, and not altruistic regard for justice alone, is behind the immunity from harm that an army is to accord to noncombatants. In fact, close scrutiny of Vattel's treatment of noncombatant immunity shows that both rationales apply throughout all the named classes, though both are not always explicitly expressed. Peasants, for example, are said to be immune because of self-interest, but they also do no harm to one's army so long as they merely work the land. Again, women are said to be immune because they "make no resistance," but obviously also no army could allow its soldiers to indulge in generalized rape and murder of women without fear of reprisal in kind. Vattel never seems to be sure which rationale he should put first, justice or self-interest. Vattel does not consider the coincidence of the two reasons a problem, however; it is a fortunate occurrence that allows him to appeal to different sorts of men with different reasons for the same thing: exemption from harm for those not directly engaged in prosecuting the war.

As a penultimate point on this subject, it is evident that Vattel is arguing in such a way as to separate *attitude* from the definition of noncombatancy. So far as his attitude toward a war is concerned, a citizen may be assumed to prefer his own country's part. In this sense all citizens are enemies and might appear to deserve treatment as persons guilty of the war their nation is fighting. But for Vattel attitude alone does not suffice to convey guilt; an individual's social function makes

[81] *Ibid.*, sect. 147.

him a noncombatant and, in turn, carries with it his immunity from the harshness of the war. Similarly, even a soldier is to receive only enough violence to cause him to submit—violence in proportion to what he is doing to prosecute the war.

Finally, there is no room for the invocation of charity in regard to the treatment to be accorded noncombatants. This treatment, whether known through considering justice or self-interest, produces a sweeping immunity, already effective in Vattel's separation of the concept of enemy from that of war guilt. The term "enemy" has here become merely a name for citizens of the country with whom one is at war, a term essentially neutral. The noncombatant and the combatant, both enemies, differ in that the former because of his social function is outside the pale of war. Vattel thus reduces the considerations necessary for granting noncombatant immunity entirely to external ones. Just as another man's hostile attitude does not necessarily make him harm me, so my attitude is not allowed to determine the way I act toward him. Thus it matters not whether I have charity; what matters are the actions of the other and whether they amount to an act of war.[82]

Together these two final points mean that ideological war is not to be allowed, but when ideological elements creep into the justification for war, they are not to be allowed to affect the prosecution of the war. Thus war is, so far as Vattel finds it to be possible, rationalized.

[82] Vattel requires that an enemy do an unjust *act* before retaliation is permitted. Locke requires only a "sedate, settled design" of enmity declared "by word or action." Locke in this matter remains closer to classic just war doctrine; Vattel has moved in the direction of the twentieth-century *jus ad bellum*. See Vattel, *Law of Nations*, bk. II, sects. 49–53; Locke, *Civil Government*, II, sect. 16.

And for him this rationalization means that the war is humanized. When disposition no longer plays a part in war, then our enemy remains a human being like us: "Let us never forget that our enemies are men. . . . Thus shall we courageously defend our rights without hurting those of society."[83]

RESTRAINING WAR'S DESTRUCTIVENESS

The prohibition of harm to certain classes of men has its counterpart in Vattel's theory in the prohibition of needless violence directed toward the lands and cities of the enemy. Vattel cites as especially savage the uprooting of vines and cutting down of fruit trees. These acts make a country desolate for many years, and no prudence can dictate such conduct, only "hatred and fury."[84] Also specifically disallowed is the bombardment, burning, spoliation, or other defacement of "fine edifices" that "do honour to human society, and do not contribute to the enemy's power." Vattel's judgment is unequivocal: "He who [destroys such edifices] thus declares himself an enemy to mankind. . . ."[85] In reference to what was in his own day "modern war" Vattel explicitly indicts bombardment of cities with red-hot cannon balls, which tended to start fires indiscriminately wherever they landed. Their use he terms "an extremity."[86]

By these restrictions Vattel enlarges the scope of his prohibition of harm to noncombatants, and a position somewhat similar to Locke's emerges. Both Locke and Vattel are opposed to counter-population warfare in both its immediate and its long-term effects. Although they differ in defining the guilt and innocence of the

---

[83] Vattel, *Law of Nations*, bk. III, sect. 158.
[84] *Ibid.*, sect. 166.   [85] *Ibid.*, sect. 168.
[86] *Ibid.*, sect. 169.

population at large, they converge in their positions on the treatment of those not actually engaged in prosecuting a war.

Let us focus the content of this convergence more sharply by concentration of the issue of harm done to the land. Locke's chief concern is that the innocent be allowed enough of the produce of the land to live on at least a subsistence level. This implies no spoliation that would render a country uninhabitable for years after the end of the war, as well as a limit on the destruction that has effects only during the period of the war. Vattel goes more directly to the point by specifically prohibiting spoliation that renders a country desolate for many years and so denies a livelihood to those inhabitants who remain. Earlier writings on just war theory do not appear to have broached this subject, suggesting perhaps that armies have become more prone to such "scorched earth" tactics in the modern period (though there are many accounts from the period of the Thirty Years' War and earlier to testify to use of such tactics then; this is not *just* a modern problem). Nevertheless, the position of Locke and Vattel on this matter not only does not contradict just war doctrine but indeed follows directly from it. The limitation on cruel treatment of noncombatants and destruction of their livelihoods during a war implies limitation on any cruelty whose effects persist after the war, when all are noncombatants. If these limits are accepted, then both types of "modern war" today—nuclear and counter-insurgency—do not escape judgment. By the criteria of Locke and Vattel, both nuclear weapons, which leave a persistent radioactivity for generations after their use, and defoliants, which severely alter the ecology of the region where they are used, must alike

252

be condemned, for both destroy the productivity of the land and thus deny those inhabitants who remain after the war what is their right by nature—a livelihood from their land.

It is both convenient and sufficient to cut off this historical investigation of just war doctrine here. It has not been the purpose of this book to offer a comprehensive history of the development of attempts to limit war in western culture, but rather to analyze thematically a crucial phase in this history, the period of approximately one hundred years when classic Christian just war doctrine becomes on one hand an ideologically narrow apology for religious war and on the other an anti-ideological, secularized just war doctrine based in natural law. In order to show the significance of what is done by both the holy war theorists and the sixteenth- and seventeenth-century secularizers, and to understand the relationships between them and both earlier and later doctrine on limiting war, the lines of development have been traced that produced classic just war doctrine by the end of the Middle Ages, and the secularized doctrine has been carried through to a point at which it is unequivocally based in nature and not grace. With Vattel this latter point has been reached, and a theory on the limitation of war is set forth that fits the presuppositions that modern man makes about himself and his world. Indeed, together the three writers treated in this chapter lay down the main lines of what remains today the controlling theory of war and its limitation, not just for the West but for the world. I wish therefore to make three retrospective observations about Christian theory on war before briefly taking up the

253

problem of ideology and the limitation of war in the Epilogue.

First, the secular theory on the limitation of war that informs relations among nations in the modern period is a *just war* theory. It derives directly, in the manner demonstrated above, from Christian doctrine on war in the sixteenth and seventeenth centuries and consists principally in the exchanging of first principles based on natural law for those based on divine law. As an accidental feature there is a tendency in secular war theory to de-emphasize the *jus ad bellum* and to give new weight to the *jus in bello*. This is not, however, a result of the essential change from one set of assumptions to another but derives from two other developments: the realization that war can ostensibly be just on both sides at once, an idea I have argued is present in Victoria's theory, and the formalization of the *jus ad bellum* criteria, a tendency I have traced to Grotius. Together these developments trivialize the *jus ad bellum*.

Second, just war doctrine does not lose intensity, effectiveness, or scope—we might say, it does not lose moral power—in the transformation from Christian to secular bases. Rather, and this is especially true for the *jus in bello*, it seems to gain as war is conceived increasingly as a *human* enterprise, subject to human controls.

Third, the history of development of just war theory that makes possible its transmutation from one base to another without loss of moral power is one of intimate and prolonged interaction between religious and secular elements in European society. The just war doctrine of the late Middle Ages was itself the product of not just Christian theology but also the secular *jus gentium*, increasingly conceived as the common body of agreements binding all men together in mutual relationships.

Holy war doctrine in its extreme form shows what can happen to Christian war doctrine when it is cut off from this dialogue, just as Vattel's conception of sovereignty gives some clues to what can happen in secular war doctrine when it stands entirely alone. Though a certain amount of independent growth is necessary for each side of the doctrine to develop fully its own wisdom, just war doctrine is at its most creative when it combines the two sets of wisdom in regard to particular circumstances. This is what happened in the late Middle Ages when the *jus in bello* came into being as an addendum to what was before that substantively a Christian position on the *jus ad bellum*. The creativity unleashed here persists in the bridge figures we have treated, from Victoria to Grotius, in their increasing interest in making what began as the war doctrine of western Christianity meaningful for the entire world.

With the resurgence of interest in a specifically Christian position on war during the post-World War II period, and with the simultaneous growth in ideological self-definition by nations and revolutionary movements—the latter a development that, understood one way, is fundamentally religious in character—there is once again a unique opportunity and need for investigation of the points of contact between secular and religious war doctrines in an attempt to forge a new synthesis. This synthesis would not last forever, any more than that which came into being during the late Middle Ages was destined to persist forever, but it would draw together for this point in time those sources of wisdom—and moral power—on the limitation of war that have largely gone their own routes for three centuries and more. The Epilogue begins consideration of one aspect of such a synthesis.

APPENDIX I

Biographical Data

It is well known that *Hugo Grotius* (1583–1645) wrote, in his *De Jure Belli ac Pacis,* one of the seminal works of modern international law. It is less well known that he studied theology, history, and philology as well as law (in which he received the doctorate from the University of Orléans in 1598). But the law and public office were his chief concerns throughout his life. Grotius practiced law in The Hague from 1599 to 1607, after which he spent eleven years in various government positions in Holland. He was tried and imprisoned for alleged treason in 1618, but in 1621 he escaped (hidden in a book-chest) to Paris, where he lived until 1631. His political troubles in Holland can be traced to his religious views, which were Arminian. In 1631 and 1632 Grotius returned briefly to his homeland but then continued his exile in Hamburg, Germany, from 1632 to 1634. Then, for eleven years, he was Swedish Ambassador to France, initially appointed by Gustavus Adolphus, who much admired Grotius' work. Grotius lived during a time of almost continuous political upheaval caused partially by religious differences and partially by conflicting dynastic claims and ambitions. The Thirty Years' War raged throughout his later life and forms a backdrop against which to understand his thought on war. But Grotius was not merely an occasional writer. He was steeped in the classics, and his use of classical allusions in *De Jure Belli ac Pacis* is apt

256

and sure. This work is also obviously influenced by Grotius' experience in practical political affairs, as well as by the interest in theology that continued throughout his life.

John Locke (1632–1704) is known for his philosophy as well as his political theories. He was *the* philosopher in England in his day, and his influence extended across the Atlantic. Perry Miller, in his biography of Jonathan Edwards, persuasively demonstrates that Edwards' profoundly affecting sermons were intended as attempts to convey simple Lockean ideas in visual, easily apprehensible imagery. Locke's concept of the social contract similarly deeply affected the form taken by the United States as it separated from England. Locke's writing on the limits of war, treated in this chapter, occupies a relatively small place in the second treatise on civil government, and it is not a portion of his thought that has received much attention. Yet it is important both as an integral element in that broad sociopolitical theory that has been so widely appreciated, and in its own right as a logical extension of the received *jus in bello* of his time.

Emmerich de Vattel (1714–67) was born the son of a Reformed clergyman in the Swiss principality of Neuchâtel. His mother was the daughter of a councilor of state and treasurer general (for Neuchâtel) of the King of Prussia. Vattel's two older brothers became soldiers, but he studied philosophy and law, and was deeply influenced by Leibnitz. The Elector of Saxony in 1749 named Vattel Minister to Berne, and during his tenure in this position he lived the life of a gentleman of leisure in Neuchâtel. The minimal demands of this office gave him time to write, and the *Law of Nations* was the result. It was published in 1758, two years after the beginning of the Seven Years' War. Augustus III of Saxony, impressed by Vattel's learning, recalled him and named him Privy Councilor of his Cabinet. This job was considerably more demanding than the ambassadorship had been, and Vattel appears to have given himself entirely to his new duties until his death in Dresden a few years later.

Ideological and Non-ideological Restraints on War

THIS book has argued that classic just war doctrine came into being as an expression of an ideology in which all Christendom partook, and that the direction taken in modern international law has been designedly to replace what was taken to be the ideological component of the classic doctrine, its value base, with one taken to be non-ideological in nature.

The fact is, of course, that what was rooted out of the inherited doctrine by the secularizers of the early modern period (including theologians as well as non-theologians) was not identical with what had supported and given meaning to the classic doctrine. In the Middle Ages the religious values incorporated into the just war doctrine of that time were an integral part of an all-inclusive system of belief and behavior, which I have termed the ideology of Christendom. In the early modern period the medieval unity of religion and culture had disintegrated: European Christianity was no longer single but (at least) dual, and religious values were no longer part of an overall structure of belief but were identified with one or the other of the faiths that comprised western Christianity after the Reformation. Religious values had become expressions of particularist ideologies. In regard to war the immediate and most significant result was holy war doctrine: the teaching that war for religion is the most just kind of war. The

259

naturalists countered by denying that religion can ever afford just cause for war, and they supported their denial by searching for a new comprehensive source of values to replace the old one that had come to pieces around them.

Whether the naturalists continued to ground natural law ultimately in the will of God or whether they in fact looked no further than to the customs and agreements among men for what was "natural," they had more in common with one another than with the proponents of holy war, as the close relation between the thought of Victoria and Grotius illustrates. Both the theologians and the secular theorists of the naturalist school abhorred holy war, war for religious cause. They understood themselves as avoiding the possibility of such war by basing their limits on war in natural reason, which all men could be expected to possess. Theirs was ostensibly and designedly a non- (or even anti-) ideological enterprise, undertaken to avoid the hated possibility of warmaking for the sake of a particularist belief. The idea of a natural religion common to all men, which came along a bit later in the modern period, points to the fallacy inherent in the enterprise of the early modern naturalist just war theorists: they were themselves dependent on the ideological structure that they were helping to establish as normative in the civilized world. This new European ideology was imposed, both in theory and in fact (through colonization) on the entire world, even though those on whom it was imposed were assumed to have the same access to its provisions as "civilized" Europeans. In reality, of course, the Indians of the New World knew nothing of this normative system, for all its dependence on such concepts as "natural reason" and later "natural religion"; it

260

was as alien to them as Christianity had been. So the attempt to create a non-ideological base for modern just war doctrine succeeded, ironically, in creating a new comprehensive ideology to replace the disintegrated one in developing war doctrine.

It is nevertheless the case that as just war doctrine became increasingly grounded in an understanding of law as rooted in man's customs and positive agreements, a more truly non-ideological set of limits on war began to emerge. The trend in this direction can be discerned, I have argued, progressively through Grotius, Locke, and Vattel. The movement of international law in the modern period has been one of increasing reliance on treaties and precedents, with the customary law still recognized but, because of its vagueness, less useful. Appeal to the natural in adjudicating international disputes is virtually unknown today, and where such appeal does appear it is given but scant attention by lawyers and policy-makers. Thus it would seem that in the long run, if not in their own time, the secularizers of just war doctrine achieved their goal: to root ideology out of the limits on war.

If a totally non-ideological doctrine limiting war has ever been attained, then it must be placed in time at the end of the nineteenth century. By this time the idea of *compétence de guerre* had supplanted the earlier concept that a just cause had to exist for war; reason of state was by definition, according to the nineteenth-century notion, such a cause. This idea persisted at least through the beginning of World War I, though by the end of that conflict the Wilsonian ideal of fighting to make the world safe for democracy had reintroduced in a powerful form the idea of a cause justified by some higher value than reason of state. The turn of the cen-

261

tury saw the attempt to limit prosecution of war by mutual agreement also reach a kind of climax in the two Hague conferences. Even though some of the moving forces behind these gatherings were present in the persons of highly idealistic men (especially Czar Nicholas' adviser de Martens, who opened a whole new era by introducing the idea of service to humanity into his draft of the Preamble to Hague Convention IV of 1907),[1] the result of the two conferences was principally to set forth by mutual agreement among the states present a set of limits on the prosecution of war. These limits, because of the method by which they were produced, did little to offset the powerful concept of military necessity, the *in bello* analogue to reasons of state. Those weapons expressly prohibited, for example expanding or "dumdum" bullets, were weapons no nation expected to use against another civilized state anyway, and the newly emerging weapons, particularly those

---

[1] The Preamble declares the High Contracting Parties to be ". . . animated by the desire to serve, even in this extreme case [of war], the interest of humanity and the ever progressive needs of civilization." Though an innovation in 1907, this notion caught on, and it finds expression again and again in the twentieth century—in the Nuremberg trials, in the 1949 Geneva Conventions for the Protection of War Victims, in the United Nations Declaration of Human Rights. It can be argued, as Colonel G.I.A.D. Draper has done (in a paper read in Newton Center, Massachusetts, September 1971, entitled "The Ethical and Juridical Status of Constraints in War"), that this is the point of entry into international law of the concept of a humanitarian law. It is also possible to trace such a concept to the latent influence of charity in the just war tradition. Whatever its source, immediate or remote, the concept of a humanitarian law in international relations is, because of its ideological nature, in strong contrast to the designedly value-free content of traditional international law.

pertaining to air warfare, were merely put off for later decision. World war postponed that decision even farther than contemplated.

The classic *jus in bello* has proven well suited for transformation into an objective, non-ideological set of limits on war. This portion of classic doctrine certainly had its ideological roots: on the religious side, Augustine's dictum that war not be prosecuted out of cruelty; on the secular side, the chivalric notion that combat is valorous only when it is between equals—knight against knight, soldier against soldier. But by the time classic doctrine took shape at the end of the Middle Ages these were no longer the controlling ideas. Instead, function as regards prosecution of war had defined certain classes of persons against whom war was not to be prosecuted; this line of reasoning was later extended, as in the thought of Locke and Vattel, to include land and even certain kinds of buildings. Vattel's plea for the sparing of "fine edifices" which "do honour to humanity" is really beside his main point, which he makes in the next breath: such buildings are not properly part of the fortifications from which and against which the war is being waged. Implicit is his agreement that when such edifices, no matter how "fine," are being used for purposes of war, their claimed immunity evaporates. Soldiers may not snipe from the walls of a magnificent cathedral and expect their enemies not to attack them for fear of damaging the building; it is the snipers who have enlarged the target and taken away the "noncombatant immunity" of the cathedral. The point, once again, is *function*. Similar considerations had earlier than Locke and Vattel modified the immunity of women, a status that reaches far back into the code of knightly conduct for its sanction. When women "play

263

the man" (as more than one writer put it), they lose their claim to protection from the ravages of war. The female sappers who dug earthworks around their cities during the Dutch War for Independence could not reasonably have expected not to be fired on by the Spanish besiegers; the women had forfeited their immunity when they had given up their feminine function.[2]

Though the criterion of function remains the principal source of limits on the prosecution of war in the twentieth century, it is no longer today an effective criterion. Little argument was needed, when armaments were primitive and scarce, to convince responsible parties to direct the killing power in the hands of their soldiers against those who were directly engaged in trying to kill them. Every bit of energy or shot wasted on peasants in their fields, women at the well, or tradesmen in the town might be needed against the real enemy in the next pitched battle. But today armaments are far from scarce, and they are devastatingly effective. A bullet shot into a peasant in his field might still be wasted in exactly the same sense as in the sixteenth or seventeenth century, but now it is hardly, if at all, missed from the vast store of bullets available to modern armies. The argument for noncombatant immunity on grounds of function, supported by considerations of necessary economy of limited force and supplies, is ineffective in a time when bullets are so plentiful that they can be sprayed by the hundreds of thousands over a sector of jungle merely on the suspicion that enemies might be there, or when bombs are so plentiful and powerful that they can be used to obliterate whole city blocks (or whole cities, in the case of nuclear bombs) instead

[2] For an example of this see Sir Roger Williams, *The Action of the Lowe Countries* (London: E. G. for John Rothwell, 1638), p. 88.

of being preserved carefully for use against targets of obvious military import. Moreover, the concept of function itself has changed when civilians working in war-connected industries are attacked directly, and functionally based restraint is entirely removed when civilian population centers are laid waste for the effect it will have on morale on what is now suggestively termed the "home front."

In the twentieth century, accordingly, the old law of war based on functional immunity of some classes of persons has been increasingly supplemented by reference to what de Martens called "the interest of humanity and the ever progressive needs of civilization."[3] That this relatively recent influence has been readily accepted is indicated by the readiness of commentators on international law to speak of a tension or a supplementary relation (alternatively) between military necessity on the one hand and the requirements of humanity/ civilization on the other. Both the latter terms are used, moreover; in their *Law and Minimum World Public Order* Myres S. McDougal and Florentino P. Feliciano refer to "compromises between military necessity and humanitarianism,"[4] and the British international lawyer Georg Schwarzenberger builds up a detailed model of the relation between "two formative agencies: the standard of civilization and the necessities of war" in his *A Manual of International Law*.[5] It is not my point here to discuss either of these formulations in detail; I wish only to indicate that whichever standard is used,

[3] See note 1, above.
[4] Myres S. McDougal and Florentino P. Feliciano, *Law and Minimum World Public Order* (New Haven: Yale University Press, 1961), p. 72.
[5] Georg Schwarzenberger, *A Manual of International Law*, 5th ed. (London: Stevens and Sons Ltd., 1967), pp. 197–99.

humanity or civilization (for it is by no means obvious that they mean the same thing), their use represents an attempt once more to find an overarching, universally acceptable ideology whose values will serve to dampen the flames of war. An ideological element has thus once again been introduced into doctrine on restraint of war, and it is no accident that this has come precisely at the point when the non-ideological thrust begun in the early modern period has reached its limit and ceased to be effective.

The twentieth century has also seen an attempt to revive the concept of limiting the right of sovereign states to make war. The requirement by the early modern secularizers that just war doctrine exclude the possibility of an ideological just cause (or conversely, that no causes allowed as just have their base in particularist ideology) led inexorably to the concept of war for reason of state and thence to the concept of *compétence de guerre*, the doctrine that there are no restraints on a sovereign's power to make war for what he deems to be the national interest. The twentieth century has held fast to the requirement of non-ideological just cause; yet it has backed away from the *laissez-faire* warmaking possible through the idea of *compétence de guerre*. The first move in this direction was made by the Covenant of the League of Nations, which attempted to substitute arbitration for war in the case of international disputes. But more to the point, since they are the principal components of international law on the *jus ad bellum* today, are the requirements of the Kellogg-Briand Pact and the United Nations Charter.[6]

[6] For fuller discussion of the contemporary *jus ad bellum* see my article "Toward Reconstructing the *Jus ad Bellum*," cited in note 6 to the Introduction, above.

In the Kellogg-Briand Pact the signatory powers are bound to "condemn recourse to war for the solution of international controversies, and renounce it as an instrument of national policy in their relations with one another" (Article 1), and to seek solution of all disputes among themselves by pacific means (Article 2). The universalistic thrust of this treaty is obvious from Article 3, which declares the treaty to be open for additional signatures for "as long as may be necessary for adherence by all the other powers of the world." The fact that this pact did not restrain even its original signatories, among whom were nations soon to begin World War II, from fighting one another does not derogate from its intent; it does, however, suggest the difficulty of abolishing war by such mutual agreement. In any event, the Kellogg-Briand Pact did not aim at restraining *all war*; it did not restrict or impair what Secretary of State Kellogg called the "inherent right of self-defense." As he further put it, "[E]very nation is free at all times to defend its territory from attack or invasion and it alone is competent to decide whether circumstances require resort to war in self-defense." This appears to declare a defensive *compétence de guerre*. Coupled with the expressed language of the Pact itself, Kellogg's clarifications, written to convince the British Government that signing the treaty did not abrogate that nation's right to wage defensive war, make the *jus ad bellum* of the Kellogg-Briand Pact a simple one: no aggressive war, but no restriction on defensive war.

This same line of approach is used, and used more explicitly, in the United Nations Charter. Article 2 prohibits members "from the threat or use of force against the territorial integrity or political independence of any state" and empowers the Security Council to preserve

267

international peace. Article 51, the other article most relevant to the matter of a contemporary *jus ad bellum*, gives all nations, whether acting individually or collectively (as in the case of action by a regional organization like the Organization of American States, the Warsaw Pact countries, or NATO), the right to resist with force an "armed attack" until the Security Council "takes the necessary measures to restore international peace and security." This is not the place to discuss the *jus ad bellum* of the Charter at any length, but a few general observations as to its content are in order.

To begin, there is a discrepancy between the language of Article 2 and that of Article 51. The former condemns "the *threat* or use of force," while the latter sanctions defense only against "*armed attack*" (emphasis added in both phrases). This would seem to rule out any response by a threatened nation to the saber-rattling of a hostile neighbor. A French commentator, Henri Meyrowitz, has argued that the language of the English text of Article 51 has removed justice from the concept of the *jus ad bellum* set forth in the Charter.[7] Under this formulation, he argues, international society has declared it cannot tolerate one particular kind of action, and that action is not war but the *first use of force*. The reason is, as Meyrowitz puts it, that "it is this act that *begins the war*" (emphasis in the text). Left out of account are the prior behavior of belligerents and value considerations as to their respective claims: "the idea of political and moral judgment, of appreciation of the pretensions of the parties and their

[7] Henri Meyrowitz, *Le Principe de l'égalité des belligérents devant le droit de la guerre* (Paris: A Pedone, 1970), p. 144, n. 5.

respective behavior before the act of armed attack."[8] The result is a *jus ad bellum* absolutely prohibiting all first use of force, while sanctioning second. This is, as Meyrowitz notes, a concept as free as possible from value considerations; we may add that it is thus as non-ideological as the framers of Article 51 were able to be. Still there remains a problem. As Meyrowitz himself points out, the Charter also sanctions the right of self-defense as recognized to exist in international customary law. This, he argues, means but one thing, that "armed attack" is *that action to which legitimate defense is the proper reaction*—that is, that "armed attack" equals "aggression."[9] This produces a second definition of the *jus ad bellum* that, because of the connotations attaching to the concept "aggression," is not entirely value-free. The ambiguity has also been noted by two American commentators, Morton Kaplan and Nicholas Katzenbach, who write of Article 51: "The wording . . . does not clearly forbid self-defense prior to armed attack but only sanctions self-defense as permissible in case of armed attack. However, the restrictive term 'armed attack' was included deliberately and most commentators would read the Article to forbid self-defense except in case of armed attack."[10] In short, these writers turn around the equation made by Meyrowitz: instead of concluding with him that "armed attack" equals "aggression," they conclude that most commentators read the Charter to declare that the customary right of

[8] *Ibid.*, emphasis in original.   [9] *Ibid.*, pp. 146–47.

[10] Morton A. Kaplan and Nicholas deB. Katzenbach, "Resort to Force: War and Neutrality," in Richard A. Falk and Saul H. Mendlovitz, eds., *The Strategy of World Order*, vol. II, *International Law* (New York: World Law Fund, 1966), p. 290, n. 3.

self-defense *has now become* the right only of self-defense against armed attack. This takes us back to the concept of a *jus ad bellum* free from value considerations (though of course the problems of ambiguity and inconsistency still remain). Such value considerations include, as noted by Meyrowitz, the question of justice.

Though the *jus ad bellum* in its value-free form (no to first use of force, yes to second) cannot be warped by particularist ideologies (like the claim that "wars of national liberation" are always just), it poses problems for even the most meritarian standard of justice. If what is evil is only force, then those predator nations that exercise their aggressive intent through economic manipulation, propaganda, and subversion are not inhibited, and the nations against which these weapons are employed have no legitimate recourse except to retaliate in kind as best they can. Furthermore, when the criterion for defining first use of force becomes the first cannon shot or the first intrusion of troops across a frontier, a predator has only to engage in a war of nerves—massing troops on the border, conducting maneuvers, sending flights of planes along what would be in wartime a line of strike, and so on—until it goads the prey into a preemptive strike. Thus the predator becomes legally the "defender" and the prey the "aggressor." Whether such a simplistic reading of the *jus ad bellum* of the Charter is likely or not, that doctrine is too simplified to be any help in clarifying right and wrong in such complex recent conflicts as the Arab-Israeli Six Day War, the October (1973) War, and the Indo-Pakistani clash over Bangla Desh.[11]

[11] Whether such a reading is likely can be judged by these examples: the United States reaction against India in the last case and the French reaction against Israel in the first. In both

When a non-meritarian concept of justice is introduced, such as the humanitarian ideal that underlies some of the twentieth-century modifications of the law of war, the result is equally out of phase with the provisions in the *jus ad bellum* conceived along a first-strike/second-strike dichotomy. It is by no means clear, for example, that a humanitarian standard of justice objectively applied would not have justified use of force to restrain Russian action against Hungarian and Czechoslovakian dissidents—even though this would have involved *first* use of force by the restraining powers against the USSR. The case of Vietnam offers another example. On the one hand, the humanitarian concern to prevent a blood bath (if Communist forces took over South Vietnam) has repeatedly been cited as a reason for United States military intervention there. Yet on the other is the claim, also frequently made, that United States participation produced a level of destruction that was, by the standard of humanity, unjustified. Leaving aside all other justifications, legal and moral, for American intervention and focusing closely on the humanitarian one, it would seem to be in conflict with the "no first resort to force" criterion. And again, if the claim (if objectively true) against American intervention is made, the case is by no means clear that other powers might not have been justified in using force to restrain the United States—even though in the particular context of the relations of these powers with the United States such action would have involved the (seeming-

---

of these cases the reasoning was the same. As Meyrowitz puts it, in the case of the Six Day War "General de Gaulle chose . . . the grossest criterion for the illicit use of force: the first cannon shot." Meyrowitz, *Le Principe de l'égalité*, p. 148, n. 10.

ly) prohibited first use of force. This last case is the equivalent, with countries changed, of the first one cited: Russia in Hungary and Czechoslovakia.

The point in all these cases is that when a non-meritarian standard of justice is in play, there may come a time when that standard implies first use of force, even when the country initiating armed action is not directly threatened but acts altruistically to defend or support another nation. This possibility is certainly provided for in classic just war doctrine through its own version of non-meritarian justice, that based in charity. But this element in the classic doctrine's concept of justice is removed when religion is excised from among the causes of war. Granted that holy war for a particularist ideology is to be avoided, the question must be asked whether the contemporary narrow construal of the *jus ad bellum*, a concept designedly as free from ideological (value) taint as possible, is not a case of throwing out the possibility of war for humanitarian or charitable reasons along with the possibility of holy or ideological war.[12]

It has not been my purpose in this Epilogue to make

---

[12] It is generally conceded that classic Christian just war doctrine was interventionist in that it gave a ruler authority, acting in the stead of God, to punish wrongdoing even among others not his own subjects. Twentieth-century Catholic moral theology, and not just international law, has backed away from interventionism to a clear stand in the concept of self-defense. Thus what I have been saying about international law applies, *mutatis mutandis*, to contemporary Catholic teaching as well. See John Courtney Murry, *Morality and Modern War* (New York: Council on Religion and International Affairs, 1959); Paul Ramsey, *The Just War: Force and Political Responsibility* (New York: Charles Scribner's Sons, 1968), chaps. 4, 10; and my own article cited in note 6 to the Introduction, above.

a definitive statement about the historical development of just war doctrine in the later modern period or about the shape, actual or desirable, of just war doctrine in the twentieth century. A study with the detail of the preceding chapters would be required for the former, and considerably more detail than I have supplied, together with more sustained argumentation, for the latter. What I have tried to do is to draw out the main lines of development of just war doctrine from the early modern period to our own time and, on the basis of that and a brief survey of the *jus in bello* and the *jus ad bellum* in contemporary international law and practice, to suggest some possible relations between ideological and non-ideological restraints on war. These need further exploration, which I hope to provide in a future study. But for now these relations can only be stated as tentative conclusions.

First, only a minimum level of restraint on war can be provided by expressed limits devoid of ideological content. The failure of a functional definition of noncombatant immunity in this century is one instance of the way in which such limits become minimalized; another is provided by the almost total evaporation of the idea of a just resort to war under the concept of *compétence de guerre*.

Second, even objective, meritarian standards of justice are not met by the minimum restraints provided for in non-ideological limits on war. The problem of the *jus ad bellum* defined by first strike versus second exemplifies this shortcoming; so also does the erosion of noncombatant immunity whereby civilians are punished with death and destruction whose sole purpose is to undermine their government's will to continue fighting.

Third, ideological constraints on war hold out a hope

273

as well as a threat. They alone seem able to support a war doctrine that can truly be called "just," both in the meritarian sense just referred to and in the higher, non-meritarian sense earlier identified as present in both Christianity and humanitarianism. But the danger is that ideological justifications can be turned around to support the waging of war for narrow, particularist reasons—whether "holy war" in the seventeenth century or "war of national liberation" in the twentieth.

The awful destructiveness of modern war in all its forms points to the need for more stringent and more workable limits on both the resort to war and its prosecution once begun. Such limits must, if morality is to be satisfied, be expressions of justice as well. If limitations free from ideology cannot meet these demands, then constraints based in ideology will also have to be employed. We are today in a far better position for incorporating such constraints into the limits on war than men have been for centuries, and that for two reasons. First, we understand perhaps better than ever before the relative nature of most of our beliefs and so are more skeptical of particularist ideologies than were the holy warriors of the sixteenth and seventeenth centuries and the fervent nationalists of the nineteenth. The theoretical work of Weber and Mannheim on ideology has further cleared the air. Second, for the first time since the Middle Ages there is a rudimentary international community that is nearly universal in membership. This suggests that a universal value system is not so far off as it was throughout the intervening centuries. We are now at a good point in history to try again the limitation of war by restraints based in ideological standards, with the hope and intent that a new and *just* war doctrine can result.

Ainsworth, Henry. *Annotations upon the Five Books of Moses*. London: John Bellamie, 1627.

Allen, William. *A True, Sincere, and Modest Defence of English Catholiques that suffer for Their Faith both at home and abrode*. London: William Cecil, 1583.

Ames, William. *Conscience, with the Power and Cases Thereof*. N.p., 1639.

Aquinas, Thomas. *Summa Theologica*. 3 vols. London: R. & T. Washbourne; New York: Benziger Brothers, 1912–22.

Arias, Franciscus. *De Bello et ejus Justitia*. In *Primum Volumen Tractatum ex Variis Juris Interpretibus Collectorum*. Lugduni: n.p., 1549.

Armstrong, John Alexander. *Ideology, Politics, and Government in the Soviet Union*. Rev. ed. New York: Praeger, 1967.

Augustine. *Basic Writings of St. Augustine*. Vol. II: *The City of God, On the Trinity*. Edited, with introduction and notes by Whitney J. Oates. New York: Random House, 1948.

——. *The Political Writings of St. Augustine*. Edited, with an introduction by Henry Paolucci. Chicago: Henry Regnery Co., 1962.

Ayala, Balthasar. *De Jure et Officiis Bellicis ac Disciplini Militari*. 3 vols. Duaci: Ioannes Bogardi, 1582.

Bacon, Francis. *Certaine Miscellany Works of the Right Honourable, Francis Lo[rd] Verulam, Viscount S. Alban*. (Contains *An Advertisement touching an*

Holy Warre and Considerations Touching a Warre With Spaine.) London: I. Haviland for Humphrey Robinson, 1629.

Bainton, Roland. *Christian Attitudes toward War and Peace.* Nashville, Tenn.: Abingdon Press, 1960.

———. "From the Just War to the Crusade in the Puritan Revolution," *Andover Newton Theological School Bulletin*, 35, no. 3 (April 1943), pp. 1–20.

Barnes, Thomas. *Vox Belli, or An alarme to Warre.* London: H. L. for Nathaniel Newberry, 1626.

Barrett, Robert. *The Theoricke and Practicke of Moderne Warres.* London: William Ponsonby, 1598.

Barth, Karl. *Church Dogmatics.* Vol. III: *The Doctrine of Creation.* Pt. 4. Edinburgh: T. & T. Clark, 1961.

Becon, Thomas. *The Governaunce of Vertue.* London: John Day, 1566.

———. *The New Pollecye of Warre.* London: John Maylerre for John Gough, 1542.

Bennett, John C. *Nuclear Weapons and the Conflict of Conscience.* New York: Charles Scribner's Sons, 1962.

Bilson, Thomas. *The True Difference betweene Christian Subjection and Unchristian Rebellion.* Oxford: Joseph Barnes, Printer to the University, 1585.

Binder, Leonard. *The Ideological Revolution in the Middle East.* New York: Wiley, 1964.

Bocer, Henrici. *De Jure Pugnae, hoc est, Belli et Duelli.* Tübingen: G. Gruppenback, 1591.

Bonet, Honoré. *The Buke of the Law of Armys or Buke of Battalis.* Translated from the French *L'Arbre des battailes.* Vol. I of *Gilbert of the Haye's Prose Manuscript*, edited by J. H. Stevenson. Edinburgh and London: William Blackwood and Sons, 1901.

———. *The Tree of Battles of Honoré Bonet.* Translated from the French *L'Arbre des battailes* and edited by G. W. Coopland. Cambridge, Mass.: Harvard University Press, 1949.

Bridge, William. *The True Souldiers Convoy. A Sermon preached . . . for the Princes good sucesse in going forth to warre.* Rotterdam: n.p., 1640.

Brzezinski, Zbigniew K. *Ideology and Power in Soviet Politics.* London: Thames and Hudson, 1962.

Bullinger, Henry. *The Decades. The First and Second Decades.* Edited by Thomas Harding. Cambridge: Cambridge University Press, 1849.

Center for the Study of Democratic Institutions. *Asian Dilemma: United States, Japan and China.* Edited by Elaine H. Burnell. Santa Barbara, Calif.: Center for the Study of Democratic Institutions, 1969.

Churchill, Winston. *The Second World War.* Vol. II: *Their Finest Hour.* New York: Bantam Books, 1962.

Churchyard, Thomas. *A Generall Rehearsall of Warres, called Churchyardes Choice.* London: Edward White, 1579.

Clark, Sir George. *War and Society in the Seventeenth Century.* Cambridge: Cambridge University Press, 1958.

Clausewitz, Gen. Carl von. *On War.* 3 vols. Translated from the German by Col. J. J. Graham. Rev. ed. London: Routledge & Kegan Paul, 1949.

Corpus Juris Canonici Gregorii XIII. 2 vols. Graz: Akademische druck-u. verlagsanstalt, 1955.

Cotereau, Claude. *De Jure et Privilegiis Militum.* Lugduni: Step. Doletum, 1539.

Cotton, John. *The Powring Out of the Seven Vials.* London: R. S., 1642.

Cox, Richard H. *Locke on War and Peace.* Oxford: Clarendon Press, 1960.

Dictionnaire de théologie catholique. Edited by A. Vacant and E. Mangeot. Vol. VI, pt. 2. Paris: Letozey et Ané, 1920.

A *Discourse of the Civile Warres and late troubles in Fraunce.* Translated from the French by Geffray Fenton. London: Henry Bynneman for Lucas Harrison and George Bishop, 1570.

The Documents of Vatican II. New York: Guild Press, American Press, Association Press, 1966.

Elton, G. R., ed. *Renaissance and Reformation: 1300–1648.* 2nd ed. New York: The Macmillan Co.; London: Collier-Macmillan, 1968.

Eppstein, John. *The Catholic Tradition of the Law of Nations.* Washington: Catholic Association for International Peace, 1935.

Erasmus, Desiderius. *Bellum Erasmi.* Translated from the Latin. London: Thomas Berthelet, 1533.

Falk, Richard A., and Mendlovitz, Saul H., eds. *The Strategy of World Order.* Vol. II: *International Law.* New York: World Law Fund, 1966.

Farer, Tom J. *The Laws of War 25 Years after Nuremberg.* International Conciliation, no. 583. New York: Carnegie Endowment for International Peace, 1971.

Finn, James, ed. *Protest: Pacifism and Politics.* New York: Vintage Books, 1968.

Fourquevaux, Raymond de Beccarie de Pavie, Sieur de. *Instructions for the Wars.* Translated from the French *Instructions sur le faict de la guerre* by Paul Ive. London: Thomas Man and Tobie Cooke, 1589.

Fulbecke, William. *The Pandectes of the Law of Nations.* London: Thomas Wight, 1602.

Fuller, Thomas. *The Historie of the Holy Warre.* Cambridge: Thomas Buck, Printer to the University, 1639.

Furniss, Edgar S., Jr. *Counterinsurgency: Some Prob-*

lems and Implications. With commentary by Charles Burton Marshall and William V. O'Brien. New York: Council on Religion and International Affairs, 1966.

Gentili, Alberico. *De Jure Belli*. Classics of International Law, no. 16. Translated from the Latin by John C. Rolfe. With an introduction by Coleman Phillipson. Oxford: Clarendon Press, 1964.

Gosson, Stephen. *The Trumpet of Warre*. London: U. (or V.) S. for I. O., 1598.

Gouge, William. *Gods Three Arrowes: Plague, Famine, Sword, In Three Treatises. I. A. Plaister for the Plague. II. Dearths Death. III. The Churches Conquest over the Sword*. London: George Miller for Edward Brewster, 1631.

Grotius, Hugo. *The Most Excellent Hugo Grotius his three Books Treating of the Rights of War and Peace*. Translated from the Latin *De Jure Belli ac Pacis* by William Evats. London: n.p., 1682.

Gyorgy, Andrew, and Blackwood, George D. *Ideologies in World Affairs*. Waltham, Mass.: Blaisdell Publishing Co., 1967.

Hale, J. R. *New Cambridge Modern History*. Vol. I. Cambridge: Cambridge University Press, 1957.

Halpern, Manfred. *The Morality and Politics of Intervention*. New York: Council on Religion and International Affairs, 1963.

Hamilton, Bernice. *Political Thought in Sixteenth-Century Spain*. Oxford: Clarendon Press, 1963.

Hugo, Herman, S.J. *The Siege of Breda*. Translated from the Latin by Henry Gage. N.p., 1627.

Johnson, James T. "The Meaning of Non-Combatant Immunity in the Just War/Limited War Tradition," *Journal of the American Academy of Religion*, xxxix, no. 2 (June 1971), pp. 151–70.

Keen, M. H. *The Laws of War in the Late Middle Ages.* London: Routledge & Kegan Paul; Toronto: University of Toronto Press, 1965.

Lacrymae Germaniae. Or, the Tears of Germany. Translated from the German. London: I. Oakes, 1638.

The Lamentations of Germany. London: E. G. for John Rothwell, 1638.

La Noue, François, Sieur de. *The Politicke and Militarie Discourses of the Lord de la Noue.* Translated from the French by E. A. London: T. C. and E. A. by Thomas Orwin, 1587.

La Primaudaye, Pierre de. *The French Academie.* Translated from the French. London: Thomas Adams, 1618.

The Law of Armed Conflicts. New York: Carnegie Endowment for International Peace, 1971.

Lawes and Ordinances of Warre, For the better Government of His Majesties Army Royall. Newcastle: Robert Barker, 1639.

Lefever, Ernest. *Ethics and United States Foreign Policy.* New York: Meridian Books, 1957.

Lippmann, Walter. "The Atlantic and America," *Life,* 10 (April 7, 1941), pp. 84–88.

Little, David. *American Foreign Policy and Moral Rhetoric: The Example of Vietnam.* New York: Council on Religion and International Affairs, 1969.

———. "Moral Discourse Under Fire," *Worldview,* 15, no. 1 (January 1972), pp. 31–38.

———. *Religion, Order, and Law: A Study in Pre-Revolutionary England.* New York, Evanston, and London: Harper and Row Publishers, 1969.

Locke, John. *Two Treatises of Civil Government.* London: J. M. Dent and Sons; New York: E. P. Dutton and Co., 1924.

Long, Edward LeRoy, Jr. *War and Conscience in America.* Philadelphia: Westminster Press, 1968.

Loque, B. de. *Deux traitez, l'un de la guerre, l'autre de la duel.* Lyon: n.p., 1589.

Mannheim, Karl. *Ideology and Utopia.* New York: Harvest Books, 1959.

McDougal, Myres, and Feliciano, Florentino. *Law and Minimum World Public Order.* New Haven: Yale University Press, 1961.

Mendoza, Don Bernardino de. *Theorique and Practise of Warre. Written to Don Philip Prince of Castil.* Translated from the Spanish by Sir Edward Hoby. N.p., 1597.

Meyrowitz, Henri. *Le Principe de l'égalité des belligérents devant le droit de la guerre.* Paris: A. Pedone, 1970.

Mornay (du Plessis-Mornay), Philippe de. *A Letter, written by a french Catholicke gentleman.* London: John Woolfe, 1589.

Mosse, George L. *The Holy Pretence.* Oxford: Blackwell, 1957.

Murray, John Courtney. *Morality and Modern War.* New York: Council on Religion and International Affairs, 1959.

National Council of the Churches of Christ in the U.S.A. *Imperatives of Peace and Responsibilities of Power.* New York: National Council of the Churches of Christ in the U.S.A., 1968.

Nef, John U. *War and Human Progress.* Cambridge, Mass.: Harvard University Press, 1950.

Niebuhr, Reinhold. *Christian Realism and Political Problems.* New York: Scribner, 1953.

———. *Christianity and Power Politics.* New York: Charles Scribner's Sons, 1940.

SELECT BIBLIOGRAPHY

Niebuhr, Reinhold. *Moral Man and Immoral Society.* New York: Charles Scribner's Sons, 1960.

——. *The Structure of Nations and Empires.* New York: Scribner, 1959.

Northrup, Filmer Charles Cuckow, ed. *Ideological Differences and World Order.* Published for the Viking Fund. New Haven: Yale University Press, 1949.

O'Brien, William V. *War and/or Survival.* Garden City, N.Y.: Doubleday and Co., 1969.

Osgood, Robert E. *Ideals and Self-Interest in America's Foreign Relations.* Chicago: University of Chicago Press, 1953.

——. *Limited War.* Chicago and London: University of Chicago Press, 1957.

Paul, Robert S. *The Lord Protector: Religion and Politics in the Life of Oliver Cromwell.* Grand Rapids, Mich.: Eerdmans Publishing Co., 1955.

Peace, the Churches and the Bomb. New York: Council on Religion and International Affairs, 1965.

Perkins, William. *A Fruitfull Dialogue Concerning the Ende of the World.* N.p.: W. Welbie, 1613.

——. *A Godlie and Learned Exposition upon the Whole Epistle of Jude.* In Perkins, *Works.* Cambridge: John Legat, Printer to the University, 1605.

Perroy, Edouard. *The Hundred Years War.* New York: Capricorn Books, 1965.

Pisan, Christine de. *The Book of Fayttes of Armes and of Chyvalrye.* Translated from the French *Les Faits d'armes et de chivalrie* by William Caxton. Edited by A.T.P. Byles. London: Oxford University Press, 1932.

Potter, Ralph. *War and Moral Discourse.* Richmond, Va.: John Knox Press, 1969.

282

Prall, Stuart E., ed. *The Puritan Revolution: A Documentary History.* Garden City, N.Y.: Anchor Books, 1968.

Raleigh, Sir Walter. *Works.* Vol. VIII. (Contains *A Discourse of the Original and Fundamental Cause of Natural, Arbitrary, Necessary, and Unnatural War* and *A Discourse Touching a War with Spain, and of the Protecting of the Netherlands.*) Oxford: Oxford University Press, 1829.

Ramsey, Paul. *The Just War: Force and Political Responsibility.* New York: Charles Scribner's Sons, 1968.

————. *War and the Christian Conscience.* Durham, N.C.: Duke University Press, 1961.

Rayner, Robert M. *European History, 1648–1789.* London: Longmans, Green and Co., 1949.

Riche, Barnabie. *The Fruites of long Experience. A pleasing view for Peace. A Looking-Glasse for Warre. Or, Call it what you list.* London: Thomas Creede for Jeffrey Chorlton, 1604.

Rohr, John. *Prophets without Honor: Public Policy and the Selective Conscientious Objector.* Nashville and New York: Abingdon Press, 1971.

Saillans, François de [Bertrand de Loque]. *Discourses of Warre and Single Combat.* Translated from the French by I. Eliot. London: John Wolfe, 1591.

Salmon, J.H.M. *The French Religious Wars in English Political Thought.* Oxford: Clarendon Press, 1959.

Sarpi, Paolo. *The Free Schoole of Warre, or, A Treatise, Whether it Be Lawfull To Beare Armes for the service of a Prince that is of a divers Religion.* Translated by W. B. London: John Bill, 1625.

Schwartzenberger, Georg. *A Manual of International Law.* 5th ed. London: Stevens and Sons, 1967.

Scott, James Brown. *The Spanish Origin of International Law.* Oxford: Clarendon Press; London: Humphrey Milford, 1934.

Segar, Sir William. *The Booke of Honor and Armes.* London: Richard Jhones, 1590.

———. *Honor, Military, and Civill.* (Commissioned by Elizabeth I and dedicated to her.) London: Robert Barker, Printer to the Queen, n.d.

Solt, Leo F. *Saints in Arms: Puritanism and Democracy in Cromwell's Army.* Stanford, Calif.: Stanford University Press, 1959.

Suarez, Francisco. *Selections from Three Works of Francisco Suarez, S.J.* Classics of International Law. Vol. II. Edited by James Brown Scott. Oxford: Clarendon Press; London: Humphrey Milford, 1944.

Sutcliffe, Matthew. *The Practice, Proceedings, and Lawes of Armes.* London: Christopher Barker, 1593.

The Swedish Discipline, Religious, Civile, and Military. London: John Dawson for Nathaniel Butter and Nicholas Bourne, 1632.

Taylor, Telford. *Nuremberg and Vietnam: An American Tragedy.* Chicago: Quadrangle Books, 1970.

Thielicke, Helmut. *Theological Ethics.* 2 vols. Philadelphia: Fortress Press, 1966 (vol. 1) and 1969 (vol. 2).

Tucker, Robert W. *The Just War: A Study in Contemporary American Doctrine.* Baltimore: Johns Hopkins Press, 1960.

———. *Just War and Vatican Council II: A Critique.* With commentary by George G. Higgins, Ralph Potter, Richard H. Cox, and Paul Ramsey. New York: Council on Religion and International Affairs, 1966.

———. *Nation or Empire? The Debate over American Foreign Policy.* Studies in International Affairs, no. 10. Baltimore: Johns Hopkins Press, 1968.

United Protestant Princes Electors and other Princes, States and Lords, of the Holie Empire. *A Publike Declaration.* Translated from the Dutch. London: John Budge, 1610.

Vanderpol, Alfred. *La Doctrine scholastique du droit de guerre.* Paris: A. Pedone, 1919.

Vattel, Emmerich de. *The Law of Nations; or Principles of the Law of Nature: Applied to the Conduct and Affairs of Nations and Sovereigns.* Translated from the French. London: n.p., 1740.

Victoria, Franciscus de. *De Indis et De Jure Belli Relectiones.* Classics of International Law. Edited by Ernest Nys. Washington: Carnegie Institute, 1917.

Walzer, Michael. *The Revolution of the Saints.* Cambridge, Mass.: Harvard University Press, 1965.

The Wars in Germany. Translated from the Dutch and the French. London: Nathaniell Butter, 1614.

Wedgwood, C. W. *The Thirty Years War.* Garden City, N.Y.: Anchor Books, 1961.

Williams, Sir Roger. *The Actions of the Lowe Countries.* London: Humfrey Lownes for Matthew Lownes, 1618.

———. *A Briefe Discourse of Warre.* London: Thomas Orwin, 1590.

Wright, Quincy. *A Study of War.* 2 vols. Chicago: University of Chicago Press, 1942.

Yoder, John. *Karl Barth and the Problem of War.* Nashville and New York: Abingdon Press, 1970.

Zahn, Gordon. *An Alternative to War.* New York: Council on Religion and International Affairs, 1963.

Taylor, Telford, 4
Thielicke, Helmut, 3
Thirty Years' War, 62, 63, 82,
83, 127
Thomas Aquinas, 26, 27 n. 1,
32, 34, 39, 40ff, 44, 46, 48,
50, 52, 54, 57, 69 n. 48, 75,
98, 100 n. 19, 150, 156, 160,
171, 172, 178, 186, 209, 210,
216, 228f
trial by combat, war as, 62f, 89,
123 n. 55, 159, 177, 189f

United Nations Charter, 17, 216
n. 11, 266ff
unlimited war, 103f, 106f, 109,
111ff, 128, 132, 137, 141ff,
223f, 226

Vanderpol, Alfred, 4, 7, 27ff,
47, 50, 53 n. 28, 78, 186, 193
Vattel, Emmerich de, 23, 89,
153, 208, 209, 211, 230,
240–53, 257f, 261, 263
Victoria, Franciscus de, 4, 19,
20, 29, 53, 81, 123 n. 55,
152, 153, 154–58, 161, 162,
163, 164, 169, 170, 173, 174,
178–95, 196ff, 204f, 208, 210,
219f, 228, 229, 230, 232, 260
vindicative justice, 27, 30, 31,
38, 39, 40, 46, 47f, 49, 50,
54, 57, 59, 69 n. 48. See also
just cause, vindication of
fault as

Vitoria, Francis de, see Victoria,
Franciscus de

Walzer, Michael, 84, 133, 134–
46, 169
war against rebels, 111, 113ff,
120, 141ff, 144, 161, 162,
212f
war as public contest, 211–13,
221f
war at Pope's command, 116f,
156, 157, 167. See also Catholic holy war doctrine
war commanded by God, 81,
98f, 100 n. 19, 104, 108,
111ff, 119, 121, 125, 127,
129, 130 n. 71, 137, 139f,
143, 157, 160, 161, 167
war for the faith, 37, 46, 48–53,
57, 58, 74. See also holy war;
just cause, religion as
war for prince, 53–63. See also
right authority; sovereignty
war in God's stead, see "minister of God"
war just on both sides, see
simultaneous ostensible justice
war ordained by God, 67ff, 73.
See also holy war; war commanded by God
Wars of Religion, French, 83,
83, 96 n. 14, 105–109, 145
Weber, Max, 12
Wright, Quincy, 5

Library of Congress Cataloging in Publication Data

Johnson, James Turner.
  Ideology, reason, and the limitation of war.
  Bibliography: p.
  Includes index.
  1. Just war doctrine—History. I. Title.
B105.W3J63   261.8'73   74-25618
ISBN 0-691-07209-4